Praise for *The Infrahuman*

"In this scrupulous and subtle book, Noam Pines shines new light on how animality, a well-worn theological figure of exclusion, can be seen afresh as a leitmotif of the intimate dialogue Jewish writers conducted with European literary traditions. With an exceptionally sure touch, Pines tracks this motif from Zionist literature through the postwar responses to Kafka's legacy. *The Infrahuman* is a profound and highly commendable achievement."

— Vivian Liska, author of *When Kafka Says We: Uncommon Communities in German-Jewish Literature* and *German-Jewish Thought and Its Afterlife: A Tenuous Legacy*

"*The Infrahuman* starts readers on an important journey from a place where we construct identities out of the cultural material that we would invent if that material had not already been provided: dichotomies (animal/human, Christian/Jew), other forms, images, things. Pines's powerful readings of Heine, Abramovitsh, Bialik, Greenberg, Kafka, Agnon, and Celan may not teach us how to remember other alternatives, but they do call us to be attentive to the identificatory incapacities that have helped us forget how to live."

— David Metzger, coeditor of *Chasing Esther: Jewish Expressions of Cultural Difference*

THE INFRAHUMAN

SUNY SERIES IN **CONTEMPORARY JEWISH LITERATURE AND CULTURE**
Ezra Cappell, editor

Dan Shiffman, *College Bound: The Pursuit of Education in Jewish American Literature, 1896–1944*

Eric J. Sundquist, *Writing in Witness: A Holocaust Reader*

THE INFRAHUMAN

Animality in Modern Jewish Literature

NOAM PINES

Cover art: Vincent van Gogh, *Old Nag*, 1883

Published by State University of New York Press, Albany

© 2018 State University of New York

All rights reserved

No part of this book may be used or reproduced in any manner whatsoever without written permission. No part of this book may be stored in a retrieval system or transmitted in any form or by any means including electronic, electrostatic, magnetic tape, mechanical, photocopying, recording, or otherwise without the prior permission in writing of the publisher.

For information, contact State University of New York Press, Albany, NY
www.sunypress.edu

Library of Congress Cataloging-in-Publication Data
Names: Pines, Noam, 1976- author.
Title: The infrahuman : animality in modern Jewish literature / Noam Pines.
Description: Albany : State University of New York Press, [2018] | Series: Suny series in contemporary Jewish literature and culture | Includes bibliographical references and index.
Identifiers: LCCN 2017040576 | ISBN 9781438470672 (hardcover)
 | ISBN 9781438470689 (e-book) | ISBN 9781438470665 (paperback)

Subjects: LCSH: Jewish literature—19th century—History and criticism. | Jewish literature--20th century—History and criticism. | Animals in literature.
Classification: LCC PN842 .P56 2018 | DDC 809/.88924—dc23 LC record available at https://lccn.loc.gov/2017040576
Further information is available at the Library of Congress.

10 9 8 7 6 5 4 3 2 1

To Yaffa,
with love and gratitude

יוֹם לְיוֹם יִשָּׂא שֶׁמֶשׁ בּוֹעֶרֶת
וְלַיְלָה אַחַר לַיְלָה יִשְׁפֹּךְ כּוֹכָבִים,
עַל שְׂפָתַי בּוֹדְדִים שִׁירָה נֶעֱצֶרֶת:
בְּשֶׁבַע דְּרָכִים נִתְפַּלֵּג וּבְאֶחָד אָנוּ שָׁבִים.

—Avraham Ben-Yitzhak,
"A Few Say"

CONTENTS

Acknowledgments   ix
Introduction: Between Figure and Creature   xi

1. Life in The Valley: The Jewish Dog in Heinrich Heine's "Prinzessin Sabbat"   1

2. A Radical Advocacy: Suffering Jews and Animals in S. Y. Abramovitsh's *Di Kliatshe*   21

3. Into the Bowels of the Earth: Prophecy and Animality in the Poetry of Hayim Nachman Bialik and Uri Zvi Greenberg   43

4. At Home in a Distorted Life: The Dog as a Constellation in the Work of Franz Kafka   73

5. After the Holocaust: Responses to the Infrahuman in the Works of S. Y. Agnon and Paul Celan   103

Postscript   131
Notes   135
Bibliography   155
Index   165

ACKNOWLEDGMENTS

I OWE THANKS to the many friends and colleagues who have offered guidance and valuable advice during the long process in which this book came to take shape. I would like to thank Michael Gluzman, who has set me on this road and has put me back on track from time to time when I needed it most. I am especially grateful for the unfailing friendship and generosity of Roland Greene, Sepp Gumbrecht, and Steve Zipperstein, with whom I came to envision this project. More recently, I have benefitted from the sharp intellectual exchange with Sergey Dolgopolski, which has greatly helped me in formulating the theoretical framework for this book.

I am indebted to Rafael Chaiken of SUNY Press, who, through his attentiveness and editorial skills, has greatly facilitated the publication of this book, as well as to the two anonymous readers whose valuable comments have greatly improved the initial manuscript.

Over the years, I have been inspired by many people who have contributed, in one way or another, to the making of this book: Michal Arbell, Henry Berlin, Karl Heinz Bohrer, Noah Burbank, Richard A. Cohen, Amir Eshel, Yair Etziony, Marisa Galvez, Anne Golomb Hoffman, Hannan Hever, Kathryn Hume, Shaun Irlam, Chana Kronfeld, Nitzan Lebovic, Vivian Liska, Alan Mintz (z"l), Dan Miron, Fernanda Negrete, Paul North, Max Pensky, Avi Pines, James Redfield, Gabriella Safran, Galili Shahar, Vered Shemtov, Ewa and Krzysztof Ziarek, and Sivan Zeimer.

I am also grateful to the graduate students who attended my course on Kafka, Benjamin, and Celan, and have offered challenging input and stimulating intellectual exchange: Josh Dawson, George Life, Dipanjan Maitra, Jake Nabasny, Eric Vanlieshout, and Hsiao Chieh Yi.

Finally, I am ever grateful to my wife Sarah, for her continued support, intellectual exchange, and infinite patience; and to Alma, my daughter, with whom I have found my lost time.

An earlier version of chapter 1 was published as "Life in the Valley: Figures of Dehumanization in Heinrich Heine's 'Prinzessin Sabbat,'" *Prooftexts* 33, no. 1 (Winter 2013): 25–47. This article is used by the permission of Indiana University Press.

Chapter 2, "A Radical Advocacy: Suffering Jews and Animals in S. Y. Abramovitsh's *Di Kliatshe*," appeared in *Jewish Social Studies*, 23.2 (Winter 2018): 24-47. This article is used by the permission of Indiana University Press.

INTRODUCTION
Between Figure and Creature

RECENT YEARS HAVE SEEN a remarkable proliferation of critical literature dealing with animals as objects of philosophical and ethical inquiry. Under the heading of "Animal Studies," this diverse critical literature challenged some of the unquestioned premises of the humanistic legacy that has dominated Western thought, such as the human–animal boundary, anthropocentrism, cruelty to animals, the limits of the human, and animal feelings and consciousness. Works in Animal Studies have built on a critical approach to Martin Heidegger's discussion of animals in *The Fundamental Concepts of Metaphysics*, and were influenced by Gilles Deleuze and Félix Guattari's notion of "becoming-animal" as well as by the late writings of Jacques Derrida in which his engagement with animality has served to question the metaphysical concept of the subject. In this context, the preoccupation with animals and animality has functioned as a critique of dominant philosophical notions and prevalent social practices that implicitly assume the centrality of humans in the world and ascribe to human beings an inherent primacy over other species. This book takes up such a preoccupation with animality not in order to offer yet another critical account of humanism and anthropocentrism, but in order to revise the terms in which the distinction between human and animal has been formulated in modern Western thought. Instead of staging a polemical philosophical dichotomy between discriminatory anthropocentric practices and a more attentive posthumanist approach, I will show how animality itself emerges as a persistent and unresolvable problem in modernity, and how this problem came to be closely associated with prevailing notions regarding Jewish identity.

As a point of departure for my inquiry I would like to take up the fundamental distinction between the presentation of Jews in literary, philosophical, and theological texts—where they play a determined role in the construction of specific arguments and positions, or assume a certain symbolic meaning—as opposed to the lived experience to which these representations refer, and which is by no means identical with them. This essential gap between *figure* and *lived experience* is proposed by Andrew Benjamin, for whom the figure is "the constitution of an identity in which the construction has a specific function that is predominantly external to the concerns of the identity itself."¹ In the case of Jewish identity, the construction of the figure of the Jew by non-Jews, which is external to Judaism, continued at the same time to influence the ways in which Jewish identity came to be internally shaped, envisioned, and affirmed, especially in modernity.

The texts to be examined in this book present various attempts by Jewish writers to negotiate the distance between figure and experience in relation to Jewish identity by means of an intermediary—a provisional figural construction that I call the infrahuman—in which this distance comes to the fore yet remains suspended and unresolved. As a literary or poetic construction, the infrahuman is above all distinguished by its universality, that is, by its capacity to integrate into contexts that are both internal and external to Judaism. And to the extent that it is universal, the infrahuman is inevitably associated with figural constructions of animality. To be sure, at stake here is not animality conceived as an ontological or conceptual category, but rather as a theological figure of exclusion from a state of humanity and Christianity alike.

Such a figural conflation of Judaism and animality is by no means new; its sources can be traced to the inception of Christianity, as far back as to Paul's designation of the Jews in I Corinthians 10:18 as "Israel after the flesh," and to the entire Pauline trope of the distinction between letter and spirit. Paul described the Jews' historical existence as carnal, physical, material, and literal. The Jews can only read according to the flesh; they do not see beyond the literal meaning of the word to the spirit behind the language.² Therefore, their place as the "children of the promise" has been taken by the new true and spiritual Israel, as Paul states in Romans 4:13: "For the promise that he would be the heir of the world was not to Abraham or to his seed through the law, but through the righteousness of faith." In Philippians 3:2–3, Paul explicitly associates the Jewish adherence to the letter of the law with dogs in his exhortation against the rite of circumcision: "Look out for the dogs, look out for the evildoers, look out for those who mutilate the flesh. For we are the circumcision, who worship by the Spirit of God and glory in

Christ Jesus and put no confidence in the flesh." Drawing on this Pauline legacy, the late fourth-century church father John Chrysostom asserted—in his interpretation of the words of Christ in Matthew 15:26: "It is not right to take the children's bread and toss it to the dogs"—that it is now the "carnal Jews" who are "the dogs", and the Gentiles have become the "children."[3] Kenneth Stow has shown how this identification of Jews with dogs continued to reverberate in the writings and sermons of Christian theologians and church leaders throughout the Middle Ages as well as in modern times.[4]

In the traditional Christian worldview Jews were thus seen as closer to animals than to humans because they lacked the spirituality and reason shared by all Christians. Consequently, medieval law codes classified sexual intercourse with Jews as bestiality, and Jews were commonly depicted as occupying a middle ground between humans and animals.[5] In this context the figure of the dog assumed a special importance, as Leonid Livak observed, since both Jews and dogs played a "dual narrative function"[6] within the traditional Christian worldview, acting both as opponents of the faith and as its helpers. As witnesses to the true Christian faith, their hostile energy was ultimately harnessed for the glorification of the church. In early modern thought this fundamentally theological construction of animality as an exclusion from Christian morality, rationality, and order of redemption came to be "secularized" in Cartesian philosophy in which humanity was posited as a distinct spiritual substance, different from and superior to the rest of the natural world. The Cartesian view, which came to inform subsequent Enlightenment thought, presents an essentialist figural construction of animality as *subhuman*: that is, as an inherent and irreversible fact of ontology or biology that renders all nonhuman species categorically inferior to humanity.

Nevertheless, the Cartesian view was not the only anthropocentric construction of animality to emerge in early modern thought. One of the characteristic formulations of an alternative figural model of animality can be found in Thomas Hobbes's dedication to *De Cive* (1642):

> There are two maxims which are surely both true: Man is a God to man, and Man is a wolf to Man. The former is true of the relations of citizens with each other, the latter of relations between commonwealths. In justice and charity, the virtues of peace, citizens show

some likeness to God. But between commonwealths, the wickedness of bad men compels the good too to have recourse, for their own protection, to the virtues of war, which are violence and fraud, i.e. to the predatory nature of beasts.[7]

For Hobbes, the natural condition of *homo homini lupus* that exists between commonwealths is also the hypothetical ground from which one begins to theorize the establishment of the Social Contract, the civil state in which people treat each other with "justice and charity." This condition of citizenship is contrasted with the lawless struggle for survival implied by life in a "state of nature." To live in a "state of nature" means to be bound by no Social Contract, to belong in no civic order, and to possess no legal rights. In this state no sovereign power guarantees human life and property, and therefore humans have recourse only to their own faculties for self-preservation. Consequently, in a state of nature, humans are reduced to the condition of beasts, a condition characterized by the single-minded and shameless pursuit of gratification of the most basic biological needs. Significantly, Hobbes does not describe the difference between the human and the animal in biological or ontological terms, but rather in terms of an inclusion in, or an exclusion from, a condition of citizenship. Thus, for Hobbes, the prerogative of humans over animals consists in the fact that humans are able to enjoy the privileges of peace, justice, and charity by virtue of a membership in a commonwealth. Beasts and savages, by contrast, are consigned to a life of peacelessness, implying that anyone can harm or kill them with impunity.

In this sense, the "state of nature" of animal life is not simply conceived by Hobbes as a biological occurrence with no relation to the law and to human community. Rather, animal life appears as "bare life," a life abandoned by the law, "exposed and threatened on the threshold in which life and law, outside and inside, become indistinguishable."[8] According to Giorgio Agamben, this relation of abandonment by the law is the original relation by which the law applies itself to life. The figure that marks this transition between law and life, a condition of citizenship and a "state of nature," is the wolf-man, *homo homini lupus*, the werewolf, whose life "is not a piece of animal nature without any relation to law and to the city. It is, rather, a threshold of indistinction and of passage between animal and man, *physis* and *nomos*, exclusion and inclusion."⁹

Although Hobbes's thought remains entirely anthropocentric in privileging "peaceful" human existence over "peaceless" natural existence, he locates the figure of the animal on a scale in which it forms a continuity with human existence. The Hobbesian construction of animality would therefore allow the existence of such transitional figures as the wolf-man, a hybrid that occupies an indeterminate position between human and animal as well as between law and nature, and which would not be conceivable in a system of thought that posits a rigid boundary between the two. In Hobbesian thought, the wolf-man thus forms a locus of the *infrahuman*: a figural construction of animality conceived as inferior to humanity, where the human–animal distinction is not formulated in essentialist biological, ontological, or racial terms, but rather in discursive terms—that is, in terms that remain culturally, politically, and philosophically negotiable.

The distinction between the figures of *subhuman* and *infrahuman* operates fully within the bounds of anthropocentric thought, and does not disrupt or challenge the traditional categories by which the difference between the human and the nonhuman has been conceived in Western thought. In this sense, my use of the term "infrahuman" differs from the way in which it was originally employed by Jacques Derrida and subsequently by Beatrice Hanssen in her book on Walter Benjamin.¹⁰ For Derrida, the term "infrahuman" carried certain taxonomical implications when he employed it in order to expand the frame of reference of the "subhuman" from animals and specific racial groups to include inanimate objects (such as stones). On the other hand, he also used the term in order to call into question the conceptual distinction between human and animal. Ultimately, both Derrida and Hanssen employ the term "infrahuman" polemically, to undermine unquestioned Western philosophical and conceptual premises regarding animality. In this book the term "infrahuman" does not exclude such a particular philosophical agenda, but it locates it within the purview of a certain literary trope—a figure—that has gone largely unarticulated and unnoticed in Western literature and thought.

As we will see, modern Jewish writers had recourse to the infrahuman in their own constructions of Jewish identity. In doing so they were not simply practicing Jewish "self-hatred," even though at times their depictions of Jews as debased animals rivaled anti-Semitic stereotypes. Instead, they employed the images of Jewish animals, with all their inherent ambiguity, as allegorical figures that could equally inhabit a Jewish as well as a non-Jewish literary setting. By appropriating these figures of exclusion from non-Jewish sources and by further elaborating and developing them, modern Jewish writers embarked on an intimate dialogue with non-Jewish literary traditions, a dialogue that eventually secured a place for certain works of Jewish literature in the modern Western literary canon as well as in the modern Jewish canon. By depicting Jews as lowly animals, Jewish authors validated some of the negative stereotypes ascribed to Jews by gentiles. Yet by framing the human–animal question in philosophical or political terms rather than in racial–biological terms, they subjected these pejorative designations to literary elaboration and to philosophical negotiation.

THE FIGURE OF THE JEW as infrahuman made its debut on the stage of modern European literature some fifty years before Hobbes published *De Cive*, in William Shakespeare's *The Merchant of Venice* (1599). In this play, a character named Gratiano accuses the Jew Shylock of possessing a wolvish character in terms that resemble Hobbes's subsequent characterization of animality in a "state of nature":

> O, be thou damn'd, inexecrable dog!
> And for thy life let justice be accused!
> Thou almost makest me waver in my faith
> To hold opinion with Pythagoras,
> That souls of animals infuse themselves
> Into the trunks of men: thy currish spirit
> Govern'd a wolf, who, hang'd for human slaughter,
> Even from the gallows did his fell soul fleet,
> And, whilst thou lay'st in thy unhallow'd dam,
> Infused itself in thee; for thy desires
> Are wolvish, bloody, starved and ravenous.[11]

The association of the Jew with an image of the wolf hanged for "human slaughter" reflects the Jew's liminal social status, recalling the old myth of the werewolf that was prevalent in many Germanic and Anglo-Saxon medieval sources, in which an outlaw banned from human society was depicted as a man with a wolf's head.[12] Traces of this menacing figure of the werewolf as the banned outlaw have found their way into *The Merchant of Venice*, and like those "peaceless" men who were excluded from human community, Shylock comes to exemplify a threshold condition between humanity and animality. As the examples from Shakespeare and Hobbes indicate, the myth of the werewolf has not disappeared from the modern Western imagination.[13] In *The Merchant of Venice*, this myth is explicitly invoked in relation to the figure of the modern Jew, who, like the banned outlaw, is an outsider to human society and lacks the spiritual and moral character shared by all Christians. Indeed, Shylock's transgressive behavior lies in his quintessentially modern attitude. For he has dared to step out of his cultural and social enclave and live among the Gentiles, conducting business with them without renouncing his religious faith and ethnic identity. His existence in Christian society therefore defies the very premises of peace, justice, and charity on which this civic order is predicated. In order to reduce the threat posed by this outsider, his exclusion from civic life must be made palpably clear. He is therefore repeatedly marked as a wolf-man, serving as a constant reminder that the foundation of civic order, in the words of Agamben, "is not an event achieved once and for all but is continually operative in the civil state in the form of the sovereign decision."[14] In the presence of the sovereign, the Duke of Venice, Shylock is ultimately reduced to a condition of bare life through the arguments of Gratiano and Portia, as opposed to the civic life incarnated by his legal adversary Antonio.[15] Nevertheless, Shylock's exclusion from civic life does not take place outside of human society or exemplify a presocial state, but instead demonstrates the active operation of sovereign power by means of an exclusive inclusion of the Jew in a "state of nature" within the bounds of the civic order.

Once contained by sovereign power and reduced to bare life, the threat posed by the Jew is effectively neutralized and he no longer appears as a wolf but rather as a lowly canine, an "inexecrable dog" whose existence is external to the civic order and yet reliant upon it. In this capacity, the Jew bears an affinity with other abject animals such as a street dog, a rat, or even a cockroach. Unlike wild beasts, these creatures dwell in human society and feed off waste products. However, since they are not domesticated and have no formal social or civic affiliation, they possess no legal rights. Consequently, they are relegated to the position of barely tolerated pests or vermin that can be harmed or killed with impunity.

In contrast to traditional Christian accounts that stress the similarity between Jews and dogs, the originality of Shakespeare's narrative lies in that it is not exclusively grounded in metaphorical or theological terms, as due punishment for adherence to the letter as opposed to the spirit. Instead, Shylock's doggishness is taken quite literally. He is not a man whose despicable behavior renders him comparable to a dog. Instead, Shylock is perceived as a creature whose desires are "wolvish, bloody, starved and ravenous." By invoking the image of the Jewish dog as a figure of exclusion from civic life, Shakespeare was not "secularizing" the theological image. Rather, that image was now reinscribed, along with its subtle theological connotations, in the sphere of modern citizenship. Thus, what originally was a figure of theological exclusion now became synonymous, in the modern context, with a figure of social and political exclusion. Moreover, such an exclusion was no longer conceived in terms of a banishment from a community, but in terms of an essential containment—an exclusive inclusion of the Jew in a "state of nature" within the bounds of civic society.

IN 1838 THE GERMAN-JEWISH POET Heinrich Heine saw Shakespeare's *The Merchant of Venice* in England and later wrote about it with an ambivalent mixture of indignation and admiration. On the one hand, he protested the attempt to present the Jew as an "unmitigated werewolf for the amusement of the crowd;"[16] yet for him the figure of Shylock ultimately provided a justification for the actions of a Jew in retaliation to the hatred on the part of Christian society, despite the author's explicit intentions. Years later, in his poem "Prinzessin Sabbat" (1851), Heine invoked the figure of the Jewish dog in order to reclaim it as an emblematic tragic hero. In this poem a cursed prince named Israel is portrayed as "a dog with doggish thoughts" who piddles through "life's excrement and rubbish."[17] It is primarily through the impact of this poem that the infrahuman enters Jewish literature in the middle of the nineteenth century. Heine's poem was not only familiar to early twentieth-century German-Jewish writers such as Else Lasker-Schüler and Franz Kafka, but also to Russian maskilic writers in the 1860s and the

1870s such as Sholem Yankev Abramovitsh, the "grandfather" of modern Yiddish and Hebrew literature. In his writings, Abramovitsh adapted the figure of the Jewish dog to his own purposes, using it to present a satiric portrayal of the shtetl Jew and to point to the urgent need for reform in both Jewish and non-Jewish Russian societies. Notably, in 1865 Abramovitsh wrote a short story about Shmulik the Ragman who lived as a "dog" during the week, and on the Sabbath was transformed into a "prince."[18] By the end of the nineteenth century the Hebrew poet Hayim Nachman Bialik likewise invoked the figure of the Jewish dog in his poem "Igeret Ktana" (A Short Letter, 1893), in which the poetic addresser, an exilic Jew writing a letter to his brother in Zion, pejoratively portrays himself as "a dog in a lost land; / driven away with sticks, feeding on crumbs, / forsaken and forgotten from heart and God."[19] The figure of the Jewish dog continued to make its appearance in Zionist literature in the years leading to the foundation of the State of Israel and thereafter, most notably in Bialik's famous pogrom poem "Be-'ir ha-haregah" ("In the City of Killings"), in Uri Zvi Greenberg's *Kelev Baiyt* (*House Dog*), and in S. Y. Agnon's 1945 novel *Temol Shilshom* (*Only Yesterday*), where it served to emphasize the discrepancy between the degenerate diasporic Jew and the proud "new Jew" envisioned by Zionism. In Yiddish literature, this figure likewise appears in the works of Sholem Aleichem and Israel Joshua Singer, and in post–World War II Jewish literature the dog continues to haunt the works of Paul Celan and Yoram Kanyuk, to name but a few examples.

The question remains in what ways these figures of dogs in Jewish literature—in their capacity as literary constructions exemplifying the unresolved gap between figure and experience—also convey the lived experience of Jews in modernity? As the figure of the dog came to be increasingly identified with the fundamentally modern Jewish condition of an exclusive inclusion in the civic order, its experiential content has been addressed in Jewish literature by means of the category of the *creaturely*. The creaturely is a corollary of the anthropocentric outlook that ascribes to human beings an inherent dominion over earthly creation. The earliest articulation of the intrinsic link between sovereignty and creatureliness is found in Genesis 1:26, where man is given divine sanction to subjugate all creatures that populate the earth. Significantly, the nature of human dominion over creation is indicated by the Hebrew word "*va-yirdu*," which stems from the root *rada*:

to rule without justice (the Hebrew word for tyrant, *rodan*, stems from the same root). From its biblical beginnings, then, the notion of the creaturely implies a subjugation to an unbounded exercise of sovereign power. This theological notion, which has traditionally served as a locus for contemplating the equivalence of human and nonhuman existence in relation to the divine, transforms in modernity into a criterion by which to assess the human capacity to succumb to political power. As Eric Santner writes:

> Creaturely life—the peculiar proximity of the human to the animal ... is a product not simply of man's thrownness into the (enigmatic) "openness of Being" but of his exposure to a traumatic dimension of political power and social bonds whose structures have undergone radical transformations in modernity. The "essential disruption" that renders man "creaturely" ... has, that is, a distinctly political—or better, biopolitical—aspect; it names the threshold where life becomes a matter of politics and politics comes to inform the very matter and materiality of life.[20]

There is perhaps no better example in modern literature of the encounter between Jewish life and the dictates of political sovereignty than in Shakespeare's *The Merchant of Venice*, where the impact of the exposure to the traumatic dimension of political power is subtly registered by Shylock toward the end of the play. Although he formally declares his satisfaction with the outcome of the trial, there is no joy or happiness in Shylock's "contentment" over the loss of his daughter, half of everything he owned, and the requirement to convert to Christianity. Yet before examining Shylock's response in detail, we must first recall the nature of his peculiar legal position vis-à-vis his legal adversary, Antonio. In the play, Venetian civic law is presented as a distinctly modern institution, a corollary of a nascent form of capitalism that would protect the rights of both parties in a commercial transaction conducted between a Venetian citizen such as Antonio, and a Venetian "alien" such as Shylock. Initially, Shylock takes Antonio to court for breach of contract. However, in the ensuing trial, Portia (who functions as Antonio's advocate) makes a deliberate move from civil to criminal law, claiming that Shylock has plotted against Antonio's life. After successfully arguing her case, the right of judgment and mercy that under Venetian law lay in the hands of the litigant, is wrenched from Shylock and delivered to the Duke of Venice, whose political sovereignty is suddenly reaffirmed.

As Julia Lupton has argued, the restoration of sovereign power at this peculiar intersection of the boundaries between civil and criminal law and between citizen and alien, is the result of a "miniature state of emergency, a situation in which someone—in this case, the Duke—must step above the merely civil law and make a decision concerning life and death, reinstituting a moment of political theology within the legal regime of Venetian constitutionalism."[21] As Lupton makes clear, the suspension of civic law and a reversion to a state of emergency is not so much a function of the murder charge, but rather a result of the threat posed by the Jewish outsider, a wolf-man whose very existence threatens the viability of the notions of peace, justice, and charity on which the Venetian civic order is predicated.[22] The suspension of civic law and the implementation of a state of emergency therefore arise out of the intrinsic necessity to protect the security of the state, to reestablish the political stability to which civic law could then apply.

This paradoxical relation between civic law and a state of emergency (also known as a *state of exception*) was famously established by Carl Schmitt in his definition of the sovereign as "he who decides on the [state of] exception."[23] According to the "decisionist" logic of sovereignty articulated by Schmitt, in a state of exception the distinction between the different powers of the State (legislative, executive, and judicial) is suspended, not in order to return to the so-called "full powers" (*plenitudo potestatis*) of sovereignty,[24] but rather to have recourse to an empty zone of the law. As Schmitt writes:

> It is precisely the exception that makes relevant the subject of sovereignty, that is, the whole question of sovereignty. The precise details of an emergency cannot be anticipated, nor can one spell out what may take place in such a case, especially when it is truly a matter of an extreme emergency and of how it is to be eliminated. The precondition as well as the content of jurisdictional competence in such a case must necessarily be unlimited.[25]

At this intersection of law and life in the state of exception it is not the absolute authority of the sovereign that is exercised, but rather a fundamental absence of the law that Agamben has aptly termed "kenomatic state."[26] In other words, the state of exception does not imply a subjection to the authority of the law, but rather a condition of utter abandonment by the law. As a result of Portia's intervention, the life of Shylock remains bound to Venetian law precisely in this relation of abandonment, and thus he stands before the law as bare life or as a mere *creature*. In his creaturely estate, Shylock is divested of the various legal, social, and civil ties that bound him as an alien to Venetian civic life. Then, in a sovereign act of Christian "mercy," the Duke offers to perpetuate Shylock's state of creaturely abandonment by means of a legal formula:

> That thou shalt see the difference of our spirits,
> I pardon thee thy life before thou ask it:
> For half thy wealth, it is Antonio's;
> The other half comes to the general state,
> Which humbleness may drive unto a fine. (4.1.366–70)

Shylock, however, rejects the Duke's offer. Refusing to be reduced to bare life, he insists instead on a qualified form of life—a *bios* as opposed to the *zoë* of animal existence[27]—by arguing that without livelihood life is not worth living:

> Nay, take my life and all; pardon not that:
> You take my house when you do take the prop
> That doth sustain my house; you take my life
> When you do take the means whereby I live. (4.1.372–75)

Only after Antonio offers to rescind the money now owed him by Shylock—on condition that he convert to Christianity and that his remaining wealth will pass to his daughter and son-in-law after his death—does Shylock finally declare he is "content" with the arrangement. Indeed, Antonio's offer aims to restore Shylock to the circle of Venetian civic life and thereby mitigate the Duke's decree. But precisely at this point, even a sharp critic such as Lupton, who examines Shakespeare's work from the angle of political theology, has failed to notice that the restoration of Shylock's legal status rests on a double act of Christian mercy: the first, which is sovereign, consigns him to a creaturely estate and acknowledges only the simple fact of his bare life; the second, which is civil, restores Shylock's civic affiliations within the framework of the Venetian polity. The crucial point is that behind the façade of restoration of ties to the civic community, Shylock has in fact forfeited his previous legal standing as an alien (whose rights are constitutionally guaranteed by Venetian law), and he now stands before the law as a creature, reduced to bare life. It is this traumatic reduction to creaturely life that explains Shylock's ambivalent reply to Portia's question: "art thou contented Jew?"

> SHYLOCK: I am content.
> PORTIA: Clerk, draw a deed of gift.
> SHYLOCK: I pray you, give me leave to go from hence;
> I am not well: send the deed after me,
> And I will sign it. (4.1.390–95)

Shylock's reply, expressing an ambivalent mixture of content and discontent, exemplifies above all an irreconcilable gap between figure and lived experience as the outcome of exposure to sovereign power in a state of exception. Shylock's formal declaration of contentment is part of a figural construction of Jewish identity by non-Jews in which "the construction has a specific function that is predominantly external to the concerns of the identity itself."[28] Specifically, it marks the moment in which the hostile wolf-man, whose desires are "bloody, starved and ravenous," is domesticized, turned into a submissive dog by virtue of sovereign decision. On the other hand, the lived experience of the Jew remains incompatible with such figural "contentment." This is not because, as Lupton argues, Shylock's characteristically Jewish "life form is altered forever,"[29] but rather because he is now condemned to face sovereign power not as a resident alien but as bare life. It is for this reason that Shylock feels "not well" in the court and in the presence of the Duke and must depart.

When considered in these terms, the court scene in *The Merchant of Venice* is remarkable because it presents us with a figural construction of Jewish identity in which the lived experience of the Jew is not suppressed. Simply put, for Shylock there is no final closure regarding the question of both civic and Jewish identity, since his formal act of religious and civic conversion is brought about by a traumatic exposure to the law as bare life. Instead of emphasizing the figural construction of Jewish identity as a form of animality, Shakespeare lays bare the fundamental unresolvedness of figure and lived experience in the case of Shylock, depicting him both as a Jewish dog and as a suffering creature. This unresolvable tension between the abject figure of an animal and the bare life that it encapsulates is the hallmark of the infrahuman, in Shakespeare as well as in subsequent Jewish literature.

THE FOREGOING ANALYSIS of the infrahuman as the site in which the gap between figure and lived experience remains suspended and unresolved stands in sharp contrast to the notion of "creaturely poetics" in the field of Animal Studies. "Creaturely poetics," as formulated by Anat Pick, is the latest attempt at harmonizing and overcoming the inherent tension between the opposite poles of the (nonhuman) figure and the creature by conflating the two into a single identity—conceived as both beautiful and vulnerable—whose essential unity is guaranteed by its underlying universal, quasi-theological character.[30] It is indeed a theological framework that underlies the nature of the symbol as a unity of spirit and matter, and for Pick symbolic form takes the shape of a postsecular unity of the beautiful with the vulnerable or the creaturely.[31] In contrast to the symbolic form that underlies Pick's "creaturely poetics," the proper form for the articulation of the infrahuman is *allegory*.[32] For in allegory, as Walter Benjamin maintained, figural meaning remains separated from creaturely existence by an insurmountable abyss:

> The greater the significance, the greater the subjection to death, because death digs most deeply the jagged line of demarcation between physical nature and significance. But if nature has always been subject to the power of death, it is also true that it has always been allegorical. Significance and death both come to fruition in historical development, just as they are closely linked as seeds in the creature's graceless state of sin.[33]

According to Benjamin, allegory exposes the essential gap between "significance" [Bedeutung] and "physical nature" [Physis], whose expressions are, respectively, "historical development" and "the creature's graceless state of sin." By establishing a conventional and arbitrary association between abstract meaning and the natural object that designates it, allegory lays bare the artificiality of the symbolic unity of spirit and matter, significance and physical nature, historical development and creaturely life, and thereby resists the sublation of lived experience to a totalizing figural scheme. Whereas the symbol imposes unity, immediacy, and harmony on the opposite poles of historical development and creaturely life—encapsulating what Benjamin calls the "idea of fulfilled historical time"[34]—in allegory these two poles remain separated by the "jagged line of demarcation" drawn by death, foreclosing the possibility of a momentary transcendence of time in the symbol that Max Pensky has adequately termed "the ironic expression of timelessness within the temporal."[35]

The form of temporality that thus emerges in allegory is not that of a teleological historical process, but is instead a manifestation of *natural history*. To be sure, natural history in Benjamin's idiosyncratic use of the term does not only designate an empty temporal continuum, but a reduction of the historical event to "spatial inauthenticity," where it comes to be encoded in a form that appears ill suited for the reception of its primary signification.[36] The allegorical displacement of historical events onto aesthetic phenomena does not imply a flight from historical time or obliviousness to history. On the contrary, the spatialization of the historical marks a specific kind of historical awareness that invests itself in figures whose meaning remains transitory and dependent upon the specific social and cultural context from within which they were articulated.

As an allegorical figure, the infrahuman is predicated on this displacement of a set of sociohistorical conditions onto aesthetic-natural phenomena. Exemplifying the spatialization of the historical, the animality of the Jew is emblematic of the cultural and historical conditions that have shaped the lives of Jews in exile and that have inscribed themselves on the very physicality of the Jew. Yet within the realm of allegory, this figural construction of Jewish identity as animality is disrupted by the emergence of that which refuses to assimilate into significance and historical development: the creaturely, whose emblematic expression is found in Shylock's "I am not well." Here the articulation of Jewish experience does not only bear witness to the unbridgeable gap from figural expression, but also threatens to unravel the figural construction of Jewish identity as animality. Jewish life thus emerges as a deficient mode of existence in which animality serves as a mark of insufficient humanity, yet at the same time this animality itself is punctuated with the dimension of the creaturely, the residue that does not assimilate into a figural construction.[37] This deficient mode of existence that is neither human nor animal recurs in subsequent depictions of the infrahuman in modern Jewish literature: Heine's Jew, "a dog with doggish thoughts," transforms into a prince on the Sabbath; Abramovitsh's mare likewise appears as a dumb animal "chewing hay, calm, nonchalant, without a care in the world,"[38] but its suffering is the suffering of Jews in the Diaspora; in Bialik's poem, the spiders on the wall provide testimony on what took place in the pogrom; and in Kafka's "Animal in the Synagogue," a marten-like creature attends the religious services in the synagogue like a practicing Jew, but it does so only because it is always startled anew by the intrusion of people into its natural habitat.

In light of such examples it is important to note that the recalcitrant form of experience that is synonymous with creaturely life is not an expression of "Jewish Thought" (in the sense of traditional forms of Jewish learning), nor should it be confused with any doctrine internal to Judaism. Instead, the articulation of the creaturely designates a notion of raw experience whose origins are found in Pauline theology. In Romans 8:19–23, Paul explicitly identifies the creaturely with a vision of earthly nature devoid of divine redemption:

> For the creation waits in eager expectation for the children of God to be revealed. For the creation was subjected to frustration, not by its own choice, but by the will of the one who subjected it, in hope that the creation itself will be liberated from its bondage to decay and brought into the freedom and glory of the children of God. For we know that the whole creation has been groaning as in the pains of childbirth right up to the present time. Not only so, but we ourselves, who have the first fruits of the Spirit, sigh inwardly as we wait eagerly for our adoption to sonship, the redemption of our bodies.

As the dimension common to both human and nonhuman existence, the creaturely implies a subjection to futility and decay, that is, to a natural-historical trajectory in the Benjaminian sense.[39] However, as Eric Santner perceptively observed, in Pauline writings the "bondage to decay" also implies a certain relation to Jewish law: "this is a relation in which law not only regulates and pacifies but also agitates and excites (to transgressive enjoyment)."⁴⁰ The transgressive enjoyment that operates in the empty time of natural-historical progression is triggered by the authoritative voice of Jewish law that commands and thereby arouses sinful passions:

> What then shall we say? That the law is sin? By no means! Yet if it had not been for the law, I would not have known sin. For I would not have known what it is to covet if the law had not said, "You shall not covet." But sin, seizing an opportunity through the commandment, produced in me all kinds of covetousness. For apart from the law, sin lies dead. I was once alive apart from the law, but when the commandment came, sin came alive and I died. The very commandment that promised life proved to be death to me. (Romans 7:7–10)

When viewed in light of these essential Pauline terms, the Benjaminian dichotomy between "historical development" and the "creature's graceless state of sin" assumes its full conceptual and theological dimensions. For it is only with the advent of the Jewish law that death emerges as a "jagged line of demarcation" between "significance" and "physical nature," and not, as Benjamin believed, with a postlapsarian state.⁴¹ From a traditional Christian perspective, natural history would then be the form of temporality synonymous with the Jewish experience of time, and creatureliness would appear as the outcome of "bondage" to Jewish law. Paradoxically, precisely these denigrated aspects of Jewish life re-emerge in Shakespeare's account of Shylock and in modern Jewish literature as disruptive elements in the figural construction of Jewish identity as animality. They point not to the suppressed humanity of the Jew, but to his exposure to a law in a state of exception. In this exposure of the Jew as a creature in a "graceless state of sin," the universal dimensions of Jewish suffering are ultimately revealed. For in the final account, Jewish life comes into its own not in the irreconcilable hostility to Christian society and morality, but in creaturely groaning—Shylock's "I am not well"—that encapsulates the wish to be liberated from the bondage to natural history. This primordial messianic impulse occupies a peculiar position within the Christian worldview, since it does not properly belong in the Christian faith, and yet it is universally shared by all of creation. Benjamin, in his essay on Kafka, called it "the natural prayer of the soul."[42] Moreover, within this constellation, the Jew occupies a special position with respect to the rest of creation: since he partakes in creaturely life and yet is able to express himself in language, he becomes—to borrow yet another phrase from Benjamin that he employed in a different context—the "advocate for all creatures, and at the same time their highest embodiment."[43] As the advocate of the creaturely, the complaint uttered by Shylock and formulated in human words is in reality an articulation of the silent language of nature, providing a glimpse into the profane yearning for redemption shared by all of creation.

The infrahuman thus emerges as the site in which the unresolved theological position of Jewish existence from a Christian perspective is allegorized as a deficient form of animality—which is at the same time construed as the highest embodiment of the creaturely. As previously mentioned, the infrahuman does not challenge prevalent anthropocentric notions, nor does it simply constitute an anti-Semitic stereotype. Although at no point is the humanity of the Jew asserted, his animality is posited as a political-theological difference rather than a racial or biological difference. Indeed, it is precisely by virtue of a latent theological dimension that the Jew's political plight assumes its universal appeal as the sigh of the oppressed creature. In this sense, the analysis of the infrahuman in modern Jewish literature provides an alternative account to the conventional debate on the "Jewish Question"—a public debate that preoccupied prominent European intellectuals, philosophers, and jurists during the eighteenth and nineteenth centuries, and dealt with the prospect of the moral and intellectual rehabilitation of the Jews and their integration into non-Jewish society. By contrast, the infrahuman exposes a relation between Judaism and European culture and society that is marked by attentiveness to the dehumanized aspects of Jewish existence. With the infrahuman, the artificiality of the figural construction of Jewish identity is laid bare not in the name of an abstract, universal ideal of humanity—that is, not by something foreign to Christianity itself—but in the name of creaturely life, a notion that emerges from the very foundations of European culture and society.

At this point it may be reasonably argued, following Andrew Benjamin, that the creaturely does not refer to authentic Jewish experience but simply to another figure in which "the constitution of an identity ... has a specific function that is predominantly external to the concerns of the identity itself."

While this argument may be true as far as the specifically Jewish content of experience is concerned, it does not apply to the general validity of experience as such. Here we must bear in mind that in the *Merchant of Venice* the reduction of Shylock to a creaturely estate is not an outcome of a theological argument between Christians and Jews, but of an exposure to sovereign power in a state of exception. Although the general validity of the experience of creaturely abandonment and bare life in a state of exception is by no means restricted to Jews, the Jew nevertheless emerges as an emblematic figure on which the effects of sovereign power in a state of exception are subtly registered. This is due not only to the Jew's marginal social status within European society, but also to the theological image of Jews within Christianity as quintessentially creaturely, which would allow for a relatively easy transition from the sphere of theology to the sphere of modern citizenship. Thus, instead of depicting a struggle for emancipation, the literature of the infrahuman depicts the individual's futile attempts to extricate himself from the empty time of natural-historical progression; instead of the prospect of integration, acculturation, or assimilation, it offers an experience of abandonment and degradation. By exploring this hitherto overlooked vector of modern Jewish existence, the infrahuman allows us to reimagine the lived experience of Jews in the modern world before World War II.

THE FIRST CHAPTER, "Life in The Valley: The Jewish Dog in Heinrich Heine's 'Prinzessin Sabbat,' " deals with the late writings of Heinrich Heine in which a "Jewish" persona emerges in response to Heine's acute physical collapse. This late persona is distinguished both from Heine's previous "Greek" persona and from the "Nazarene" mentality with which he polemicized. Emblematized in the figure of a dog in the poem "Prinzessin Sabbat," Heine's late adoption of a "Jewish" identity marks a perspective that is reconciled with the inevitable transience of happiness, yet remains opposed to the "Nazarene" denial of corporeality and earthly pleasures.

The second chapter, "A Radical Advocacy: Suffering Jews and Animals in S. Y. Abramovitsh's *Di Kliatshe*," focuses on the novella *Di kliatshe* by S. Y. Abramovitsh (also known as "Mendele the Book Peddler"), in which the dehumanized figure of a mare is invoked as an allegory for the political and social conditions of Jews in tsarist Russia. By reconstructing the social and historical context in which this work emerged, I show how it came to promote a radical ethical position on the question of human and animal suffering, and engaged in a subtle literary dialogue with non-Jewish authors.

The third chapter, "Into the Bowels of the Earth: Prophecy and Animality in The Poetry of Hayim Nachman Bialik and Uri Zvi Greenberg," addresses the tension between prophecy and nature in Bialik's pogrom poem "In The City of Killings," and in Greenberg's *House Dog*. In both cases the Zionist poet-prophet delves into the profane realm of nature in order to extract from it a redemptive historical meaning for the Jewish collective. In the context of Bialik's pogrom poem, this prophetic function affirms the irreducible humanity of the poet, whereas in Greenberg's poems this prophetic function is the hallmark of the "house dog," contrasted with the figure of the diasporic "street dog."

The fourth chapter, "At Home in a Distorted Life: The Dog as a Constellation in The Work of Franz Kafka," explores the role of the dog in Kafka's writings and its relation to Jewish identity. In Kafka's writings the figure of the dog is associated with a subjection to an obscure law, the product of an ambiguous desire. Kafka's protagonists, who are burdened by the impenetrable mystery that surrounds their existence, ultimately embrace undisclosedness of meaning as a form of earthly redemption in which their humanity is reconciled with animal life.

In the final chapter, "After The Holocaust: Responses to The Infrahuman in The Writings of S. Y. Agnon and Paul Celan," I chart the development of the infrahuman in Jewish literature after World War II in response to Kafka's legacy, by focusing on S. Y. Agnon's novel *Only Yesterday* and on Paul Celan's "Meridian" speech. Both works explore a relation between artifice and the creature, and outline the terms in which the dichotomy between history and nature will be staged in Jewish literature after the Holocaust.

1 LIFE IN THE VALLEY
The Jewish Dog in Heinrich Heine's "Prinzessin Sabbat"

HEINRICH HEINE HAS OFTEN BEEN CITED as an exemplary figure of "Jewish self-hatred" in nineteenth-century European culture, partly due to the twofold nature of his alienation from his Jewish identity. On the one hand, Heine seems to have entertained a negative stereotypical view of the Eastern, non-German Jew as a dirty wretch, speaking a bastardized form of German; on the other, he also attacked assimilated German Jews, intellectuals such as Eduard Gans and Ludwig Börne, who like Heine himself opted for a formal conversion to Christianity over a nominal belief in Judaism. Whereas the negative image of the Eastern Jew had been part and parcel of the cultural legacy of German anti-Semitism during the first half of the nineteenth century,[1] Heine's originality came to be expressed in the terms by which he decried the political, aesthetic, and religious attitudes of assimilated Jewish intellectuals. The most paradigmatic example of this intellectualized form of "Jewish self-hatred" can be found in Heine's famous distinction between "Hellenes" and "Nazarenes" in his essay on Ludwig Börne. By reviewing the terms in which this distinction came to be formulated, and in light of subsequent developments in Heine's poetry, I would like to reassess the somewhat simplistic designation of "Jewish self-hatred" with which Heine has often been credited, and arrive at a radically new formulation of Jewish identity that he espoused during the last years of his life.

In his book on Jewish self-hatred, Sander Gilman essentially describes this phenomenon in terms of a substitution of lived experience for a figural construction of identity: "self-hatred results from the outsiders' acceptance of the mirage of themselves generated by their reference group—that group in society which they see as defining them—as a reality."[2] Self-hatred thus appears as the outcome of a demand for assimilation that is based on a suppression of one's own lived experience. However, once the outsider assumes the demand for identification with the figural construction whose function remains external to the concerns of his own identity, he encounters a resistance in the form of a hidden qualification that emerges from the reference group: namely, that his identity is nothing but a contrived attempt, an artificial façade that betrays his ineradicable otherness. This double bind can be summed up with the convergence of two contradictory demands—"Be like me! You can't be like me!"—that assimilated German Jews have experienced throughout the nineteenth century.

In Heine's case, this ineradicable Jewish difference emerged in various literary and critical contexts, such as in August von Platen's *Der Romantische Oedipus* (*The Romantic Oedipus*) (1829), in which Platen sarcastically remarked about Heine: "I would be his friend, but not his lover; for his kisses stink of garlic."[3] The reference to the stench of garlic was a commonplace association with the image of the "Jew" in nineteenth-century German culture, and it also appeared in Heine's own depiction of Polish Jews in the essay *Über Polen* (*On Poland*) from 1822.[4] Along with such ad hominem attacks was the more general accusation directed against Heine and other assimilated German Jews, that they represent a specifically "Jewish" direction in culture and politics whose aim is to undermine the religious and political order in Germany. Along these lines, in 1836 Wolfgang Menzel listed the four qualities that he identified as quintessentially "Jewish": "the idea of a universal concept of man that opposes nationalism; the advocacy of a revolutionary future for Europe aimed at the destruction of the class system; opposition to religion and stress on materialism; and immorality."[5] Such political, religious, and cultural attitudes were deemed to be markedly "un-German" in character, and were, in fact, closely associated with the idea of France and with the values of the French Revolution.[6] On the other side of the debate, Menzel's Jewish opponents actually agreed with Menzel's assessment of writers such as Börne and Heine, except that they laid stress on their baptism as the act that separated them from the core values of Judaism. In this perspective, Heine's political and cultural positions were not indicative of his Jewish worldview, but rather of a Christian mindset.[7] Such conflicting views on the nature of Heine's "Judaism" ultimately contributed to the problematic status of his work within modern Hebrew literature and the modern Jewish literary canon.[8]

Heine came to formulate his political, religious, and aesthetic positions against such repeated attacks on his Jewish identity, which compelled him, in a way, to produce a public persona that would be distinct from German, Jewish, and assimilated Jewish mentalities. Thus, during the 1830s and the 1840s Heine embraced a "Hellenic" persona that he explicitly contrasted with a "Nazarene" tendency in Western culture. To be sure, the fascination with Hellenism was already evident in Heine's first essay "Die Romantik" ("Romanticism") from 1820, in which his perception of antiquity was informed by the basic distinction between the sensuality of Greek culture and the spiritualized culture of Christians.[9] This distinction continued to reverberate in various forms throughout Heine's writings. It came to be expressed in his poems, as, for example, in "Die Götter Griechenlands" ("The Gods of Greece," 1827), in which the poet mourns the passing of the Greek gods and decries "the new sad gods . . . that gloat over woe, in sheep's clothing of meekness."[10] But more importantly, the distinction between "Hellene" and "Nazarene" also carried subtle philosophical resonances shaped by Heine's encounter with Saint-Simonism, a philosophically based utopian doctrine that called for the "rehabilitation of matter," and involved the emancipation of the sensual-material dimensions of human existence. This philosophical doctrine influenced Heine's analysis of current affairs in Germany in two of his most famous critical works, *Die Romantische Schule* (*The Romantic School*, 1835) and *Zur Geschichte der Religion und Philosophie in Deutschland* (*On the History of Philosophy and Religion in Germany*, 1835). Both essays revolve around the contrast between a sensual, "Hellenic" direction in culture and a spiritual, "Nazarene" conception.[11] Yet the distinction between "Hellene" and "Nazarene" appeared in its most fully articulated form in Heine's essay on Ludwig Börne, published in 1840:

> As in his statements about Goethe, Börne also always betrayed his Nazarene narrowness in his judgment of other writers. I say Nazarene in order to employ neither the expression "Jewish" nor "Christian," although both expressions are synonymous for me and I use them not to denote a belief but rather a temperament. "Jews" and "Christians" are for me quite homologous words, in contrast to "Hellene," with which I also do not mean a particular people, but a mentality and viewpoint both congenital and cultivated. In this connection I would like to say: all men are either Jews or Hellenes, men with ascetic drives, hostile to images, and addicted to spiritualization, or men

with a realistic nature, with a cheerful view of life, and proud of evolving. Thus there were Hellenes in German pastors' families, and Jews who were born in Athens, possibly descended from Theseus.[12]

As can be seen here, the distinction between "Hellene" and "Nazarene" was clearly an attempt to conflate the mentalities of Christian and Jew, bind them both together under the rubric of "Nazarene" mentality. However, in the Börne essay this distinction also serves to distinguish Heine's cultural and political sensibilities from those of the assimilated Jew, personified in Börne. Like Heine, Börne was a converted German Jew who had been living in Parisian exile. Both men belonged in a community of German exiles and were committed to revolutionary politics and to the critique of prevailing forms of government in Germany. The anti-royalist tendency they both shared was hardly surprising, since as Jews they enjoyed equality under the law during the Napoleonic occupation of Germany (1806–1814). Under Napoleon, the region around Heine's native Düsseldorf was renamed the Grand Duchy of Berg, a French state with a written constitution, and Heine was able to attend a lycée on the French model. Börne, who was older than Heine, was able to complete a doctoral degree in *Kameralistik* (administrative science) in 1808, due to relief of Jewish disabilities under Napoleon. In 1811 he obtained a position as a police actuary in Frankfurt, but was dismissed in 1815 after the reinstitution of Jewish disabilities in the post-Napoleonic era. Shortly after the July Revolution of 1830 Börne moved to Paris, where he became increasingly radicalized, abandoning his liberal monarchism for republicanism, and began publishing articles in which he advocated a German republican revolution. His witty invectives against the political establishment in Germany established him as the leading spokesman for German radical political activists and for thousands of German emigrés in Paris, who were mostly comprised of artisans and workingmen.

Heine, too, was sharply critical of the political establishment in Germany, but he rejected the republicanism preached by Börne. Apart from his preference for monarchies, Heine believed that in the years following the French Revolution, French character and culture had become essentially republican in nature—that is, irreverent and disrespectful toward traditional forms of political authority. The Germans, on the other hand, still paid respect to royalty. This essential cultural difference,

Heine argued, rendered any attempt to institute republican forms of government in Germany futile and obsolete. The republican idea was compelling for German radicals like Börne who would doggedly pursue its consequences regardless of its relevance to the actual political and cultural conditions in Germany.[13]

When considered in the context of European culture and politics of the 1830s, Heine's distinction between "Hellene" and "Nazarene" in the Börne essay implies an opposition between two different types of revolutionary worldviews. Whereas the dogmatic view of the "Nazarene" implies a self-abnegating, single-minded pursuit of an idea for its own sake, the "Hellene" embraces his sensuality, and is not restricted by a traditional ethical code or by the confines of social etiquette. Accordingly, Heine envisioned the dimensions of "Hellenic" revolutionary activity not in terms of a narrowly defined political sphere, but as encompassing every dimension of human experience. For him, politics would ultimately inform a religion that will propagate liberation from the spiritual tutelage of traditional churches, espouse an artistic practice that will celebrate the sensual dimension of human life, and cultivate a morality that will be free from hypocrisy.[14] While the dualistic worldview of the "Nazarenes" consists in the rigid separation of spirit and flesh, a tenacious adherence to abstract principles, a self-righteous denial of sensual pleasures, and a repression of sexual desire, the opposing mentality of "Hellenic" monism embraces sensual fulfillment, aesthetic cultivation, and political emancipation as corresponding aspects of a single source of human experience and knowledge.

In these terms, Heine's critique of a "Nazarene" mentality is important, not as an early manifestation of Jewish self-hatred, but as one of the first sustained attempts at analyzing the phenomenon of self-hatred. By identifying the basic drive of the "Nazarene" mentality as the abnegation of lived experience for the sake of an abstract ideal, Heine anticipated Gilman's subsequent definition of self-hatred as the acceptance of the individual's mirage of himself generated by the reference group. For Heine, to be "Greek" meant to ultimately reconcile figure and experience, whereas for the self-abnegating "Nazarene" the figural construction of identity will always overshadow lived experience. Paradoxically, the only way that Heine could articulate such a critique of the self-hating, assimilated Jew was by projecting a "Greek" figure in which the gap between the figural construction of identity and lived experience would no longer exist. It is precisely this redeeming "Greek" figure that is abandoned in Heine's late works.

IN AN ARTICLE published in the *Augsburger Allgemeine Zeitung* in April 1849, Heine publicly announced that he was suffering from a chronic debilitating illness that had led him to forsake his former "Greek" persona and return to "Judaism":

> I am no longer a divine biped, nor am I "the freest German after Goethe," as Ruge once called me in healthier days; nor am I the Great Pagan No. 2 who was likened to Dionysus wreathed in vine leaves while my colleague Goethe, the Great Pagan No. 1, was given the title "Jupiter of the Grand Duchy of Weimar"; nor am I a well-fleshed Hellene who enjoys his life and smiles down on melancholy Nazarenes—all I am now is a poor Jew sick unto death, an emaciated image of wretchedness, an unhappy man.[15]

Here Heine quite clearly frames the emergence of his late "Jewish" persona against the distinction between "Hellene" and "Nazarene." Given the close association between these terms, the question arises in what ways Heine's late return to "Judaism" is related to the "Nazarene" mentality that he rejected in his earlier "Greek" phase. Surprisingly, critical literature has failed to address this relation. If Heine's late adoption of "Judaism" was identical with a "Nazarene" mentality, then this would imply a concession to the very attitudes against which Heine sought to distinguish himself as a poet and thinker. On the other hand, if "Nazarenism" is not identical to Heine's late "Judaism," then the question remains in what ways they differ.

As we come to address this question, we must take into account that Heine's renunciation of his "Hellenic" persona was by no means an ideological move on his part, but a result of a debilitating physical condition. Or to put it in other words, the demise of the "Hellenic" persona took place because the "Hellenic" pursuit of a comprehensive sensual fulfillment implied a modicum of physical health that was lost to Heine in 1848. Heine's health had never been robust: in 1832, at the age of thirty-five, he developed a paralysis of two fingers of the left hand from which he never recovered; from 1837 through 1841 he suffered from intermittent spells of vision disorders; during 1842 and 1843 he suffered from a facial palsy and from facial paralysis.[16] In April 1843 he wrote to his brother Maximilian that "almost the whole of my left side [of the face] is paralyzed as regards feeling, the mobility of the muscles is still preserved.... Moreover the left eye is feeble and hurts, does not agree with the right, and this causes a confusion of sight which is much more intolerable than the darkness of full blindness."[17] Heine continued to suffer from such fits of visual failure, facial palsy, and partial paralysis, and by 1847 his condition had become so severe that in a letter to Caroline Jaubert he remarked that "the beautiful ladies turn away when I pass them on the streets; my closed eyes (the right one can only open up to an eighth), my hollow cheeks, my wild beard, my staggering walk, all these give me an appearance of a dying man that suits me perfectly!"[18]

It is not clear whether Heine's condition was a result of syphilis,[19] multiple sclerosis,[20] or a brain tumor,[21] as various scholars have suggested. But the illness took a turn for the worse in May 1848, as Heine became completely and permanently paraplegic. In early July 1848, he wrote to his publisher, Julius Campe: "for a week I have been completely paralyzed, so that I am always in my armchair or in bed. My legs are like cotton wool and I am carried like a child. Terrible cramps. My right hand is beginning to die, and God knows whether I can write to you. Dictating is painful from the paralysis of my jaws. My blindness is the least of my troubles."[22] In September of that year he wrote to his brother: "for 48 hours I have been rolling about in the most awful cramps ... which have now reached the hands ... which bring about contortions and distortions. [. . .] My lips are paralyzed like my feet, the tools of eating are also paralyzed as well as the channels of excretion. I can neither chew nor shit, and have to be fed like a bird."[23] In this pitiful state Heine was to spend the remainder of his life, paralyzed, blind, and suffering from terrible cramps, in his "mattress-grave" ("Matratzengruft"), which he described as "a grave without rest, a death without the advantage of the dead, who do not have to pay money, write letters or books."[24]

Under such an acute physical condition, it was no longer possible for Heine to sustain a "Hellenic" persona that involved a distinctive "cheerful view of life"—as he wrote in the Börne essay. In the afterword to his volume of poetry *Romanzero* (written in 1851, after his physical collapse), Heine presented a symbolic account of the physical collapse he had suffered in 1848, which was likewise couched in terms of a departure from a "Greek" persona:

> In May, 1848, on the day when I went out for the last time, that I bade farewell to the sacred idols whom I worshiped in my days of good fortune. I dragged myself painfully as far as the Louvre, and nearly dropped exhausted as I trod the lofty room where the blessed goddess of beauty, our beloved lady of Milo, stands on her pedestal. I lay a long time at her feet, and wept so bitterly that it would have moved a stone. The goddess looked kindly down on me, but hopelessly, as if she would have said, "Do you not see I have no arms, and cannot help you?"[25]

While it would be safe to assume that this picturesque account of a collapse at the foot of the Venus de Milo is far from authentic, Heine nevertheless delivers here a powerful allegory of his departure from the "Greek" persona. To begin with, this departure takes place in the realm of art, the Louvre, at the foot of the goddess of beauty. The collapse at the foot of the statue symbolizes the poet's inability to attain the "Greek" ideal of aesthetic beauty and sensuality, but at the same time it subtly registers the futility of such an attempt. The sentence uttered by the stone goddess—"do you not see I have no arms, and cannot help you?"—implies an essential identity between statue and poet. Their "Greekness" is a thing of the past, irrevocably lost. The deteriorated physical condition of the statue is equated with the poet's deteriorated health; both are, in fact, personifications of ruined Greek beauty. Heine's late "Jewish" persona is thus not a moral or ideological antithesis to his former "Greek" self, but rather a mentality or a worldview that emerges at the point in which the "Greek" persona unravels and collapses altogether under the burden of natural history.

In his autobiographical *Geständnisse* (*Confessions*), published in 1854, Heine came to formulate the narrative of his illness as a fall from a meaningful historical life into a natural-historical trajectory with a clearly evident Pauline mindset:

> But the expenses of playing the role of a God, for whom it were unseemly to go in tatters, and who is sparing neither of body nor of purse, are enormous. To play such a role respectably, two things are above all requisite—much money and robust health. Alas! it happened that one day—in February 1848—both these essentials failed

me, and my divinity was put to halt. [. . .] Like many other divinities of that revolutionary period, I was compelled to abdicate ignominiously, and to return to human private life. [. . .] I came back into the lowly cradle of God's creatures [Ich kehrte zurück in die niedre Hürde der Gottesgeschöpfe], and again I bowed in homage to the almighty power of a Supreme Being, who directs the destinies of this world, and who for the future shall also regulate my earthly affairs. The latter, during the time I had been my own Providence, had drifted into anxious confusion, and I was glad to turn them over to a celestial superintendent, who with his omniscience really manages them much better. [. . .] I am no longer careful for the general good; I no longer ape the Deity; and with pious humility I have notified my former dependents that I am only a miserable human wretch, a sighing creature [eine seufzende Kreatur] that has naught more to do with governing the world.[26]

Significantly, even though Heine's physical collapse took place in May 1848, in this passage Heine dates it back to February of that year so as to coincide with the revolutionary events in Paris that led to the overthrow of King Louis-Philippe. By comparing himself to "other divinities of that revolutionary period" who were compelled to abdicate and return to a "human private sphere," Heine indicated where his political affinities lay: with a champion of constitutional monarchy such as François Guizot, the French prime minister whose political career ended in the aftermath of the February Revolution. For Heine, the "godlike" existence that Guizot had led was a life in the public sphere that was marked by a commitment to an autonomous shaping of historical events. Heine identified a similar commitment in his own revolutionary approach to the improvement of human nature during his "Greek" phase. Yet it was precisely this autonomous capacity to lead a meaningful historical life that was irreparably compromised after Heine's physical collapse. Subsequently, he writes about himself as being reduced from an active, autonomous historical agent to the passive position of a mere creature whose fate lay entirely in the hands of God. The reference to the "sighing creature" [seufzende Kreatur]—that is, to creation suffering under the burden of futility and decay—invokes a theological context, but Heine writes about God with little reverence or devotion. Here, as elsewhere in Heine's late writings, God is mostly imagined as a being essentially no different from the poet himself, endowed with markedly human characteristics, who is nevertheless infinitely powerful. In his late poems Heine rebukes God, presents questions and demands, and blasphemes. Indeed, in Heine's conversations with God, the emphasis is laid on the creature's suffering rather than on the glory of the Creator. It seems that, for Heine, God serves as a poetic ruse by which he came to explore the various aspects of creaturely life. The figure with which he identified was not God, but the sighing creature from Romans 8:23.

Aside from invoking a theological context, Heine's reference to the "sighing creature" also alludes to the radical critique of institutionalized religion. The phrase "seufzende Kreatur" refers not only to Pauline theology, but also to Karl Marx's famous statement on religion in his *Critique of Hegel's "Philosophy of Right"* (1844):

> Die Religion ist der Seufzer der bedrängten Kreature, das Gemüt einer herzlosen Welt, wie sie der Geist geistloser Zustände ist. Sie ist das Opium des Volkes.
>
> Religion is the sigh of the oppressed creature, the heart of a heartless world and the soul of soulless conditions. It is the opium of the people.[27]

Marx's statement itself contains a reference to Heine's Börne essay, in which Heine characterized the compensation that religion offers for the "Nazarene" abnegation of the senses as "soporific drops" of "spiritual opium" (geistiges Opium).[28] The religious sensibility that Heine cultivated toward the end of his life could hardly be seen as offering such a compensation for the decay and futility associated with natural history. Rather, Heine's religion was a "natural" religion that occurred within a theological context, but outside the purview of institutionalized religion, and was therefore entirely undogmatic in character. In this sense, Heine's religion, as Ritchie Robertson remarked, "was home-made, not the property of any church or denomination, and not wholly discontinuous with the beliefs he had explored earlier."[29] Its universal validity did not stem from an appeal to spirituality or to a redeemed state of human existence, but from an acknowledgment of the irreconcilable gap between "significance" and "physical nature." In his turn to religion, Heine replaced the symbolic unity of his "Greek" vision of the world, which projected a state of human fulfillment on a trajectory of historical development, with an allegorical vision of the world as a vale of suffering, a dimension of transience and futility hopelessly separated from any form of historical or religious consummation. Heine's religion therefore did not offer an alleviation of earthly suffering, but merely afforded an opportunity for the creature to voice its complaints. The articulation of these complaints was perceived by Heine to be a quintessential "Jewish" matter. His "Jewish" persona therefore does not belong in an institutionalized "Nazarene" dogma, but in a profane religion of the creature whose sighs have acquired a distinctive poetic quality.

IN THE EPIGRAPH to the final cycle of poems in *Romanzero*, titled "Hebräische Melodien" ("Hebrew Melodies"), Heine presents the tenets of his newly espoused "Jewish" outlook in two emblematic stanzas:

> O laß nicht ohne Lebensgenuß
> Dein Leben verfließen!
> Und bist du sicher vor dem Schuß,
> So laß sie nur schießen.
>
> Fliegt dir das Glück vorbei einmal,
> So faß es am Zipfel,
> Auch rat ich dir, baue dein
>   Hüttchen im Tal
> Und nicht auf dem Gipfel.

> O let your life not drain away
> Without having tasted life's
>   enjoyment!
> And when you are safe from harm,
> Let them shoot at their pleasure.
> If happiness should pass you by,
> Then grab it by the tail.
> Build your little hut in the valley,
>   I say,
> And not on the peak.
> ("Hebrew Melodies," 97;
>   translation modified)

In these lines the poet implores the reader to catch whatever enjoyment he can in life, using rhetorical means of injunction and advice ("O laß nicht" . . . "Auch rat ich dir" . . . "O let not" . . . "I say"). Since it is possible to infer from the title that the speaker here is a Jew, the similarity to Heine's former "Greek" persona is striking as the poet seems to retain a commitment to the pursuit of happiness and sensual pleasure. However, whereas the "Greek" persona advocated the cause of individual happiness and enjoyment as part of a comprehensive revolution in human consciousness, the "Jewish" persona seems to retreat into a corner of good living amidst the chaos of the world, advocating enjoyment solely for its own sake. To be sure, this doctrine is not directed against a "Greek" mentality, but against the mentality of those who choose to build their "little hut" (Hüttchen) on the "peak" (Gipfel). These two key terms—"hut" and "peak"—are unmistakable hallmarks of German romantic poetry, made famous in Goethe's "Wandrers Nachtlied" (1780) which begins with the line "Über allen Gipfeln" (above all summits); and in Novalis's *Hymnen an die Nacht* (*Hymns to the Night*, 1800) in which the poet builds "huts of peace" (Hütten des Friedens) on the "mountain frontier of the world" (Grenzgebürge der Welt).[30] However, both allusions to romantic poetry are satirical: Goethe rhymed the word "Gipfeln" with the equally lofty "Wipfeln" (treetops), whereas Heine debases the metaphor by rhyming "Gipfel" with a "tail of a coat" ("Zipfel"). Similarly, Novalis's sublime "huts of peace" built on the "mountain frontier of the world" are reduced to "a little hut in the valley." Far from being an expression of a "joyous philosophy,"[31] Heine's metaphors provide us with a critical reaction to German romantic poets whose "Nazarene" world-abnegation now served as a fresh target for his "Jewish" scorn.

What precisely were the romantic ideas against which Heine reacted? Here it would be useful to consider a principal work that implicitly served as a target for Heine's criticism: Novalis's *Hymns to the Night*. Novalis's work revolves on an epiphany that the poet experienced while lamenting the death of his beloved Sophie. The nature of his revelation was such that he was suddenly able to renounce the world and its riches as well as its woes: "Away fled the earthly glory, and with it my mourning—the longing flowed together into a new, unfathomable world."[32] The terms in which Novalis articulated his romantic vision were in fact inversions of common Enlightenment metaphors such as illumination, forward movement, and clarity. Instead, Novalis affirmed mystery, unfathomable depths, stillness, and primordial night: "he who has tasted it, he who has stood on the mountain frontier of the world, and looked across into the new land, into the abode of the Night—verily he turns not again into the tumult of the world, into the land where dwells the Light in ceaseless unrest."[33] Ultimately, the poet attains peace and is able to reunite with his beloved in eternity, finding strength in the knowledge that he will also die one day. But in the meantime, and for as long as he still lives, the poet must stand on the "mountain frontier of the world," and on these heights build for himself "huts of peace" from which he will continue to long and love, and serenely gaze across at the tumultuous world below, until "the welcomest of all hours"[34]—the hour of death—arrives. Novalis's use of the metaphor of a "mountain frontier," which signals detachment from the world, refers to the realization that earthly desire and the longing for a lost love's presence can be overcome and sublated into a pious, eternal Christian love. As Novalis concludes in the final stanza of *Hymnen an die Nacht*: "down to the sweet bride, and away / to the beloved Jesus."[35] In turning away from earthly life and renouncing the world, the poet contemplates death and salvation in Christ.

From Heine's perspective, Novalis's romantic ideal of detachment from the world would have undoubtedly been seen as an expression of a "Nazarene" tendency to deny corporeality and sensual pleasures. However, this "Nazarene" detachment from the world is not only opposed to the "Greek" affirmation of sensuality, but also appears to be contrasted with the "Jewish" affirmation of existence in the "valley" of earthly life. In the epigraph to "Hebräische Melodien" Heine suggests that the attempt to detach oneself from the futility of the natural-historical trajectory would deprive one of "life's enjoyment." Only by descending into the valley of earthly life would it be possible to experience a fleeting form of happiness. "Jewish" life, then, as Heine envisions it, involves a pursuit of happiness not in order to elevate human life to a higher plane of existence, but for its own sake, against a backdrop of transience and futility. Therefore, the poet advises the reader to grab happiness "by the tail" at every opportunity. The "Jewish" pursuit of happiness is colored by a foreknowledge of its inevitable demise.

At the core of "Hebrew Melodies," then, lies a resigned awareness of the inevitable decay and futility to which all corporeal things are subjected, including the poet himself. This position is implicitly contrasted with that of Novalis, for whom man is a "lordly stranger" (Herrliche Fremdling),[36] a spiritual being who does not belong in the earthly world and who is potentially able to overcome transience. Novalis describes man's relation to the world solely in terms of detachment and mastery. Yet it is precisely in this realm of futility that Heine recommends to "build your little hut." It is where man, too, becomes subject to the pleasures as well as to the existential uncertainties that plague the animals. Building a little hut in the valley, man no longer sets himself apart from nature as a "lordly stranger," but rather becomes one with it, partaking in the suffering and enjoyment immanent to earthly life. In contrast to the sovereign, detached figure of the romantic poet, Heine invokes the pathetic figure of the "Jew," wholly embroiled in the degradations and comforts of the creature. In this respect, perhaps, Heine's "Hebrew Melodies" may also be seen as quintessentially "Jewish": in its embrace of simple, fleeting pleasures and in the refusal to accept an otherworldly redemption for earthly suffering.

THE FAMOUS OPENING POEM of "Hebrew Melodies," "Prinzessin Sabbat" ("Princess Sabbath"), presents an Arabian Nights tale about a prince changed by an evil spell into a hairy monster. However, it quickly turns out that the tale of the cursed prince serves only as an allegorical backdrop to illustrate the manifest tension between figure and lived experience informing Jewish identity:

In Arabiens Märchenbuche	In Arabia's book of fables
Sehen wir verwünschte Prinzen,	We can see cursed princes
Die zuzeiten ihre schöne	Who at times regain
Urgestalt zurückgewinnen:	their former beautiful form:
Das behaarte Ungeheuer	Once again the hairy monster
Ist ein Königsohn geworden;	Changes back into a prince;
Schmuckreich glänzend angekleidet,	Dressed in brightly jeweled splendor,
Auch verliebt die Flöte blasend.	Enamored, he plays the flute.
Doch die Zauberfrist zerrinnt,	But the magic hour expires,
Und wir schauen plötzlich wieder	And suddenly we see again
Seine königliche Hoheit	His royal highness
In ein Ungetüm verzottelt.	Degraded into a brute.
Einen Prinzen solchen Schicksals	Of a prince of such fortune
Singt mein Lied. Er ist geheißen	Sings my song. He is called
Israel. Ihn hat verwandelt	Israel. He was changed
Hexenspruch in einen Hund.	By a witch's spell into a dog.
	("Hebrew Melodies," 97–98; translation modified)

In this allegorical depiction of the Jew, Heine posits the figures of prince and dog, both separated and conjoined by an irreconcilable gap that corresponds to the contrast between the particular dignity of Jewish religion as Heine came to envision it, and the prevalent negative stereotype of the Jew. The depiction of the Jew as a dog probably testifies to the influence of Shakespeare's *The Merchant of Venice*, which Heine saw in England in 1838. After seeing the play, he recalled "the pale British beauty who wept violently at the end of the fourth act and frequently cried out, 'The poor man is wronged!' Hers was the face of the noblest Grecian cut, and her eyes were large and black. I could never forget them, those great black eyes, that wept for Shylock" ("Hebrew Melodies," 83). Ironically, in Heine's assessment of the *Merchant of Venice*, it was precisely the "Greek" sensibility that took note of the suppressed humanity of the Jew. From the "Greek" perspective, Shylock's doggishness appeared to be an essential part of his tragic fate, since it came to emblematize his human dignity in the face of the Gentile oppressor, his refusal to bow down to ill treatment and requite hatred with love. Such an obsequious "Nazarene" response would have truly rendered Shylock a lowly dog.

In the poem "Prinzessin Sabbat," the depiction of the Jew as a dog is cast in more ambiguous terms. To begin with, the Jew is not presented as a human being in the guise of a beast, with a repulsive outer shell that belies an inner human character (like Quasimodo, the hunchback of Notre Dame). No, the Jew is "a dog with doggish thoughts," thoroughly dehumanized from within and from without. He does not inhabit the intellectual and emotional world of human beings and remains a stranger to European civilization, detached from common cultural concerns:

Hund mit hündischen Gedanken,	A dog with doggish thoughts,
Kötert er die ganze Woche Durch des Lebens Kot und Kehricht, Gassenbuben zum Gespötte.	All the livelong week he piddles Through life's excrement and rubbish, Mocked by street boys. ("Hebrew Melodies," 98; translation modified)

This negative depiction of the Jew resembles in certain respects Heine's own impression of Polish Jews on a trip he took to the Eastern provinces of Germany in 1822, in which he came to describe the Polish Jews—along the lines of a widespread Jewish stereotype—as dirty, stinking wretches speaking a degenerate form of German, whose thoughts were articulated in a false, corrupt logic:

> The external appearance of the Polish Jew is terrible. A shudder runs down my spine when I remember my first experience ... of a Polish village inhabited mainly by Jews. Not even the "Berlin Weekly" under Wadzeck's editorship, stewed, physically, into a porridge, could have nauseated me as utterly as the sight of those filthy and ragged apparitions. [. . .] But compassion soon shouldered out disgust when I took a closer look at the way these people lived; when I saw the pigsty-like hovels which they inhabit and in which they jabber [*mauscheln*], pray, haggle—and are miserable. [. . .] They failed, clearly, to keep pace with European civilization, and their spiritual world sank into a morass of unedifying superstition squeezed into a thousand grotesque shapes by a super-subtle scholasticism.[37]

The figure of the Jewish dog, then, evidently appears in "Prinzessin Sabbat" as an expression of "Jewish self-hatred," a pejorative figural construction of Jewish identity that became firmly entrenched in German political, academic, and cultural institutions throughout the nineteenth century. However, the reference to the mockery of the street boys does not seem to have been part of the stereotypical depiction of Jews in German culture. It belonged in a depiction of marginal social figures in French society. Thus, for example, the scene that depicts the mockery of street boys recurs in a poem written by Charles Baudelaire around the same time as "Princess Sabbath," titled "Châtiment de l'orgueil" ("Punishment of Pride").[38] The poem is an adaptation of the story of Faust that recounts the tale of a revered doctor who fell from glory due to his "satanic pride" (orgueil satanique). Thinking himself greater than Jesus, the doctor was stricken with madness. Baudelaire's description of the madman bears a striking resemblance to Heine's depiction of the Jewish dog:

Dès lors il fut semblable aux bêtes de la rue,	Henceforth he was like the beasts in the street,
Et, quand il s'en allait sans rien voir, à travers	And when he went along, seeing nothing, across
Les champs, sans distinguer les étés des hivers,	The fields, distinguishing nor summer nor winter,
Sale, inutile et laid comme une chose usée,	Dirty, useless, ugly, like a discarded thing,
Il faisait des enfants la joie et la risée.	He was the laughing-stock, the joke, of the children.[39]

Mocked by street boys, Baudelaire's madman, like Heine's Jewish dog, is a quintessential "street beast" that occupies a threshold position between human and animal. While street boys can still claim a place on the lowest echelon of human society, the Jew and the madman appear to be located on "the other side," living on the threshold of nature and civilization, or more precisely, in a "state of nature" within the bounds of civic society. The mockery of street boys, then, is the distancing gesture that marks the boundary between human and the nonhuman. In this sense, the existence of the Jew served a specific social function, as Martha Nussbaum pointed out: the Jew "stands between us and our own animality." According to Nussbaum, privileged groups in society used to define their superior human status by comparing themselves with Jews, to whom they ascribed "certain disgust properties."[40] The mad served a similar social function in eighteenth- and early nineteenth-century France, as Michel Foucault pointed out. It was customary to put the mad on public display, and notorious spectacles were organized in Paris in which the mad played the role of actors. Their unusual behavior provoked mockery and laughter, as well as the insulting pity of the audience.[41] "Madness had become a thing to be observed," Foucault writes in *The History of Madness*, "no longer the monster within, but an animal moved by strange mechanisms, more beast than man, where all humanity had long since disappeared."[42] The animalization of the mad "dispossessed man of his humanity, not so that he might fall prey to other powers, but rather to fix him at the degree zero of his own nature."[43] This "degree zero" of human nature is precisely what Baudelaire's madman shares with Heine's Jewish dog. As literary figures, both are allegorical representations of humanity at its vanishing point.

Despite the uncanny similarity between Heine's Jewish dog and the madman in Baudelaire's poem, the figures differ in one important respect: Heine's Jew periodically regains his humanity on the Sabbath, transforming into a "human, with human feelings / With head and heart uplifted" ("Hebrew Melodies," 98; translation modified), whereas the madman's condition is permanent. In Heine's account, the two contradictory aspects of Jewish existence are not reconciled but are juxtaposed in the representation of the Jew as infrahuman. Similarly, the transformation from prince to dog and vice versa does not take place in the realm of historical reality, but in an atemporal dimension that belongs in the realm of allegory. Heine ironically contrasts this timeless dimension with the temporality of myth or the fairy tale, precisely by framing the allegory of Jewish life in the diaspora as an Arabian Nights tale. Instead of a retreat from history, at stake here is a deliberate spatialization of the historical, an encoding of the historical in a form that is ill suited for the reception of its primary signification. Thus, the legend of the cursed prince belies the historical conditions that have rendered the Jew a dog, not in order to suppress them, but to point to the irreconcilable gap between figural representation and lived experience. Just like Heine himself, the Jew is exiled from the realm of historical existence, and his fleeting humanity can be preserved only in the realm of religion.

This unresolvable tension between history and religion inherent to Jewish life corresponds to an earlier depiction of a Jewish figure in Heine's *Die Bäder von Lucca* (*The Baths of Lucca*) from 1829, in which a Jew named Moses Lump (in German: rogue), "an old Jew with a long beard and a torn cloak who cannot speak an orthographic word and is a bit mangy,"[44] undergoes a similar transformation with the coming of the Sabbath.

> A man called Moses Lump, also called Moses Lümpchen, or Lümpchen for short. He runs around during the entire week, through wind and weather with his pack on his back, in order to earn a couple of marks. When he comes home on Friday evening, he lays down his bundle and all his cares, and sits down at his table with his misshapen wife and yet more misshapen daughter, partakes with them of fish cooked in garlic sauce, sings the most splendid psalms of King David, rejoices wholeheartedly at the exodus of the children of Israel from Egypt, rejoices also that all the miscreants

who behaved wickedly toward them died in the end, that King Pharaoh, Nebuchadnezzar, Haman, Antiochus, Titus, and all such people are dead, while Lümpchen is still alive and partaking of fish with his wife and child.—And I tell you, Herr Doktor, the fish is delicious and the man is happy, he does not have to worry about culture, he sits wrapped contentedly in his religion and green dressing-gown like Diogenes in his tub, he gazes cheerfully at his candles . . .[45]

Moses Lümpchen, like the Jew from "Prinzessin Sabbat," is a deformed creature, but on the Sabbath he lays down the hunch that he has been carrying all week long and rejoices in his religious beliefs. Remarkably, Heine's description of the Jew's religion provides no positive internal content, but remains confined to the realm of the creature and of natural history. Thus, the religious blessings of the Jew simply consist in rejoicing over the fact that Jews have outlived their ancient enemies; and the Sabbath rituals are described primarily in terms of consumption of traditional Jewish food. The emphasis on Jewish food as one of the defining traits of Jewish life also occurs in "Prinzessin Sabbat":

Schalet ist die Himmelspeise,	Schalet is the food of Heaven,
Die der liebe Herrgott selber	And the recipe was given
Einst den Moses kochen lehrte	By the Lord himself to Moses
Auf dem Berge Sinai,	One fine day upon Mount Sinai,
Wo der Allerhöchste gleichfalls	On the very spot where likewise
All die guten Glaubenslehren	God revealed his moral doctrines
Und die heil'gen Zehn Gebote	And the holy Ten Commandments
Wetterleuchtend offenbarte.	In the midst of flames and lightning.
Schalet ist des wahren Gottes	Schalet is God's bread of rapture,
Koscheres Ambrosia,	It's the kosher-type ambrosia
Wonnebrot des Paradieses,	That is catered straight from Heaven;
Und mit solcher Kost verglichen	And compared with such a morsel,
Ist nur eitel Teufelsdreck	The ambrosia of the pagan
Das Ambrosia der falschen	Pseudogods of ancient Hellas,
Heidengötter Griechenlands,	Who were devils in disguise, is
Die verkappte Teufel waren.	Just a pile of devils' *dreck*.
	("Hebrew Melodies," 100–101)

As in *Die Bäder von Lucca*, the consumption of Jewish food is presented here as the authentic form of Jewish experience, independent of any intellectual or halachic influences. In these terms, Heine comes to celebrate the sensual, material aspects of Judaism as a religion that occupies a profane realm within the Christian universe. In this realm the Jew can indulge in a creaturely "enjoyment of life," which is, of course, contrasted with the Christian promise of eternal life. The enjoyment of the Sabbath is fleeting, and as the Sabbath expires the prince "lets out a sigh" (Es seufzt der Prinz) ("Hebrew Melodies," 101) before his fateful transformation. The emblematic sigh unequivocally links the material aspects of Jewish religion to the creaturely yearning for liberation from the bondage to futility and decay. Here, the crucial point is that the creaturely religion of the Jew is not reconciled with the figural construction of the Jew as a dog, but is profoundly contrasted with it. In these terms the Jew in "Prinzessin Sabbat" emerges as the infrahuman, a figure that emblematizes the unresolved gap between the experiential content of Judaism (reduced to its bare aesthetic and material components) and the figural construction of Jewish identity as abject animality. The Jewish dog, like the dying man writing from his "mattress-grave," is confined to the futility of natural-historical progression along with the rest of creation. But the "Nazarene" who remains on the path to eternal life will never know the simple pleasure of a momentary respite, an earthly happiness, salvaged from the mouth of impending catastrophe.

2 A RADICAL ADVOCACY
Suffering Jews and Animals in S. Y. Abramovitsh's *Di Kliatshe*

DI KLIATSHE (THE MARE), a Yiddish novella published in 1873 by Sholem Yankev Abramovitsh and largely forgotten today by the general Jewish reading public, marks a turning point in Haskala literature. In literary scholarship, *Di kliatshe* has been credited as one of the first works to register the failure of the Haskala to achieve integration into Russian society and secure legal rights for Jews in tsarist Russia.[1] Consequently, it paved the way for a Jewish national revival in both Yiddish and Hebrew literatures. *Di kliatshe* was also the literary piece that first established Abramovitsh as a popular writer in the Yiddish literary scene, and Abramovitsh himself has always considered it to be one of his finest works,[2] even though it was subsequently eclipsed by *The Travels of Benjamin III* (1878) and *Fishke the Lame* (1869). As Ruth Wisse has observed, one of the major obstacles in the subsequent reception of *Di kliatshe* and its inclusion in the modern Jewish literary canon was its inaccessibility to future generations of readers. In order to be appreciated and enjoyed as a literary work, *Di kliatshe* requires a knowledge of Russian political history and the history of Jews in the Pale of Settlement, as well as an intimate familiarity with the Bible, with contemporaneous Jewish and Russian literature, and with the exegetical curriculum of Lithuanian yeshivas.[3] As a result, this work fell into a "vague intermediate zone," as Dan Miron puts it, between "an artistic vitality of a classic literary work, and decrepitude through age."[4] Here I wish to revisit *Di kliatshe* not in order to reassess its impact on Zionism or Yiddishism, but to examine its role as one of the seminal works in modern Jewish literature that advocated an awareness to nonhuman suffering. Such an awareness was indicative of new social and cultural sensibilities that emerged in tsarist Russia during the 1860s and early 1870s. By allegorically depicting the Jew as a beaten mare, Abramovitsh deployed these sensibilities in order to conflate them with the fundamental uncertainty of diasporic Jewish existence.

According to Abramovitsh, *Di kliatshe* was inspired by a scene he witnessed in which a mare suffered cruel mistreatment at the hands of her Jewish master. This later, rather dubious, account of the circumstances that led Abramovitsh to write *Di kliatshe* appears in an essay published in 1908 by Sholem Aleichem, titled "Fir zenen mir gezesn" ("The Four of Us Were Sitting"), in which Sholem Aleichem documented the conversations he had with Abramovitsh during his stay at a Swiss Alpine retreat with two other celebrated figures of Jewish literature: Ben-Ami, a Zionist novelist and pamphleteer who wrote mostly in Russian, and Hayim Nachman Bialik, who in the coming years would be crowned the national poet of Hebrew revival.[5] Abramovitsh himself noted that Sholem Aleichem's account was riddled with distortions and inaccuracies.[6] However, for the purposes of the argument presented here, the factual account of the genesis of *Di kliatshe* matters less than the seminal role accorded to the literary representation of the figure of the beaten, downtrodden mare. This figure, as will become apparent, carried a special importance not only in Jewish literature but also in Russian literature of that time.

The plot of the story is set in motion by a seminal scene in which the protagonist—a young maskil named Isrolik—confronts a group of Russian bullies mistreating a weak, defenseless mare:

> I stood up and followed the turmoil, until I came to a large grassy meadow, where I witnessed a terrible scene. Young, wild bullies were harassing a skinny, haggard mare on all sides, pelting her with stones, siccing whole packs of dogs on her. [. . .] I couldn't simply stand there as a silent observer to such misdeeds. A human capacity for compassion cannot put up with such cruelty. And besides, disregarding compassion, the mare had a right to my assistance, what with my being a member in good standing of the Society for the Prevention of Cruelty to Animals [*tsa'ar ba'alei hayim*], which prohibits tormenting or hurting any living creatures, for they are flesh and blood and have the same right to live in God's world as we do. I don't want to launch into that venerable and profound discussion about human beings and beasts. Let us grant, as some maintain, that I, a human being, am the crown, the ornament, the apex of creation; that all other creatures live on this earth only for my sake,

for my needs and my pleasure, for me the acme. Let us even grant that I, the acme, am the king, the overlord, of all animals, and that they are meant to serve me, wear the yoke, and sacrifice their lives for me. Nevertheless, I felt that the mare, such an ordinary drudge, had a right to my assistance. I would have to fulfill my duty toward her, if not by compassion than [sic] at least by law.[7]

Remarkably, this passage conflates a Jewish maskilic identity with a concern for the well-being of nonhuman animals. What accounts for this peculiar conjunction of Haskala and animal-protection societies in *Di kliatshe*? The pervasive concern for animal rights was part of a trend that swept the Russian intelligentsia during the 1860s, a time in which significant social and political reforms took place in the Russian Empire. Chief among these reforms was the emancipation of peasants in 1861, and the legal reforms of 1864 that sought to create a system of uniform statute law for all citizens of the Russian empire. These legislative reforms also facilitated the establishment of a Russian Society for the Protection of Animals (RSPA) in 1865, which expanded quickly to become the largest and most influential voluntary organization in tsarist Russia. Animal protection societies sprang up across the country and pursued broad agendas such as the improved treatment of carriage horses and stray dogs, the establishment of humane slaughtering procedures, abolition of cruel hunting practices, education of youth with an ethos of kindness to animals, and the establishment of legal penalties for abusing domestic animals.[8]

In Russia, animal protection was a fashionable concern for traditional social elites and for the emerging middle class, and it was popular among those who subscribed to the cause of the Enlightenment and advocated the Westernization of Russian culture. Those who were engaged in animal protection shared with the Russian state a concern for the moral improvement of the newly emancipated lower classes. Thus, the efforts of animal-protection societies consisted mainly of attempts to restrain certain behaviors associated with the lower classes and to ban popular pastimes that involved cruelty to animals.[9] In 1871, two years before the publication of *Di kliatshe*, the Russian Ministry of Internal Affairs ratified a law stipulating that "for causing domestic animals 'wanton torment,' the guilty is subjected to a fine of no more than ten rubles."[10] The RSPA's charter authorized members of the organization to require and receive assistance from "government instances, as well as from local police authorities" in order to enforce this law. Members of animal-protection societies carried cards signed by the town governor, and the police were supposed to help these individuals when they were presented with the membership cards.[11] This awareness of animal rights and of animal suffering forms a central concern in *Di kliatshe*. Throughout the story, the legal authority of the RSPA is explicitly invoked, and for this reason Isrolik feels that the mare "had a right to [his] assistance. [He] would have to fulfill [his] duty toward her, if not by compassion than [sic] at least by law."

Even though Isrolik clearly identifies with the progressive social agenda of Russian enlighteners, his affinity with the mare extends beyond mere ideology and is rooted in a specifically Jewish experience of life under the restrictive statutes of Russian imperial law. As a young maskil, Isrolik detests the constrictive traditional Jewish life of the shtetl and seeks to integrate into Russian society through the study of medicine. Like the mare, he longs for a formal arrangement that would secure his legal rights in the Russian empire:

> Like all other Jews, [I would] have to put up with insults and injuries from the rest of the world. I would remain a *luftmensch*; up in the air for the rest of my life, force without fuel. I would feel the energy to do something, but have no way of activating my energy, applying it to something useful. I would be like so many pitiful failures among us Jews ... I would be a Jew and not a human being ... an enigma! (M, 205)

A possible way out of this daunting existence seemed to open up for Russian maskilim after the legislative reforms of Alexander II in the 1860s. These reforms primarily addressed the humanitarian crisis of the Russian peasants who had been beyond the law as the personal subjects of their landlords, ending their long exploitation under the tsarist regime. Concurrently, the Russian government also alleviated some of the existing restrictions on Jewish rights of residence. The Jews, who were confined for the most part to the Pale of Settlement (the western borderlands of Russia),[12] were now allowed to reside in the Russian interior lands if they obtained university degrees. The emancipation of peasants and subsequent emergence of animal-protection societies in the Russian state seemed to herald a new awareness of the cause of universal suffering, and consequently hopes were raised among maskilim that Jewish suffering would eventually be reckoned with, as a first step toward the emancipation of Russian Jews. These hopes, however, were quickly proven false. The first visible cracks in the long-standing maskilic belief in the benevolence of the Russian authorities, in the eventual enlightenment of the non-Jewish masses, and in the support of liberal non-Jewish intellectuals in the cause of Jewish emancipation became apparent in the aftermath of the Odessa pogrom of 1871.[13] This pogrom was the culmination of a series of escalations that gradually eroded the hopes of maskilim—including Abramovitsh himself—that the Great Reforms of Alexander II would bring about a substantial improvement in the legal and social standing of Jews in Russia.[14] This realization is allegorically figured in *Di kliatshe* by the RSPA's response to Isrolik's written request to aid the mare, in which the attitude of Westernized Russian intellectuals and liberals—the so-called champions of suffering animals—is exposed in its duplicity:

> First of all, the mare ought to have her elflocks removed. Let her become more presentable. In order to avoid a great measure of conflict on this issue and to improve her condition in the future, it is, in our opinion, necessary to do something about her dreadful ignorance. She has to be led onto the right path, she has to be trained and educated, taught how to walk properly, etc., etc. Then, when she has learned all the tricks required of a trained horse, she will be worthy of our commiseration, and our society will stand by her and not permit any maltreatment of her. (M, 264)

These corrective measures, of course, might apply equally to the shtetl Jew as to the mare, evoking the frequent debates on the "Jewish Question"—the putative conditions under which Jews would be eligible to become members of Russian society. In these terms, *Di kliatshe* registered the disappointment among maskilim with the government and with non-Jewish liberals and intellectuals who advocated such progressive social causes. The degree to which non-Jewish intellectuals and social elites had been estranged from the plight of Jews became apparent during the 1871 Odessa pogrom, as described by Steven Zipperstein:

> Even as the pogrom was raging, the city's non-Jewish intellectuals openly maintained that the Jews themselves were to blame for the

uprising, since the Jewish community had created the oppressive economic atmosphere in which such action was the only avenue for self-defense (gymnasium teachers had even told this to their classes). The upper classes proved indifferent, and often openly hostile, to the plight of the Jews: one well-dressed woman was seen riding in a carriage in the midst of the pogromists, pointing out to the mob the houses of wealthy Jews. Friendships and business partnerships between Jews and non-Jews dissolved: one Jew, for instance, who had planned to hide his valuables in the apartment of a non-Jewish business associate during the pogrom was greeted by his acquaintance with violent curses and abuse.[15]

Such incidents appear even more paradoxical in light of the intense engagement with animal-rights organizations among Odessa elites, intellectuals, and bourgeoisie precisely during the same years. It is not unlikely that many of the intellectuals and noblemen who were indifferent, or who were assisting the pogromists to carry out their vicious attacks, were members of the Odessa Society for Sympathy to Animals—an organization that played a major role in anticruelty legislation during the late 1860s and early 1870s.[16] Thus, by the time Abramovitsh was writing *Di kliatshe* in 1873, the political and social reality of Jews in Russia had become palpably clear: whereas the condition of peasants and animals improved, the social and legal status of Jews deteriorated. The hypocrisy of those Russians who prided themselves on being Westernizers or members of a non-Jewish liberal movement was characteristically decried by literary critic David Frishman in the mid-1880s, following yet another wave of pogroms directed against Odessa Jews:

> O, how I always loved all these sensitive souls, the members of animal-rights organizations, who simply cannot bear to watch the suffering of a small animal or a little bird! I once knew a man of such good nature, generosity, and honesty, who was very fastidious with regard to any animal and bug.... But when came the time of great deed and action, to drive stakes through the brains of human beings with a sledgehammer, or to hack to pieces the intestines of people while they were still alive, or to stick burning files into the eyes of quivering children, this good and kind soul suddenly forgot for three

days that he is a loyal member of those fine organizations that uphold mercy and compassion.[17]

In *Di kliatshe*, the duplicity of Russian intellectuals toward the Jews is not only allegorized in the RSPA's response letter to Isrolik, but also implied in Isrolik's futile attempts to enter the Russian university. Although Isrolik is legally allowed to apply to the university, he is thwarted by the demand that he master Russian folklore. The justification for this requirement is presented as an anti-Semitic procedure that seems to have been put in place solely to discourage and disqualify Jewish students. Frustrated with useless attempts to memorize haphazard details of Russian folktales, Isrolik begins to experience a series of mental breakdowns in which he becomes subject to strange hallucinations. Despairing of emancipation, the maskil who has become alienated both from his Jewish community and from gentile Russian society can no longer find a place for himself in the human world. Consequently, he goes mad.

INASMUCH AS ISROLIK'S MADNESS signals the historical failure of the Haskala in tsarist Russia, it also serves as an important poetic device throughout *Di kliatshe*. Indeed, madness is the medium through which the historical conditions that have shaped the lives of Jews in Russia acquire spatial dimensions in the work. Through Isrolik's hallucinations, the mare assumes an allegorical function in the story, and her degradation is revealed to be emblematic of the suffering of the Jewish people in diaspora:

> And suddenly, two eyes were gazing at me, expressing sorrow and weariness, as well as an entreaty and an infinite kindness, the eyes of a sick, downtrodden, browbeaten person, who gazes at everyone in utter silence, and whose every gaze reveals his innermost sufferings; every gaze talks, cries fury, pleads for mercy, and tears out a piece of your heart. I stared and stared. Was this a horse? I saw a human face before me. How did a human being get here so suddenly, where did he come from? This freak! ... And as I stared, transfixed, at this creature, it held out a hand from somewhere below, and taking it courteously, I felt: a hoof! (M, 210–11)

In this uneasy mixture of hallucination and allegory, the dehumanized figure of the mare comes to the fore as the historical trajectory of Jewish emancipation begins to recede from view. Allegory thus comes to replace the historical account in Abramovitsh's so-called fantasy tale, which contains multiple references to the deplorable conditions of Jews in nineteenth-century tsarist Russia, encoded in descriptions of suffering animals. Such depictions of animal suffering are imbued with substantial lyrical depth, which at times threatens to undermine allegory's representative power. In this sense, *Di kliatshe* appears as a unique literary achievement that could best be described as a lyrical form of allegory. The unique lyrical function of allegory finds one of its most powerful expressions in a scene that depicts the song of the nightingale. The scene takes place in a pastoral, sylvan setting that contains a highly colorful description of a spring morning that is likened to a nuptial between earth and sky: "everything was festive and scented, and the air was filled with the sweet, lovely perfumes of spices. How beautiful is the dawn of a spring morning in the forest!" (M, 244–45). As Gidi Nevo has shown, this sylvan topos manifests itself frequently in the works of Abramovitsh and is constituted through a set of repeating elements that include a forest clearing in which sunlight can shine through and a soft, rounded topography, covered with grass and inhabited by small, harmless animals such as ants or birds.[18] However, despite this pastoral and tranquil surroundings, Isrolik detects a sad note in the song of the nightingale:

> Oh, I can read your heart, my dear, sweet nightingale! A poet's heart feels the sorrow of the world. It can sense what is lacking—and he plays what he feels, he always remembers it at feasts and celebrations. You sing a fresh and lilting lovesong for your wife, and then right in the middle of it—a sigh, an echo from a terrible winter when you were wanderers, strangers in a strange land! You serenade the forest, radiant in his new green cap, and yet in your friendly wishes there is a tearful strain, a dirge for last year's leaves, which are rotting at the foot of the trees. And then, for our earth in her bridal flowers, you utter funeral prayers in memory of her children, whom she bears and buries year after year. How I like you, my world-famous singer, my nightingale! That sad note in your sweet melody touches me more than all your songs. For my mother bore me in torment and

anguish, and she cradled me in sorrow, and her lullaby of suffering has remained the song of my life! What does a hapless fellow like myself have in common with spring? What does a lonesome creature like myself have to do with the festive crowd, the beautiful forest, freshly blossoming Nature? The joy of the world is not for me. When others live in happiness, anguish is my fate. When they celebrate, I face violence, blood, fire, flames, and smoke. When the land turns green and the birds start chirping then my days are full of fasting, grieving, and lamenting. (M, 245)

At first glance, the melancholic singing of the nightingale appears to be an allegory for the spirit of poetry and for a poetic weltschmerz in a condition of exile.[19] However, upon closer inspection it becomes apparent that the real cause of anguish in the midst of the spring festivities is only hinted at, not explicitly stated. The lament over last year's leaves that lie "rotting at the foot of the trees" frames the sadness within a cyclical, natural occurrence that belies the reference to a particular historical event. Yet the painful memory, invoked in the midst of the spring bloom, refers to an event that involved "violence, blood, fire, flames, and smoke" and took place in the springtime. Such an event is undoubtedly the pogrom. Pogroms have traditionally taken place around the time of the Easter festival or of Passover. The 1871 Odessa pogrom was no exception, and subsequent pogroms in 1881 and 1903 would repeat the pattern of springtime slaughter.[20] Although certainly not all pogroms took place near Easter, the paradoxical association of springtime and slaughter became an important theme in Russian Jewish literature, and would later recur in Bialik's famous pogrom poem "Be-'ir ha-haregah" (In the City of Killings, 1903).

The discrepancy between literal and allegorical meaning in the forest scene—that is, between the serene, timeless appearance of blooming nature in spring and the violent historical event that it signifies—is a constitutive feature of the spatialization of the historical. Here nature appears as a cipher, in a profoundly unhistorical form, that encapsulates a latent historical meaning. Encoding the historical event in the natural phenomenon within the field of allegorical representation is an act of deliberate obfuscation in *Di kliatshe*, a displacement that renders the text accessible only to those who possess sufficient cultural or historical knowledge for deciphering its encoded meanings. This strategy, in which history "merges into the setting"[21] has complicated the work's reception and ultimately prevented its inclusion in the modern Jewish literary canon. On the one hand, many historical testimonies indicate that *Di kliatshe* was widely read and enjoyed in common Jewish households as well as by yeshiva students, intellectuals, and maskilim both in and outside of Russia.[22] On the other hand, some Jewish authors—foremost among whom was Yankev Dinezon[23]—criticized *Di kliatshe* precisely for being too highbrow, and claimed that its veiled allegorical references and its lofty, artistic language rendered the work inaccessible to the uneducated Jewish masses.[24] Recent studies of the reception history of Yiddish literature in Eastern Europe corroborate Dinezon's assessment of the popularity of *Di kliatshe* among Jewish readers. As Alyssa Quint argues, "*The Nag* [*Di kliatshe*] appeared 'popular' because it appealed to Russifying Jews of every shade of cultural assimilation ... It did so because it played out the very compelling anxiety of the breakdown of the Russian-Jewish symbiosis on which these Russian Jews staked their lives."[25] Thus, references to the political and social conditions of Russian Jews allegorically encoded in *Di kliatshe* proved to be opaque not only to future readers who lacked the original cultural and historical context of these references.[26] They were likewise indecipherable for the majority of contemporaneous Jewish readers and remained so for a long time thereafter.

DESPITE THE THEMES of suffering and degradation commonly associated with the allegorical portrayal of the Jewish people as a kliatshe, this figural construction merits an examination in its own right, as it extends beyond the purview of Jewish sources, marking a cultural dialogue with contemporaneous Russian literature. Indeed, the key term *kliatshe* does not originate in the Yiddish language but is imported from Ukrainian, where it also means *nag*, a worn-out old mare. But the etymology of the word sheds light on its usage in the specific context of abuse and degradation. The original Ukrainian term *kl'áča* stems from the root *kliakat*, which indicates the servile act of bending the knee. *Kliatshe* is thus not simply a zoological designation but a figural construct that connotes debasement under conditions of slavery.[27] This term made its appearance in Russian literature seven years prior to the publication of *Di kliatshe*, in Dostoevsky's

Crime and Punishment (1866). Not surprisingly, it appears in a scene that depicts the harsh and brutal treatment of a mare.[28] The scene takes place in Raskolnikov's symbolic dream, in which he returns as a child to the small town where he grew up, walking with his father past a tavern where "drunken and horrible-looking figures were hanging about."[29] Near the entrance of the tavern stands a big cart, one of those usually drawn by heavy dray-horses, but instead of a sturdy horse the child Raskolnikov sees

> [a] thin little sorrel beast, one of those peasants' nags (*kliacha*) which he had often seen straining their utmost under a heavy load of wood or hay, especially when the wheels were stuck in the mud or in a rut. And the peasants would beat them so cruelly, sometimes even about the nose and eyes, and he felt so sorry, so sorry for them that he almost cried, and his mother always used to take him away from the window.[30]

In Raskolnikov's dream, a group of drunken, rowdy peasants comes out of the tavern and climbs onto the cart to the sound of the crowd's laughter. Mikolka, the owner of mare and cart, assisted by others, whips the mare repeatedly, in cruel jest, as if to make her drag the full cartload at a gallop. When the poor creature fails to do so, the peasant flies into a rage and beats her as if she has willfully disobeyed him. When someone in the crowd points out that he is going to kill the mare, Mikolka replies angrily: "[D]on't meddle! It's my property. I'll do what I choose."[31] Then, to the sound of the crowd's jeering, the mare is flogged with six whips and thrashed with a thick pole; finally, Mikolka deals her a ferocious deathblow with a crowbar. Upon witnessing this, the child Raskolnikov runs screaming through the crowd to the mare.

> He put his arms round her bleeding dead head and kissed it, kissed the eyes and kissed the lips ... Then he jumped and flew in a frenzy with his little fists out at Mikolka. At that instant his father, who had been running after him, snatched him up and carried him out of the crowd. "Come along, come! Let us go home," he said to him. "Father! Why did they ... kill ... the poor horse!" he sobbed, but his voice broke and the words came in shrieks from his panting chest.[32]

Here the authentic reaction of the child to animal suffering is still untainted by artificial notions of property adopted in adulthood, an empathy based on a shared creaturely estate. The artificiality implied by the alienated notion of property imposed on living beings was likewise decried and defamiliarized by another famous Russian horse: Tolstoy's Kholstomer.[33] In *Crime and Punishment*, the killing of the "useless" mare foreshadows the killing of the "useless" old moneylender in the name of a utilitarian notion that excludes any feeling of compassion for "useless" individuals who can be sacrificed for the greater good of society.[34] Yet it is not only social inutility that justifies the cruel treatment that the mare receives from Mikolka. The mare's essential nature as *kliatshe* is determined not simply by her equine form but rather by her exploitation and degradation as a senseless piece of property. To be sure, public scenes of wanton cruelty against animals were common not only in Russia but throughout most of the Western world in the nineteenth century, but in Russia it was also possible to observe human beings publicly treated as animals. This was especially evident in the notorious spectacle of "public coachmen" (*izvozchiki*) in St. Petersburg, who according to common accounts lived the lives of "dogs."[35] These coachmen were peasants who had recently arrived in the city or seasonal migrants from the countryside. Deprived of any legal status, they were subjected to the extreme violence of the conductors or guards of the mail coach.

One such incident of public cruelty involving one of the izvozchiki and his horse left an indelible mark on the teenage Dostoevsky who witnessed a government courier changing carriages at the station house across the street from the inn where his family was staying in St. Petersburg. As he later recalled:

> The courier at once flew out of the inn, ran down the steps, and got into the carriage. Before the coachman could even start the horses, the courier stood up and, silently, without any word whatsoever, raised his huge right fist and dealt a painful blow straight down on the back of the coachman's neck. The coachman jolted forward, raised his whip, and lashed at the shaft horse with all his might. The horses started off in a rush, but this did nothing to appease the courier. He was not angry; he was acting according to his own plan, from something preconceived and tested through many years of

experience; and the terrible fist was raised again, and again it struck the coachman's neck and then again and again; and so it continued until the troika disappeared from sight. Naturally the coachman, who could barely hold on because of the blows, kept lashing the horses every second like one gone mad; and at last his blows made the horses fly off as if possessed.[36]

In the notebooks of *Crime and Punishment*, Dostoevsky jotted down the words "my first personal insult, the horse, the courier,"[37] suggesting that the scene that depicts the beating of the kliatshe relates to his formative experience with the government courier, the izvozchik, and his horse. As Dostoevsky's biographer Joseph Frank points out, Dostoevsky saw in the courier a symbol of the "brutal, oppressive government that he served—a government whose domination over an enslaved peasantry by naked force incited all the violence and harshness of peasant life."[38] This experience played a formative role in Dostoevsky's subsequent political radicalization during the 1840s. As he later admitted, this scene appeared to him "as an emblem, as something very graphically demonstrating the link between cause and effect. Here every blow dealt to the animal leaped out of each blow dealt at the man."[39] In Dostoevsky's account, the form of political oppression associated with the figure of the kliatshe thus appears as an outcome of a traumatic exposure to the law in a state of exception. The kliatshe emerges as a paradigmatic expression of the infrahuman, a constellation in which both peasant and horse are reduced to a condition of bare life.

The adaptation of the figure of the kliatshe from contemporaneous Russian literature into a markedly Jewish context entailed—in addition to the denunciation of the oppressive Russian government—a condemnation of corrupt Jewish leadership. The internal critique of Jewish society is implied in Abramovitsh's account of the genesis of *Di kliatshe* in "Fir zenen mir gezesn," where he recalls that his inspiration for the story came about after witnessing a scene in which a mare was cruelly treated by her Jewish master:

> Once, on a summer night, I was sitting at an inn in Glupsk, looking pensively outside through an open window when I saw a worn-out, sweaty Jew, the laps of his torn caftan tucked in, standing and lashing a poor, worn-out, sweaty mare (*kliatshe*) with a bitten skin,

harnessed to a cart full of bricks. He was hurling deadly curses at the mare, at himself, and at the entire world: — "I should have burned your skin off, you dismal mare you!" And she, the mare, turned that wasted blackened chin of hers towards the Jew, looked at him as one would look at a sinner, and then I seemed to hear her say to him: — "Fool! He calls me a nag! You yourself are a nag! Take a look there, where I pull the bricks, then you will see that you are all nags, dark wasted nags, then everything will become a great sorrow for you too!"

Thus, it seemed to me, spoke the mare, and I raised my eyes to that place where she had indicated with her chin, and I saw a familiar soul, one of those fine creatures who stood out in Glupsk by virtue of fighting their way with five fingers up a wall made of kosher Jewish money, of kosher Jewish sweat and blood, and then up another such wall ... This good person, this fine creature, kept his hands down, his cap lay crooked on his head, his forehead produced sweat and made plans, and around him gathered poor Jews who, like slaves, submissively surrounded him. They looked into his eyes like faithful dogs, and when he smiled they were happy, and when he gave them an evil look they shook, terrified. — It was then that the meaning of the verse from the Song of Songs occurred to me: Le-susati be-rikhvei parʿoh—to a mare among Pharaoh's chariots—dimitikh raʿayati—I compare you, the Jewish people![40]

As in Dostoevsky's description of the government courier, the izvozchik, and his horse, Abramovitsh, too, presents the Jew's cruelty toward the mare as a result of his own exploitation by a "familiar soul" from Glupsk. The reference here is, of course, not to a real town but to a recurring topos in Abramovitsh's work, modeled after the fictional town of Glupov in Mikhail Saltykov's series of satirical feuilletons published in the radical Russian journal *Sovremennik* in 1861 and 1862.[41] As some scholars have pointed out, Glupsk also bears a strong resemblance to the real Ukrainian town of Berdichev, where Abramovitsh resided for ten years of his life (1858–1868) and with which he was intimately acquainted.[42] The town of Glupsk (literally, "Fooltown" in Russian) served as an important artistic device in Abramovitsh's critique of Jewish life during the 1860s, combining representations of contemporary social and historical realities with abstract or exaggerated satirical portrayals. In the play *Di takse* (1869), which preceded the original publication of *Di kliatshe* by four years, the town of Glupsk is inhabited by corrupt benefactors taking advantage of a population of poor, passive Jews. This was not a fictional situation but a real one faced by Russian Jewry in the 1860s, after the traditional Jewish community councils (*kahal*) had been abolished at the beginning of Tsar Alexander II's reign in 1856, leaving the Jews with virtually no authoritative governance.[43] In *Di takse*, the maskilic reformer Shloyme Vekker (whose surname literally means "awakener") confronts the corrupt benefactors who step into the vacuum left by the demise of the *kahal* to exert their influence in Glupsk through their control of the kosher meat tax (also known as *di takse*). The reference to the "familiar soul" from Glupsk in "Fir zenen mir gezesn," then, clearly establishes a link between the exploitation of the common Jew by his benefactors and the Jew's own mistreatment of the mare, identified with the allegorical figure of the kliatshe.

Just like the "familiar soul" from Glupsk, the figure of the horse-beating common Jew alludes to one of Abramovitsh's earlier works, *Fishke the Lame*, which depicts the lives of poor Jews in the Pale of Settlement. Throughout this work, poor Jews are depicted in close proximity to their worn-out, decrepit mares. Reb Alter's horse, for example, is described as "an old, tall and withered mare with a scratched, bitten back and udders, with big ears and a mane tangled in elflocks," clearly recalling a poor Jew in appearance.[44] And conversely, too, Reb Alter utters incoherent noises that resemble the sound of a braying donkey.[45] Remarkably, in the first edition of the story, published in 1869, the word *kliatshe* does not appear. Instead, Abramovitsh employed the Yiddish word *shkape* to designate the beaten-down mare. Thus, even though the figure of the shkape was clearly an allegory for the Jewish poor in this early work, it still lacked the association with economic and political exploitation that appeared four years later in *Di kliatshe*. In the greatly expanded edition of *Fishke the Lame*, published in Odessa in 1888, a nearly identical description of a mare can be found, except that the crucial word *shkape* has now been replaced with *kliatshe*.[46] As might be expected, the designation of the mare as *kliatshe* is accompanied by added vivid descriptions of brutality toward the animal: "and straightway I made for that broken-down bonerack of a she-nag he calls his mare; and I took my whip to her, and lay into her good."[47]

Here and throughout Abramovitsh's oeuvre, Jews appear both as victims of oppression and as petty tyrants in their own right. These two aspects of Jewish mentality encapsulate the dehumanized condition of the "homo economicus" that Gershon Shaked has identified in the writings of Abramovitsh.[48] According to Shaked, on the one hand, Jewish existence in Abramovitsh's writings is described as a debased state in which petty materialist gain is elevated as a supreme value in life; on the other hand, this condition itself illustrates the arbitrary and unfortunate circumstances to which Jews were subjected under the oppressive tsarist regime. In *Di kliatshe*, both aspects of dehumanized Jewish existence are allegorized in the figure of the mare: the tragic tale of a cursed prince struggling to maintain his human dignity converges with a satirical portrait of a creature that indulges in shameless gratification of basic biological needs.

The convergence of these two categories of dehumanized existence is demonstrated in an emblematic scene in which Isrolik hears the mare let out a sigh that he interprets as the expression of an oppressed creature: "[Her] sighs reveal the unhappy prince struggling with all his might to achieve a human shape. Your sighs contain his voice shouting: I'm still alive! I still feel everything like any human being!" (M, 214). However, a moment later Isrolik discovers that it was not cosmic grief that prompted the sigh but simply a lack of hay to consume. It then occurs to him that the mare "didn't care what happened—as long as she had a mass of oats and a full belly" (M, 214). In this emblematic scene, the two aspects of dehumanized existence are linked not by an underlying historical reality, as Shaked argues, but by an internal rift. Put in other words, the figure of the kliatshe does not foreground the internal coherence of dehumanized existence but instead places the emphasis on the gap between the calculated, materialist aspect of Jewish existence, and the creaturely exposure to the law as bare life. By emphasizing the overarching social and historical conditions of Jews in tsarist Russia in his analysis of dehumanization, Shaked fails to address self-alienation as the core problem in Russian Jewish mentality that Abramovitsh never ceased to analyze and criticize, in *Di kliatshe* and in his other works. Ultimately, it is not political or economic exploitation but self-alienation that emerges as the direct cause of the brutal treatment of the mare in the passage from "Fir zenen mir gezesn." Accordingly, Abramovitsh articulated the animal's silent rebuke in the following terms: had the abusing Jew realized that he himself was a kliatshe and recognized the mare as his equivalent, he would not have subjected her to brutal mistreatment. Like Balaam, he would have been forced to admit that he had sinned against the animal by wantonly venting his anger against a helpless creature. The righteous man, according to Proverbs 12:10, is always mindful of the needs of his beasts.

IN LIGHT OF THESE CONSIDERATIONS, we can begin to identify in Abramovitsh's writings a unique approach to the suffering of animals that exceeds a mere preoccupation with legal rights. This approach is exemplified, for instance, by the figure of *Isrolik dem meshugenem* (Isrolik the madman), who despite being mad is not self-alienated. Isrolik is disturbed by the mistreatment of the mare not because it constitutes an infraction of the law but because he can perceive the animal's pain and identify it as his own. Despite the evident correlation between the suffering of the mare and Isrolik's personal predicament (which also encapsulates the general predicament of the Haskala), this is a question not of Jewish pain allegorically represented by an animal but rather the opposite: a quintessentially animal or creaturely pain is felt and expressed by the maskilic Jew. The mad maskil, who has lost any meaningful connection to the human world, thus emerges as the "advocate of the creaturely" who articulates the silent language of nature.[49] In *Di kliatshe*, this attention to the creaturely aspects of the natural world emerges as an ethical position that is somewhat misleadingly labeled *tsaʿar baʿalei hayim*. The Talmudic notion of tsaʿar baʿalei hayim—a Hebrew phrase that literally means "the sorrow of living beings"—concerns a broad principle of prevention of pain and suffering to animals, and its relevance to the context of *Di kliatshe* is demonstrated by its appearance as the subtitle to the story. The question at stake is to what degree Abramovitsh's advocacy of the creaturely is indebted to this Jewish legacy.

In order to assess the ways in which Abramovitsh's use of the term *tsaʿar baʿalei hayim* corresponds to the traditional Jewish notion, we must briefly clarify its status within Jewish thought. To begin with, the principle of tsaʿar baʿalei hayim was conceived as a legal criterion. Rabbinical legislators set up restrictions for the appropriate handling of animals and further decreed that these restrictions were of biblical and not rabbinical origin, thereby rendering them irrevocable.[50] In the writings of some of the most prominent Jewish philosophers and rabbis, such as Maimonides, Nahmanides, and Joseph Caspi, it is possible to find attitudes that demonstrate an awareness of the suffering of animals.[51] Thus, for example, Maimonides explains the biblical restriction on slaughtering a young calf in front of its mother by the fact that the female animal is attached to its offspring just like the human mother is attached to her child:

> For in these cases animals feel very great pain, there being no difference regarding this pain between man and the other animals. For the love and tenderness of a mother for her child is not consequent upon reason, but upon the activity of the imaginative faculty, which is found in most animals just as it is found in man.[52]

In a similar vein, Nahmanides has interpreted the biblical restriction on the consumption of animal blood as a result of certain traits shared by both humans and animals. According to Nahmanides, since all living beings were saved from the flood by Noah, God permitted man to use animals' bodies for his benefit and needs,

> because their life was on account of man's sake, and that their soul [i.e., blood] should be used for man's atonement when offering them up to Him, blessed be He, but not to eat it, since one creature possessed of a soul is not to eat another creature with a soul, for all souls belong to God. The life of man just as the life of the animal are all His.[53]

The traditional Jewish standpoint thus maintained that even though man must show consideration toward animals, this by no means implies equality in stature. But this is certainly not the kind of attitude found in the work of Abramovitsh. At stake in *Di kliatshe* is not an attitude of "consideration" toward animals from a superior human position but one of identification from a position of a shared creaturely estate. Literary critic Fishel Lachower did not fail to observe this attitude and accord it a position of seminal importance in his assessment of Abramovitsh's work:

> Abramovitsh presents before us man and beast, as well as the living, the vegetative, and the inanimate in one stroke and with a single motion of his painterly brush. In his portrayals, he does not ascribe a special status to man and does not consider him to be the "lord of creation." He does not crown man and does not consider him superior to other animals that populate his tales. . . . On the contrary,

humans are often compared in his mind to beasts and when he discusses beasts in The Book of Cattle and in other works, he sometimes includes human beings in this category. When he is moved to love and compassion toward the Jewish people, when he sees them beaten and broken, they resemble a mare in his eyes . . .[54]

In light of this assessment, we can distinguish Abramovitsh's approach from the traditional core of Jewish thinking, which has always remained essentially anthropocentric and perceived animals as intended for the use of mankind. Instead, Abramovitsh presents a heterodox position that equates human and animal existence in terms of a shared capacity for lived experience. As Lachower observed, the overwhelming identification with animal life is nowhere as evident as in Abramovitsh's late autobiographical piece *Sefer ha-behemot* (*The Book of Cattle*, 1902/1912).[55] In this work Abramovitsh recounts how as a boy he felt great pity for a young, orphaned heifer and protected it from harassment by members of his household. By placing himself as a buffer between the heifer and its human tormentors, he subjected himself to ridicule and to the same mistreatment suffered by the heifer. After experiencing the cruelty of the household members, he wondered:

> [w]hether man and cattle, made of the same flesh and blood, might also share the same spirit. And all animals, since they are endowed with spirit, heart, and senses, feel sorrow and joy, suffering and pleasure, like human beings do. This contemplation was not a mere passing thought that arises for a moment like a cloud and then fleets away, but was fixed in my heart. Later, when I grew up and acquired knowledge, I realized that animals have various spiritual possessions. They have discourse, manners in familial and social life, individual and public requirements, and contrivances whereby they acquire food and escape death; they have rules and customs, all according to their different ways. . . . But man has hardened his heart toward animals, and his own self-interest requires him to think of them as mindless oafs deprived of feelings, created only for his sake. When they serve him for his own benefit they are called useful animals, and if he cannot make use of them, he calls them pests and considers them redundant in this world.[56]

The Book of Cattle, as well as another notable work by Abramovitsh, *Mi-sefer ha-zikhronot* (*From the Memoir Book*, 1915),[57] are riddled with vivid and disturbing descriptions of suffering animals: a calf separated from its mother as it is led to slaughter, a horse left dying on the road after having outlived its usefulness to its owner, a cow vainly searching for its slaughtered newborn calf, and so on. These heart-rending descriptions portray time and again the mute despair of domestic animals under the yoke of human oppression. Above all, such descriptions demonstrate that the designation of animals as livestock, a commodity, is incompatible with their essential constitution as sentient beings capable of experiencing the same range of emotions felt by humans. By acknowledging the shared capacity for experience inherent in creaturely life, Abramovitsh came to formulate a radical position on the question of the human and the animal, namely, that animals possess *lives* as opposed to a mere zoological existence.[58] In thinking about animals in terms of *bios* as opposed to *zoë*, Abramovitsh anticipated contemporary writers such as J. M. Coetzee, whose novels *The Lives of Animals* (1999) and *Elizabeth Costello* (2003) marked a shift from anthropocentric, rights-based approaches regarding the question of animal suffering to an awareness of the bodily vulnerability shared by humans and animals alike, an awareness that Anat Pick has termed "creaturely thinking."[59] Nevertheless, Abramovitsh's descriptions of suffering animals do not manifest an awareness of the vulnerability of the creature only to imbue it with the "beauty of necessity."[60] Nor does he equate the love of nature—as in romantic poetry—with its aesthetic appreciation. Instead, Abramovitsh's depiction of suffering animals lays bare the irreconcilable gap between the figural construction of animality and lived experience. By stressing the incompatibility between the beauty of nature and its infinite capacity for degradation and corruption, Abramovitsh resisted the sublation of lived experience to a totalizing figural scheme.

The natural world in Abramovitsh's work is thus predicated on a strict separation of figure and lived experience, to the degree that at certain points this world begins to resemble an Ovidian universe, where all appearances are deceiving and identities are obscured. In the plight of animals, at stake is not simply a demand for justice, for inalienable universal natural rights, or even for compassion. Instead, the identification with animal suffering is the mark of self-awareness, an attentiveness to the creaturely that arises from the insurmountable gap between the ideal and the real. Here, Walter

Benjamin's observation about the character of Bucephalus in Kafka's "The New Attorney" might equally apply to Abramovitsh's attitude toward animals: "whether it is a man or a horse is no longer so important, if only the burden is removed from the back."[61] Such an ethical approach, which remains radical even today in its reconceptualization of the boundary between human and animal (and by extrapolation, also between Jew and non-Jew), would have been entirely foreign even to the most enlightened Russian maskil in the 1870s. That is perhaps why Abramovitsh chose to place his radical message in the mouth of a madman, *Isrolik dem meshugenem*.

3 INTO THE BOWELS OF THE EARTH
Prophecy and Animality in the Poetry of
Hayim Nachman Bialik and Uri Zvi Greenberg

ON THE LAST DAY OF THE PASSOVER HOLIDAY, April 19, 1903, a pogrom took place in the Bessarabian city of Kishinev. The Kishinev pogrom lasted for two days, and was the first major pogrom to erupt in the Russian Pale of Settlement since the wave of pogroms of 1881 to 1882 that followed the assassination of tsar Alexander II. The destruction in the aftermath of the Kishinev pogrom was considerable: 47 Jews had been murdered, 424 wounded, seven hundred houses were burned, six hundred shops looted, and the total damage to property was estimated at three million roubles.[1] As soon as the news of the pogrom reached the Jewish communities across the Pale of Settlement, a "historical committee" of inquiry was formed in Odessa by prominent intellectual figures such as the historian Simon Dubnow, the publicist and essayist Ahad-Ha-am, and S. Y. Abramovitsh. The committee dispatched Hayim Nachman Bialik, a Hebrew poet of some renown, to Kishinev in order to collect evidence and testimonies from the pogrom's victims. Bialik was given detailed instructions on the manner in which he was to collect evidence, such as "to be present at the magistrate courts" or to document "the number of people buried," and "interrogate the victims in their homes" in order to produce a report that will provide "an ordered historical picture of the event from its inception until the present moment."[2]

Bialik left soon thereafter to Kishinev, where he followed the committee's instructions to the letter. During his stay, which lasted five weeks, he recorded numerous testimonies from eyewitnesses, visited hospitals and cemeteries, and took photographs of the pogrom's victims and of destroyed property. Nevertheless, the five large notebooks that he had filled with factual accounts were never published during his lifetime. Instead, Bialik published two poems on the Kishinev pogrom: "Al ha-shechita" (On the Slaughter, 1903) and "Be-'ir ha-haregah" (In the City of Killings, 1903).[3]

"On the Slaughter" was a spontaneous poetic reaction to the impact of the news of the pogrom prior to Bialik's departure to Kishinev, whereas "In the City of Killings" was composed after his stay there. Both poems address the death of Jews in the pogrom, albeit from two different perspectives. In "On the Slaughter" it is God who is emphatically accused of becoming deaf to the prayers of the people, and the poet expresses absolute identification with the victims. By contrast, in "In the City of Killings" the accusation is paradoxically leveled at the victims themselves. Furthermore, as Dan Miron remarked, an important stylistic difference distinguishes the two poems. "On the Slaughter" presents an attempt to situate the massacre in multiple frames of reference: theological, moral, and national, as well as that of Zionist ideological struggle. But in "In the City of Killings" Bialik attempted to make the event palpable for the reader in the style of journalism: " 'to be there,' to see up close, to feel with the hands, to absorb, fixated, the unbearable sights, to smell the blood mingling with the perfume of acacia buds."[4]

It is hard to think of a single poem that exerted a more decisive influence on the formation of Jewish history and Zionist identity in the twentieth century than "In the City of Killings." After the publication of this poem Bialik was officially recognized as the national poet of modern Hebrew revival. The poem, even in the censored form in which it initially appeared, made an enormous impact on Bialik's contemporaries, ranging from enthusiastic responses of literary critics such as Yosef Klozner and Fishel Lachower, to the unreserved admiration of Yiddish poets and authors such as Y. L. Peretz and Peretz Hirshbein. Zionist leaders such as Yitzhak Ben-Zvi and Ze'ev Jabotinsky likewise praised the poem, and Jabotinsky promptly translated it into Russian. He later claimed that Bialik's poem "played an enormous role in the formation of Jewish social movements. It inspired all actions of self-defense."[5] Moreover, countless books and articles were written about this single poem, covering and analyzing almost every aspect associated with it, from its historical background to the way in which Bialik's suppressed childhood trauma informed the process of writing.[6]

Inasmuch as Bialik's two poems about the Kishinev pogrom differ from each other in significant ways, both nevertheless foreground a disturbing figure that the diverse critical literature of Bialik's oeuvre has failed to sufficiently address. This figure is that of a decapitated dog, and it plays a significant role in both poems, appearing to be in some way metonymical to the event of the pogrom itself. In "On the Slaughter" the reference to the decapitated dog marks the reduction of the life of the Jew is to a condition of bare life in the pogrom, a life that can be taken with impunity:

> Hangman! Here's a neck—come slaughter!
> Decapitate me like a dog, you have the axe-arm.
> and all the earth is to me a scaffold—
> and we—we are the few in number!
> My blood is outlaw—hack skull, let murder's blood leap,
> Let the blood of a suckling newborn and the elderly stain your garb—
> Stain to endure forever, forever.

> הַתַּלְיָן! הֵא צַוָּאר—קוּם שְׁחָט!
> עָרְפֵנִי כַּכֶּלֶב, לְךָ זְרוֹעַ עִם-קַרְדֹּם,
> וְכָל-הָאָרֶץ לִי גַרְדֹּם—
> וַאֲנַחְנוּ—אֲנַחְנוּ הַמְעָט!
> דָּמִי מֻתָּר—הַךְ קָדְקֹד, וִיזַנֵּק דַּם רֶצַח,
> דַּם יוֹנֵק וָשָׂב עַל-כֻּתָּנְתְּךָ—
> וְלֹא יִמַּח לָנֶצַח, לָנֶצַח.

As David Roskies has shown, in this stanza Bialik subverts the traditional formulas that glorify God's majesty and power on earth, specifically in Psalms 89:14 and in Kallir's hymn recited on Rosh Hashana.[7] By appealing to the hangman to take action rather than to God, the poet emphasizes the absence of divine intervention in the world. In this godforsaken world, devoid of redemption and divine justice, Jews are led to slaughter like animals. This is implied by the title of the poem, which is itself excerpted from the traditional blessing uttered prior to the kosher butchery of animals.

Bialik's evocation of the metaphor of kosher butchery (*shechita*) in the context of the Kishinev pogrom by no means implies a concern for the welfare of animals, such as we find in the writings of Abramovitsh. On the contrary, the metaphor of *shechita* acquires its potency only once we assume the implicit distinction between a form of killing sanctioned by moral and religious law and a form of killing that is rendered illegal. *Shechita* is thus contrasted with murder (*retzach*) as the killing of those who have been set outside the law, a permissible killing. Bialik plays on the ambiguity implied by the concept of *shechita* as an act implying both the humanization and dehumanization of the victims. Essentially, *shechita* is the Jewish ritual through which the impure flesh of animals is rendered admissible for human consumption. In this sense, *shechita* implies a humanization, a process through which the nonhuman becomes part of the human world. But since a dog can never be slaughtered in a kosher way, the oxymoronic *shechita* of a dog is pointless, profane, and merciless, for it serves no purpose other than bloodlust, thus exposing the arbitrariness inherent in the act of killing. In this sense the poet calls on the hangman to "decapitate [him] like a dog," that is, to kill him without committing homicide. However, this appeal to the pogromist can only be understood antiphrastically, for even though Jewish life may be taken with impunity, we are assured that the guilt of "murder's blood" (*dam retzach*) will never be obliterated. The insistence on murder as opposed to *shechita* in this context must be taken as the poet's ultimate affirmation of the victims' humanity.

IN THE SUBSEQUENT POEM, "In the City of Killings," the image of the decapitated dog appears once again as an emblem of a senseless, degrading death, yet here it is embedded in a far more complex, dramatic setting:

> And you will flee and come upon a yard with a mound in it —
> Upon this mound two were decapitated: a Jew and his dog.
> A single axe decapitated both and onto a single rubbish heap they were thrown
> And in their mingled blood pigs shall rummage and roll;
> Tomorrow the rain will fall and wash it into one of the wasteland's streams —
> And the blood shall cry no more from the gutters and the rubbish heaps,
> For it will be lost in the great deep or feed the thornbush—
> And all shall be as nothing, and all shall go on as if it never was.

> וּבָרַחְתָּ וּבָאתָ אֶל־חָצֵר, וְהֶחָצֵר גַּל בּוֹ—
> עַל הַגַּל הַזֶּה נֶעֶרְפוּ שְׁנַיִם: יְהוּדִי וְכַלְבּוֹ.
> קַרְדֹּם אֶחָד עֲרָפָם וְאֶל־אַשְׁפָּה אַחַת הוּטָלוּ
> וּבְעֵרֶב דָּם שְׁנֵיהֶם יְחַטְטוּ חֲזִירִים וְיִתְגּוֹלָלוּ;
> מָחָר יֵרֵד גֶּשֶׁם וּסְחָפוֹ אֶל־אַחַד נַחֲלֵי הַבָּתוֹת—

וְלֹא-יִצְעַק עוֹד הַדָּם מִן הַשְּׁפָכִים וְהָאַשְׁפָּתוֹת,
כִּי בִתְהוֹם רַבָּה יֹאבַד אוֹ-יַשְׁקְ נַעֲצוּץ לִרְוָיָה—
וְהַכֹּל יִהְיֶה כְאָיִן, וְהַכֹּל יָשׁוּב כְּלֹא-הָיָה.

Two elements that originally belong in the decapitation scene from "On the Slaughter" reappear in this stanza: the decapitated dog (Bialik uses the same verb, *araf*, for the act of decapitation in both poems), and the axe (*kardom*), the tool of slaughter. Moreover, the two decapitation scenes are linked temporally, with the one from "On the Slaughter" supposedly occurring during the "real time" of the pogrom and addressed to the pogromist from the victim's perspective just before he is beheaded "like a dog." The scene from "In the City of Killings," on the other hand, portrays the external perspective of an investigator who arrives late at the pogrom site, observing the headless bodies of a Jew and his dog in a decapitation scene that resembles the one described in "On the Slaughter." Most strikingly, "In the City of Killings" marks the poet's disillusionment with the earlier tragic pathos with which he accused the pogromists of murder. "Murder's blood" that was supposed to endure forever will soon be washed away, "lost" in the great deep and would no longer "cry" from the gutters. The crying of blood refers to the first act of murder, alluding to God's words to Cain in Genesis 4:10: "What have you done? The voice of your brother's blood is crying to me from the ground." The successful suppression of the cry of "murder's blood" implies, then, that in the aftermath of the pogrom *shechita* has taken precedence over murder, and that counter to the poet's initial expectations, the act of homicide, in its deep moral sense, will be obliterated.

As we will see, the terms that depict the obliteration of the act of murder in Bialik's "In the City of Killings" will prove to be vital for subsequent manifestations of the infrahuman in Jewish literature. The victim's human blood (which in Judaism is equivalent to the soul) is defiled by mingling with the blood of a dog and by its imminent dilution with rainwater. Thus, the dehumanization of the pogrom's victims is signaled by the assimilation of their blood into the cycles of profane nature, cycles that are implicitly contrasted with the endurance of murder in time: "and all shall be as nothing, and all shall go on as if it never was." The absorption of "murder's blood" into the earth is equivalent to the obliteration of murder, and nature here becomes emblematic of a timeless state that remains external to and unaffected by the catastrophic events of history. The essential dichotomy between nature and history informs the entire poem, particularly the first stanza, where the poet becomes painfully aware of the incompatibility between the reality of the massacre and the spectacle of spring in bloom:

> And the acacia trees bloom before you and pour their
>   perfume in your nose,
> And half their buds are feathers, and their smell is the smell of blood;
> And despite your resistance their foreign incense shall bring
> The spring's delight into your heart—and you shall not detest it;

וְלִבְלְבוּ הַשִּׁטִּים לְנֶגְדְּךָ וְזָלְפוּ בְאַפְּךָ בְּשָׂמִים,
וְצִיצֵיהֶן חֶצְיָם נוֹצוֹת וְרֵיחָן כְּרֵיחַ דָּמִים;
וְעַל-אַפְּךָ וְעַל-חֲמָתְךָ תָּבִיא קְטָרְתָּן הַזָּרָה—
אֶת-עֶדְנַת הָאָבִיב בִּלְבָבְךָ—וְלֹא-תְהִי לְךָ לְזָרָא;

The conflict in the poet's psyche is engendered by two contradictory manifestations of nature: on the one hand nature appears as an emblem of the pogrom, displaced into "spatial inauthenticity" in the allegorical image of the acacia trees that exude the "smell of blood" and bud feathers from torn pillows. At the same time, nature also emerges as a self-sufficient totality that is not compromised by the historical event to which it serves as a background. As "pure" nature, it is not perceived through the allegorical gaze that extracts from "spring's delight" the melancholy note of suffering. On the contrary, in its self-sufficient autonomy, nature discloses "spring's delight" *despite* the historical context in which it is embedded. The absolute separation between the two spheres of nature and history allows the poet to celebrate nature in its purely aesthetic form while suppressing its allegorical character.

Nevertheless, the overcoming of allegorical nature and its replacement by a romantic notion of a pure, self-sufficient nature is by no means presented as an established fact in the poem. Allegorical nature has not yet disappeared from the pogrom site but is rather encountered at its point of departure, before it is covered up entirely by a nature that remains entirely indifferent to historical meaning. Significantly, at the particular point in time from which the poem is articulated (the deictic "now" of the poem), murder's blood has not yet been washed away, and evidence of the mass murder was still lying about in plain sight. Although we are told that "tomorrow the rain will fall and wash it into one of the wasteland's streams" and all shall be forgotten, at present the scene of carnage still bears the marks of a spatialization of the historical, where nature shows traces of the historical, and the historical, in turn, bears traces of the natural. Thus, as the poet wanders through the ruins and scenes of devastation that riddle the pogrom site, he is struck by the uncanny resemblance of broken artifacts to mutilated bodies:

> The bare black stone and the naked burnt brick,
> And they seem like the gaping mouths of black, mortal wounds
> That can no longer heal, cannot be cured,

> מַחֲשֹׂף הָאֶבֶן הַשְּׁחֹרָה וְעָרוֹת הַלְּבֵנָה הַשְּׂרוּפָה,
> וְהֵם נִרְאִים כְּפִיּוֹת פְּתוּחִים שֶׁל־פְּצָעִים אֲנוּשִׁים וּשְׁחֹרִים
> אֲשֶׁר אֵין לָהֶם תַּקָּנָה עוֹד וְלֹא־תְהִי לָהֶם תְּרוּפָה,

The exchange of properties between the organic and inorganic, nature and artifact, marks the pogrom as the uncanny site in which a monstrous breach of boundaries has taken place. Above all, this breach is epitomized by a comprehensive dehumanization of victims, perpetrators, and survivors alike. Whereas the gentile pogromists are bestialized as "wild boars" (*chazirei ya'ar*) and "centaurs" (*susei adam*) in their brutal rape and *shechita* of Jewish women, the victims are associated with dogs, and the survivors of the pogrom are depicted as cursed, abominable creatures:

> Under this bench and behind that barrel
> Lay husbands, fiancés, brothers, peeping out of the holes
> As holy bodies quivered under the flesh of donkeys,
> Suffocating in their impurity and gagging on their own throat's blood,
> And like pieces of meat the loathsome gentile carved their flesh—
> And their kindred lay in disgrace and watched—and they did not stir nor move,
> And they did not pluck their eyes out and did not lose their minds—
> And perhaps then each had it in his heart to pray:
> O Lord, grant me a miracle—and spare me from harm.
> And those who lived off their impurity and awoke from their blood—

They were damned for the rest of their lives and the light of their
    world has been tainted
Eternal abominations, impurity of body and soul, inside and
    out—

תַּחַת מְדוֹכַת מַצָּה זוֹ וּמֵאֲחוֹרֵי אוֹתָהּ חָבִית,
שָׁכְבוּ בְעָלִים, חֲתָנִים, אַחִים, הֵצִיצוּ מִן-הַחוֹרִים
בְּפַרְפֵּר גְוִיוֹת קְדוֹשׁוֹת תַּחַת בְּשַׂר חֲמוֹרִים,
נֶחֱנָקוֹת בְּטֻמְאָתָן וּמְעַלְעוֹת דַּם צַוָּארָן,
וּכְחַלֵּק אִישׁ פַּת-בָּגוֹ חִלֵּק מְתֹעָב גּוֹי בְּשָׂרָן—
שָׁכְבוּ בְּבָשְׁתָּן וַיִּרְאוּ—וְלֹא נָעוּ וְלֹא זָעוּ,
וְאֶת-עֵינֵיהֶם לֹא-נִקְּרוּ וּמִדַּעְתָּם לֹא יָצָאוּ—
וְאוּלַי גַּם-אִישׁ לְנַפְשׁוֹ אָז הִתְפַּלֵּל בִּלְבָבוֹ:
רִבּוֹנוֹ שֶׁל-עוֹלָם, עֲשֵׂה נֵס—וְאֵלַי הָרָעָה לֹא-תָבֹא.
וְאֵלֶּה אֲשֶׁר חָיוּ מִטֻּמְאָתָן וְהֵקִיצוּ מִדָּמָן—
וְהִנֵּה שִׁקְּצוּ כָּל-חַיֵּיהֶן וְנִטְמָא אוֹר עוֹלָמָן
שִׁקּוּצֵי עוֹלָם, טֻמְאַת גּוּף נֶפֶשׁ, מִבַּחוּץ וּמִבִּפְנִים——

As this passage makes explicitly clear, the cowardly, selfish behavior of Jews in the face of atrocities may have helped them survive the pogrom, but at a terrible cost: they had to watch their wives and daughters get beaten, raped, and killed without lifting a finger to help them. Consequently, their very humanity was tainted. In Bialik's poem, the dehumanization of victims and perpetrators marks their expulsion from a meaningful historical context, and their exposure in the futility of natural-historical progression. In the pogrom, primordial violent impulses that normally remain submerged in everyday life are suddenly unleashed onto its surface. The subsequent animalization of victims and perpetrators can occur only within a temporary suspension of the law, in a "state of nature" that offers a glimpse into the anarchic, brutal forces held in check by sovereign power. As an eruption of natural forces within the boundaries of the civic order, the pogrom affords no room for moral conduct; ultimately the only reality is that of perpetrators and victims, victors and vanquished, and both are dehumanized in the process.

In his account of the pogrom, the poet thus testifies to the insurmountable abyss between the reality of the pogrom and the historical perspective from which it is represented in retrospect. Within the bracketed temporal and spatial coordinates of the pogrom, everything that transpires is destined to fall into oblivion as nature itself leaves no traces of the atrocity: "and all shall be as nothing, and all shall go on as if it never was." In these terms, nature appears in the poem as the prehistorical condition that lies outside justice, morality, and memory. By refusing to grant a redemptive historical meaning to the death of the victims and to the life of those who survived the pogrom, Bialik was working against a well-established Jewish tradition of cultural reactions to catastrophes that perceived the destruction, in the words of Alan Mintz, "as a deserved and necessary punishment for sin, a punishment whose magnitude is in proportion to the transgressions committed."[8] The basic paradigm of explanation of national catastrophes laid out in Deutronomic and biblical prophetic traditions that continued to reverberate in various forms thereafter ensured that the destruction visited upon Jews throughout history was not a sign of God's abandonment of His people, but rather an expression of His concern for them. The sacrifice of the victims made amends for the sins that supposedly provoked the catastrophe and allowed the surviving members of the community to reestablish a relationship with God. The Jewish victims of atrocities were thus traditionally martyrized, and their death was considered to have been for the sake of *kiddush hashem*, the sanctification of God's name. It is precisely this redemptive theological impulse that is resisted in "In the City of Killings," and the death of the victims, which occurs within the bracketed temporality of natural-historical progression, may not be used to exculpate the Jewish collective and redeem it of its sense of historical suffering.[9]

In contradistinction to the tradition that interpreted catastrophes as punishments for the sins of the people, the pogrom is presented in Bialik's poem not as an outcome of a divine plan, but rather as a product of random, blind circumstance. The poetic addresser, who is none other than God himself, readily admits to His failure to render the death of the victims meaningful:

> Forgive me, you wretched of the earth, your God is as poor as you
> Poor is He in your life and all the more so in your death,
> Tomorrow, when you knock at my door and ask for your reward—
> I shall open wide, lo and behold: I have been pauperized!
> And I grieve for you, my children, I pity you:

Your dead have died in vain, and neither I nor you
Know why you died and for whom and wherefore you died,
And your deaths are as pointless as your lives.

סִלְחוּ לִי, עֲלוּבֵי עוֹלָם, אֱלֹהֵיכֶם עָנִי כְמוֹתְכֶם,
עָנִי הוּא בְחַיֵּיכֶם וְקַל וָחֹמֶר בְּמוֹתָכֶם,
כִּי תָבֹאוּ מָחָר עַל-שְׂכַרְכֶם וּדְפַקְתֶּם עַל-דְּלָתָי—
אֶפְתְּחָה לָכֶם, בֹּאוּ וּרְאוּ: יָרַדְתִּי מִנְּכָסָי!
וְצַר לִי עֲלֵיכֶם, בָּנַי, וְלִבִּי לִבִּי עֲלֵיכֶם:
חַלְלֵיכֶם—חַלְלֵי חִנָּם, וְגַם-אֲנִי וְגַם-אַתֶּם
לֹא-יָדַעְנוּ לָמָּה מַתֶּם וְעַל-מִי וְעַל-מָה מַתֶּם,
וְאֵין טַעַם לְמוֹתְכֶם כְּמוֹ אֵין טַעַם לְחַיֵּיכֶם.

In this passage, God's rejection of responsibility for the death of the victims is explicitly identified with the obliteration of murder and the affirmation of *shechita*. Stripped from an overarching symbolic meaning, the death of the victims appears as untranscended, bare death, emblematic of the natural history of the individual and the collective to which he belongs. Moreover, this death reveals the limited scope of God's law as a law that applies to the sphere of history, but not to nature. The pogrom as a site of natural-historical destruction therefore remains outside the purview of the divine scheme and instead appears as an arbitrary occurrence, an outcome of a temporal movement without telos.

Once the pogrom site is thus excluded from the purview of historical development and divine providence, the stage is set for the reception of the testimony of the atrocities.

And when you lift your eyes to the roof—its tiles shall also fall mute,
Shade you in silence, and you shall ask the spiders;
Living witnesses they are, eyewitnesses, and they shall tell you all
    that has transpired:
A tale of a cloven belly filled with feathers,
A tale of nostrils and nails, skulls and hammers,
A tale of slaughtered men hung from beams,
And a tale of a babe, found sleeping beside the body of its stabbed
    mother

And in its mouth the cold nipple of her breast;
And a tale of a child who cried mama!" as he was ripped open,
And his eyes, too, are here, demanding me to account.
And such tales and others the spider shall recount
Deeds that pierce the brain, and suffice to
Eternally kill your spirit and soul—

וְנָשָׂאתָ עֵינֶיךָ הַגָּגָה—וְהִנֵּה גַם רְעָפָיו מַחֲרִישִׁים,
מַאֲפִילִים עָלֶיךָ וְשׁוֹתְקִים, וְשָׁאַלְתָּ אֶת-פִּי הָעַכְּבִישִׁים;
עֵדִים חַיִּים הֵם, עֲדֵי רְאִיָה, וְהִגִּידוּ לְךָ כָּל-הַמּוֹצָאוֹת:
מַעֲשֶׂה בְּבֶטֶן רְטֻשָׁה שֶׁמִּלְאוּהָ נוֹצוֹת,
מַעֲשֶׂה בִּנְחִירַיִם וּמַסְמְרוֹת, בִּגְלְגָלוֹת וּפַטִּישִׁים,
מַעֲשֶׂה בִּבְנֵי אָדָם שְׁחוּטִים שֶׁנִּתְלוּ בְּמָרִישִׁים,
וּמַעֲשֶׂה בְּתִינוֹק שֶׁנִּמְצָא בְּצַד אִמּוֹ הַמְדֻקָּרָה
כְּשֶׁהוּא יָשֵׁן וּבְפִיו פִּטְמַת שָׁדָהּ הַקָּרָה;
וּמַעֲשֶׂה בְּיֶלֶד שֶׁנִּקְרַע וַיָּצְאָה נִשְׁמָתוֹ בְּ"אִמִּי"—
וְהִנֵּה גַם עֵינָיו פֹּה שׁוֹאֲלוֹת חֶשְׁבּוֹן מֵעִמִּי.
וְעוֹד כָּאֵלֶּה וְכָאֵלֶּה תְּסַפֵּר לְךָ הַשְּׁמָמִית
מַעֲשִׂים נוֹקְבִים אֶת-הַמֹּחַ וְיֵשׁ בָּהֶם כְּדֵי לְהָמִית
אֶת-רוּחֲךָ וְאֶת-נִשְׁמָתְךָ מִיתָה גְּמוּרָה עוֹלָמִית—

Like Abramovitsh's mare or Heine's Jewish dog, the talking spiders in Bialik's poem are clearly no ordinary spiders. Rather, they are the infrahuman products of the natural-historical process. Although they initially appear as conventional metonymies for ruin and abandonment, these spiders function in the poem as spatialized allegorical forms in which the testimonies of the survivors have been displaced. Paradoxically, although the poet collects the spiders' testimonies, they are nevertheless withheld, almost not heard at all, and only through the mediation of the poet is a factual account of the atrocities hinted at, though not directly told.[10] It would seem that one reason for withholding the details of the pogrom lies in its potential danger for those who hear it. The poet wishes to spare his audience from "deeds that pierce the brain, and suffice to / eternally kill your spirit and soul." Instead, he alludes to them only by means of metonymical figures (for example, "a tale of a cloven belly filled with feathers / a tale of nostrils and nails, skulls and hammers," etc.). This catalogue of common pogrom topoi, ranging from the Book of Lamentations to contemporary journalistic accounts, strips the Kishinev pogrom of its historical specificity, and renders the spiders' testimony inadequate as historical evidence, while retaining its intense dramatic effect.

In certain respects, the poet functions here as an advocate of the creaturely, articulating in human speech the silent lament of the creature, and thus salvaging an account of the atrocities from the oblivion of the natural-historical process. But the poet also maintains strict editorial control over the factual information relating to the pogrom that he releases to his audience. The figurative (mis)representation of the spiders' testimonies and their mediation by the poet is made all the more conspicuous in view of the fact that Bialik held in his possession five notebooks of detailed accounts of the pogrom that he refused to publish during his lifetime. In "In the City of Killings," the infrahuman is thus implicated in a poetic strategy that aims at marginalizing the survivors' testimonies and undermining their witness-position, replacing it with Bialik's own poetic account of the pogrom. Bialik establishes the supremacy of poetic creativity over the passivity of historical testimony, indicating that his decision to suppress the five notebooks with the testimonies is a deliberate choice entirely consistent with the values, poetics, and general worldview set forth in "In the City of Killings."

The poet's superiority over those he purports to represent is likewise emphasized by the epithet "son of man" (*ben adam*) that recurs no less than five times throughout the poem. Although this term alludes to the prophecy in the book of Ezekiel, as literary scholars have pointed out,[11] its recurrence in the poem suggests that it also functions as an emphatic term that distinguishes the poet from his fellow Jews, who are depicted as a crowd of groaning "broken men" (*shivʻrei adam*) who plead for the mercy of gentile nations. Significantly, it is not the poet who relates to himself as a "son of man" in a sovereign act of self-affirmation. On the contrary, the poet remains a silent addressee throughout the poem, and his direct intervention, as we have seen, comes to be expressed through his editorial censorship. It is rather God himself who refers to the poet as "son of man," an appellation that unequivocally validates the poet's superior human status as well as the authenticity of his prophetic mission.

THE MUTUAL RELATIONSHIP between the poet-prophet and the dehumanized collective that he is charged with representing is given a significant allegorical expression in the seventh stanza of the poem, in a scene that takes place at the cemetery where the pogrom victims are buried. In the vicinity of the graves a seemingly inconspicuous patch of grass arrests the poet's attention:

> And when you turn to leave the graves of the dead,
> Your gaze shall linger for a moment on the surrounding carpet of grass
> And the grass is soft and moist, as in the beginning of spring:
> The sprouts of death and the fodder [*hatzir*] of graves you see with your eyes;
> And you shall pluck a handful and cast it behind your back,
> Saying: the people is uprooted grass [*hatzir*]   is there hope for the uprooted?

> וּפָנִיתָ לָלֶכֶת מֵעִם קִבְרוֹת הַמֵּתִים, וְעִכְּבָה
> רֶגַע אֶחָד אֶת-עֵינֶיךָ רְפִידַת הַדֶּשֶׁא מִסָּבִיב,
> וְהַדֶּשֶׁא רַךְ וְרָטֹב, כַּאֲשֶׁר יִהְיֶה בִּתְחִלַּת הָאָבִיב:
> נִצָּנֵי הַמָּוֶת וַחֲצִיר קְבָרִים אַתָּה רוֹאֶה בְעֵינֶיךָ;
> וְתָלַשְׁתָּ מֵהֶם מְלֹא הַכַּף וְהִשְׁלַכְתָּם לַאֲחוֹרֶיךָ,
> לֵאמֹר: חָצִיר תָּלוּשׁ הָעָם—וְאִם-יֵשׁ לַתָּלוּשׁ תִּקְוָה?

In this scene a complex link is established between the peculiar manifestations of nature in Bialik's poem and the biblical prophetic tradition (here, specifically to the prophecy of Isaiah), as well as to the prophetic persona that Bialik had established in some of his earlier poems. To begin with, the image of the uprooted grass alludes to Isaiah 40:6–8, where it serves as a metaphor for the transience of flesh, as opposed to the endurance of the word of God: "All the flesh is grass, and its constancy is like the flower of the field. The grass withers, the flower falls for the spirit of God blows upon it; surely the people is grass. The grass withers, the flower falls; but the word of our God shall endure forever." The common translation of the key metaphor for the transience of flesh in the biblical text as "grass" is misleading. The actual term *hatzir* means "hay," that is, dried grass used for the consumption of livestock. The term *hatzir*, which also recurs in the above quoted lines, connotes the idea that in nature nothing is lost but is instead recycled and reconverted for other purposes through a process of displacement and metamorphosis. If "murder's blood" lingered unnaturally at the scene of the crime in "On the Slaughter," then *hatzir kvarim*, the fodder of graves, implies the opposite: the flesh and blood of the victims had been assimilated into natural processes, serving as fertilizer for the lush carpet of grass that surrounds the graves.

The depiction of the grass sprouting from the graves of the pogrom victims thus echoes the description of the thornbush that feeds on the mingled blood of the decapitated Jew and his dog at the beginning of "In the City of Killings." And, as in the beginning of the poem, a sharp contrast is drawn between the inhuman death of the victims and the spectacle of spring in bloom. But the grass does not simply mark a profanation of the death of the pogrom victims and the assimilation of their blood into natural processes. Rather, the essential ambiguity of the phrase *hatzir kvarim* indicates the curious overlapping of both literal and metaphorical meanings. Thus, it is possible to interpret the prophetic judgment "the people are uprooted grass" as a metaphor for the condition of the Jewish people in the Diaspora; but at the same time, it can also be interpreted literally as referring to the grass that grows around the graves that thrives on the flesh of the victims. Instead of an elevating metaphor, the image of the plucked grass functions here as a degrading metamorphosis.

The plucking of the grass exemplifies the active intervention of the poet in biblical prophecy, by which his prophetic persona is implicitly contrasted with the passivity of the people. By plucking the grass that *is* the people, the poet-prophet affirms his own creative agency. And while in Judaism nature has traditionally been perceived as a manifestation of God's active power and deemed consonant with the fate of the nation, in "In the City of Killings" nature is portrayed as indifferent and complicit in the obliteration of murder. In this constellation, the poet-prophet can no longer have recourse to nature as an allegorical expression of the calamities of the Jewish people, as was the case with Abramovitsh. Instead, in order to present a poetic account of the pogrom, the poet himself must assume active agency and leave his own mark upon nature.

Finally, the graveyard scene also alludes to one of Bialik's earlier prophetic poems, "*Akhen hatzir ha-am*" (Surely the People is Grass), which was published in 1897. This was the first major poem that Bialik published in the prophetic style of admonishment in which he used the biblical metaphor of *hatzir* to denounce the impotence and passivity associated with Jewish diasporic existence. However, the phrase *akhen hatzir ha-am* (surely the people is grass) as it appears in the 1897 poem differs from the expression *hatzir talush ha-am* (the people is *uprooted* grass), as it appears in "In the City of Killings." The word *talush* (uprooted), which has been added to the original prophetic allusion, refers to the characteristic homelessness associated with the figure of the diasporic Jew. *Telishut* was often ascribed to individuals who could not find a place for themselves in either Jewish or gentile societies. It implied not only a loss of a native land but also a lack of a clear sense of national and individual identity. The Hebrew term *telishut*, as Eyal Chowers pointed out, "could be translated as disconnectedness and being apart. Literally, it means being separated from something, as when a leaf is detached from a tree. *Telishut* is the Hebrew word most resembling homelessness, but it does not evoke directly the idea of home but rather being apart, alone, disconnected, nonembedded; it is more all-engulfing than homelessness."[12] In "Surely the People is Grass" the passivity of the Jewish people in the face of national catastrophes is described as the passivity of the dead. Throughout the poem the people are portrayed as "dry," "slain," and "rotten" and described in terms that strongly convey lethargy and inaction. The poem ends with rhetorical questions: "Shall the dead awaken? Will the dead be shaken?" An equivalence is established in "In the City of Killings" with a rhetorical flourish that similarly follows the portrayal of the Jewish people as "uprooted grass": "Is there hope for the uprooted?" The essential difference between the two poems consists in that the dead in "Surely the People is Grass" can at least rest in peace, whereas in "In the City of Killings" no rest is granted to the uprooted, not even in death.

An additional important difference between the two prophetic poems involves the depiction of the figure of the poet as the man of God who will lead the people out of exile. In "Surely the People is Grass" the poet-prophet is described in the following terms:

> Surely the people wither, full of vileness and venom
> From the foot to the head, all of it rotten and worthless!
> Seeing it raised not a man from its midst in the day of anguish,
> One that was mighty in works, living, whose heart should impel him;
> One in whose heart should burn a spark to enkindle the life-blood,
> One from whose brow a flame should light up the path of the people;

One who would treasure the name of his God and the name of the
    nation
Far over wealth and the glitter of gold—the false idols;
His would be some burden of the heart, much truth, and power
A fierce hate of the lot of his people, its life of scorning and bondage,
Pity as vast as the sea, compassion that ever grows
With the disaster of his poor people, with the weight of its burden—
All this would surge in his heart, surge and rage like the sea,
All this will burn like a fire, burn in the blood till it kindles,
All this would thunder as an echo, day and night unceasing:
"Arise and work, arise and act, for the hand of God is with us!"[13]

אָכֵן נָבַל הָעָם, מָלֵא נְקֻלָּה וָרוֹשׁ,
כֻּלּוֹ רָקָב וּמְסוֹס מִכַּף רֶגֶל עַד-רֹאשׁ!
שֶׁלֹּא הֵקִים מִקִּרְבּוֹ בְּיוֹם נַחֲלָה וּכְאֵב,
רַב פְּעָלִים, אִישׁ חַי, אֲשֶׁר יִפְעַם בּוֹ לֵב,
וּבַלֵּב יִבְעַר זִיק, זִיק מַרְתִּיחַ הַדָּם,
וּבָרֹאשׁ יַגַּהּ שָׁבִיב מֵאִיר דֶּרֶךְ הָעָם;

אֲשֶׁר יֵקַר לוֹ שֵׁם כָּל-הַגּוֹי וֵאלֹהָיו
גַּם מֵהוֹן וּמִפָּז—מֵאֱלִילֵי הַשָּׁוְא;
אֲשֶׁר מְעַט מַשָּׂא-לֵב, הַרְבֵּה אֱמֶת, עֱזוּז,
שִׂנְאָה עַזָּה לִמְנָת חַיֵּי עַבְדוּת וּבוּז,
חֶמְלָה גְדוֹלָה כַיָּם, רַחֲמִים רַבִּים כִּגְדָל
שֶׁבֶר עַמּוֹ הָאֻמְלָל וּכְכֹבֶד הָעֹל—
כָּל-זֶה יֶהֱמֶה בַלֵּב, יֶהֱמֶה יֶחְמַר כַּיָּם,
כָּל-זֶה יִבְעַר כָּאֵשׁ, יִבְעַר יַצִּית הַדָּם,
כָּל-זֶה יִרְעַם כַּהֵד תָּמִיד יוֹמָם וָלֵיל:
"קוּם עֲבֹד, קוּם עֲשֵׂה, כִּי עִמָּנוּ יַד-אֵל!"

Although in this early poem Bialik was careful to disassociate his autobiographical self from the prophetic persona he portrayed, the same cannot be said of the figure of the prophet that appears in "In the City of Killings." In the later poem, the prophetic mission issued by God is made identical with the task given to Bialik by the "historical committee" in Odessa. The Kishinev pogrom thus provided an extra-textual ruse for the complete fusion of the autobiographical poet with the prophet, situating the poem itself at the intersection of individual biography and national history. With the fusion of the prophetic persona and the autobiographical self, the mission of the poet-prophet is likewise changed. He is no longer required to express his rage and stir the people to action. Instead, the poet-prophet is expressly ordered by God to stifle his rage and refrain from giving it any kind of verbal expression. The time has not yet come for him to fulfill his prophetic mission. What, then, is the nature of the poet's mission, if he is barred from arousing the people to action? His mission consists, instead, in giving poetic testimony to their degradation. It is only because the poet-prophet remains quintessentially human, *ben adam*, that he is able to serve as the primary reference point against which the infrahuman can be weighed in moral and historical terms.

As previously mentioned, the human reference point finds its expression in the poem by means of a correspondence between natural occurrences and historical events. The first three stanzas of the poem end in lines that ironically draw parallels between nature and history. At the end of the first stanza an analogy is drawn between the cyclical recurrence of spring and the *shechita* of Jews: "For God called up the spring and the massacre together: / The sun shone, the acacia bloomed, and the slaughterer slew." The second stanza ends with the poet's return to the sunlight from the dark attics where rape and killings took place, noticing that "the sun shall waste its radiance upon the earth, as in every other day." At the end of the third stanza, the pogrom survivors rush to the Rabbi's house to inquire whether their raped wives will now be permitted for sexual intercourse, and with that "all shall return to the way it was, and everything shall fall into line." In short, everything in nature and in Jewish collective behavior conspires to cover up the atrocities of the pogrom in order to resume a natural-historical progression. The awareness to the complicity of nature in the obliteration of the catastrophe marks the ground zero of the poet-prophet's moral and political agency.

On the other hand, the human perspective developed in "In the City of Killings" also encounters nature as an aesthetic phenomenon that is enjoyed regardless of the historical context in which it appears. As Dan Miron has pointed out, in "In the City of Killings" Bialik incorporates familiar themes from his earlier poetry, which celebrated various aesthetic aspects of nature such as the optical wonder of sunlight breaking through shiny objects in the poem "Zohar" (Radiance, 1900), or the grandiose sunset depicted in "Ba-arov ha-yom" (Through Clouds of Fire, 1895).[14] The same sense of wonder at the beauty of nature is retained in "In the City of Killings," albeit under entirely different circumstances. The "sevenfold rays from each shard of glass that rejoice at your sorrow" are the shards from the shattered glass windows of the houses of Jews, and the sun that descends in the west "wrapt in bleeding clouds and girt with flame" serves as a background to a scene of carnage. Throughout the poem, aesthetic descriptions of nature are set against manifestations of nature impregnated with ominous historical meaning, producing the effect of a sharp cognitive dissonance. The poet-prophet traverses this ambivalent landscape, torn between his allegiance to the beauty of nature and its allegorical function.

In this sense, the claim made by David Roskies that in "In the City of Killings" "Bialik's higher purpose was to desacralize history in God's own name"[15] misses the mark. The desacralization of history and its replacement by a profane, natural-historical order had already begun in the late Haskala literature of Abramovitsh, as we have seen in the previous chapter. Bialik's achievement in "In the City of Killings" was instead to link natural-historical occurrences to the Jewish prophetic tradition, producing in turn a desacralization of the figure of the prophet itself. In other words, the literary persona of the prophet no longer relied on the sanction of God in order to set itself up in the role of a leader and representative of the people. The prophet could now be the advocate of the people solely through overcoming his own inherent creatureliness, his own *telishut*. In this sense, Miron rightly claimed that Bialik's romantic view "fundamentally humanized and thus psychologized the concept of prophecy, which now indicated a discourse emerging not from the transcendental Other but rather from the psychic core of the human self as it strove for contact with the transcendental."[16] The poet-prophet is a human being with very human sensibilities, but he also accounts for the infrahuman. He can delve into the bowels of the earth, track the course of murder's blood, follow its metamorphosis into a thornbush or grass, and at the same time is able to enjoy these spatialized allegorical forms as pure aesthetic objects. Such attention to aesthetic surface details, paradoxically accompanied by an evocative allegorical power that stems from the deep recesses of the subject is, according to Paul de Man, one of the elusive yet singular traits of romantic poetry.[17]

THE DEGREE TO WHICH the figure of the prophet has been desacralized in modern Hebrew poetry can be gauged in the writings of the most prominent exponent of the prophetic tradition after Bialik: Uri Zvi Greenberg. This tendency is especially conspicuous in a collection of poems titled *Kelev Bayit* (*House Dog*), which was published in 1929, more than twenty-five years after the publication of Bialik's "In the City of Killings." By that time, the young Greenberg had already established himself as a prominent expressionist poet in both Hebrew and Yiddish, and as one of the leading voices of the Zionist labor movement in mandatory Palestine. However, from 1926 a growing rift has developed between Greenberg and labor Zionist leadership. This rift was occasioned by the decline of Jewish immigration to Palestine, which subsequently halted the demand for new houses on the market. The extensive construction projects that up until then sustained most of the Jewish workers in the cities were discontinued, and many of the unemployed suffered from poverty, depression, and hunger. A prevailing mood of despair took over the Yishuv,[18] and some distinguished Jewish groups and associations left for Europe. The Zionist labor leadership responded to the crisis by urging the workers to practice self-restraint and persist in their Zionist belief until economic conditions improved. It was then that Greenberg claimed that the crisis was not economical but rather conceptual in nature, and that the lack of strong leadership in the labor movement generated a lack of interest in the Zionist project itself. During the years 1928 and 1929 Greenberg had radicalized politically and espoused a new poetic style, essentially different from his earlier expressionism. At the same time, he cut his ties to both the labor movement and to the modernist group that included prominent Hebrew poets such as Avraham Shlonsky and Avigdor Hameiri, and drew closer to the right-wing Zionist Revisionist party headed by Ze'ev Jabotinsky.

The poems of *House Dog* constituted Greenberg's early attempts to forge a clear political statement out of his expressionist leanings, in which the political message was often obfuscated. To accentuate the new political turn of his poetry, he made use of the persona of the house dog, which serves throughout the book as an allegorical figure for the politicized poetic addresser. As Greenberg declared in "Levai le-sifri kelev baiyt" (Addendum to My Book House Dog), the poems in the book are "an assortment of barks in the form of punctuated letters; thus I played the part of a dog in the homeland."[19] The faithful dog senses the danger to his home, and warns with his barks against the spiritual corruption of the Yishuv's leadership and the eradication of messianic hopes by a group of "professional authors, without vision, who serve as typewriters to the 'profession' of Zionism" (CW, 38). With this remark Greenberg referred to contemporaneous Zionist poets such as Shlonsky and David Shimonovitch who, following A. D. Gordon and Y. H. Brenner, either rejected or satirized the prophetic posture in literature as grandiloquent and essentially out of touch with the realities of life in Palestine and the hardships of the Zionist pioneers.[20] In *House Dog*, Greenberg was intent on rehabilitating the status of prophecy in Hebrew poetry. His aim was to show that prophecy, while it remained latent, was never more indispensable than at the present moment. Hence the motto that appears in the poem that serves as an epigraph to *House Dog*:

> Prophecy has not strayed from Israel,
> And if its voice like the sword is not brandished at crossroads—
> That's no sign.[21] (CW, 45)

הַנְּבוּאָה לֹא סָרָה מִיִּשְׂרָאֵל
וְאִם קוֹלָהּ כַּחֶרֶב לֹא יוּנַף בְּאֶם רְחוֹב—
אֵין זֶה סִמָּן.

After affirming the persistence of prophecy in the present, Greenberg predicts the inevitable clash between prophecy, armed with "divine rage," and its mortal enemies. As Hannan Hever has pointed out, Greenberg's concentration on the opposition between the prophet and his enemies at the beginning of *House Dog* foreshadows the principal aim of the book: the elaboration of the figure of the warrior-prophet through the poetic persona of the house dog.[22] The act of barking, however, does not only carry political implications but poetic ones as well. Barking connotes raw, unadorned poetic expression, contrasted with the romantic image of the poet as a songbird:

> "I do not sing as a bird," for I am no descendent of the noble poet from Weimar and my letters are not *gothic*. For I am the child of the scaffold in Europe, the grandson of the burned, butchered, tortured prisoners of Rome and martyrs [*harugei malchut*] among the gentiles. I came from Jewish exile as one who had plunged in and arose from rivers of blood and tears, and in Eretz-Israel the stars are

still not singing gothic confidence and classic love to my ear, for the kingdom of Israel is not fully there. It is still a battlefront to be conquered. (CW, 44)

Remarkably, the question of poetic style is posed here as a confrontation between two animals—the songbird and the dog—that symbolize the poetry of two national cultures: German as opposed to Jewish. The German poet who feels safe in his homeland can sing like a carefree bird, enjoying poetry for poetry's sake, whereas the homeless Jew, who is susceptible to violence everywhere, writes poetry as a series of barks. The Jew's barking serves both as a warning signal to his people from impending catastrophes, and as an expressive sigh of the creature. It is the Jewish idiom par excellence, a product of the collective experiences of exile, humiliation, and persecution suffered by generations of Jews in Europe. The figure of the dog is thus metonymically associated with scenes of atrocities and with the profane suffering and degradation of Jewish victims. As Hever rightly points out, such a figural construction of Jewish identity links Greenberg's *House Dog* with previous poetic manifestations of Jewish dogs in Heine's "Prinzessin Sabbat" and in Bialik's "Igeret Ktana."[23] But in *House Dog*, Greenberg attempted to do more than just establish a poetic genealogy. His aim was to elaborate and expand the forms of experience associated with the figure of the Jewish dog.

In an earlier collection of poetry *Eyma gdola ve-yare'akh* (*A Great Fear and the Moon*, 1924), Greenberg already employed the image of a barking dog as a poetic symbol for creaturely suffering. In the poem "Ha-elef hashelishi" (The Third Millennium), the act of barking serves as an alternative communicative outlet for the expression of anguish when ordinary human speech has failed:

> If words are lighter for they expired in the markets like sick dogs,
> And prayers that the wind devoured did not reach God—
> Why should the distressed man still be ashamed to tear the garb from his flesh
> *And bark like a dog*, the man as a dog, and God shall understand him and answer.
>
> Yes, *perhaps* God will listen to him and in the quiet sky angels will tremble.

> For God, too, shall rise and howl his woe if the horror should increase in the valley
> *And man in His image barks like a dog from the burden of his days in the world.*
> (*Collected Writings*, vol. 1, 20; emphases in the original)

אִם קַלּוּ הַמִּלִּים כִּי נַפְשָׁן הוֹצִיאוּ בִּשְׁנָקִים כַּכְּלָבִים הַחוֹלִים,
וּתְפִלּוֹת שֶׁטָּרְפָה הָרוּחַ בְּפִיהָ עֲדֵי אֱלֹהִים לֹא הִגִּיעוּ—
מַדּוּעַ עוֹד יֵבוֹשׁ הָאָדָם הֶהָמוּי לִקְרֹעַ שִׂמְלוֹתָיו מִבְּשָׂרוֹ
וְנָבַח כַּכֶּלֶב, הָאָדָם כַּכֶּלֶב, וְאֵל יְבִינֵהוּ וְיַעֲנֶה.

כֵּן, אוּלַי לוֹ יַאֲזִין הָאֵל וּבַשַּׁחַק הַשֶּׁקֶט מַלְאָכִים יִרְעָדוּ.
כִּי יָקוּם וְיִשְׁאַג גַּם אֵל אֶת אֲבוֹיוֹ, אִם רָבְתָה הַזְּוָעָה בָּעֵמֶק
וְאָדָם בִּדְמוּתוֹ כַּכֶּלֶב נוֹבֵחַ מֵעֲקַת יְמוֹתָיו בָּעוֹלָם.

In the poems of *A Great Fear and the Moon* as well as in the later *House Dog*, barking refers to what Deleuze and Guattari called "an asignifying intensive utilization of language," which opens the word onto "unexpected internal intensities."[24] It is an expressionist formulation of shock and indignation in the face of existential hardships, either as experienced by Jewish pioneers in Palestine in *A Great Fear and the Moon*, or when facing the corruption of Zionist leadership in *House Dog*. In both cases, barking fulfills the dual function of a warning signal and an authentic expression of creaturely suffering. The warning applies to the concrete political situation in which the poem is written, whereas the aspect of creaturely suffering serves as the implicit theological framework against which the poetic addresser comes to terms with a reality in which messianic redemption fails to appear in history. In this context, the act of barking bypasses ordinary human speech and establishes an unmediated channel of communication with God. This communication, however, is one-sided, for God does not answer back ("*perhaps* God will listen to him"); nor does God intervene in history. Such an essentially Pauline understanding of creaturely life is affirmed in *House Dog* in the following lines:

> Nowhere in the universe, only here I have seen:
> The earthly "inanimate" lives a deep life
> Painful and wise, without prayer of lips,
> And awaits redemption like the corpse of man. (CW, 61)

בְּשׁוּם מָקוֹם בַּיְקוּם, רַק פֹּה רָאוּ עֵינַי
הַ"דּוֹמֵם" הָאַרְצִי חַי חַיִּים עֲמֻקִּים
כְּאוּבִים וַחֲכָמִים, בְּלִי צִקּוּן שְׂפָתַיִם
וּמְצַפֶּה לִגְאֻלָּה כִּגְוִיַּת הָאָדָם.

The wordless bark that arises from suffering creation to God ultimately gives rise to a collective cry of suffering that is picked up by the dog with his keen senses. It thus legitimates a profane form of prophecy:

I am no prophet in Zion, but this:
Part house-dog, part jackal,
That smells disaster and barks on time— (CW, 79)

אֵינֶנִּי נָבִיא בְּצִיּוֹן, אֶלָּא כָּךְ:
סָפֵק כֶּלֶב-בַּיִת וְסָפֵק תַּן,
הַמֵּרִיחַ לְאָסוֹן וְנוֹבֵחַ בִּזְמַן—

Paradoxically, the house dog does not derive his authoritative prophetic voice from a transcendental source, but rather from a sense of impending disaster prompted by the occasion of spilled blood. As stated in the lines that follow: "It was not the voice of God in heaven that suddenly called me: go prophesy in this Beth Jeshimoth / ... Not the voice of God, but the voice of the blood of my brothers and sisters, which is the sound of my own roaring blood" (CW, 79). The spillage of Jewish blood prompts the occasion of prophecy as barks, and the dog tracks the course of blood in the "depth of time," which is Greenberg's metaphor for the present moment as it incorporates parts of the past.[25] Indeed, the dog's keen intuition consists precisely in that he is able to pick up the trail of blood, even blood that has been spilled two millennia ago.

What man does not see
And the spade of man has not dug
The dog sees with its own eyes:
What remains covered for two
Millennia under the earth.
He therefore wanders and whines
Where people pass

Without hearing with their leg and hand ...
The dog tarries and lingers
Where blood has been spilled
Listening to the depth that grew silent. (CW, 123)

מָה שֶׁבֶּן אָדָם לֹא רוֹאֶה
וּמְעֻדָּר הָאָדָם לֹא חָפַר
רוֹאֶה בְּעֵינָיו הַכֶּלֶב:
מָה שֶׁמְּכַסֶּה זֶה אֶלֶף
שְׁנֵי בַשָּׁנִים בֶּעָפָר.
וְעַל־כֵּן הוּא צוֹעֶה וּפוֹעֶה
בַּמָּקוֹם שֶׁעוֹבְרִים בְּנֵי־אָדָם
בְּלִי שֶׁמַע בְּרַגְלָם וּבְיָדָם ...
מִתְעַכֵּב הַכֶּלֶב וְשׁוֹהֶה
בַּמָּקוֹם שֶׁשָּׁפַךְ הַדָּם
וּמַאֲזִין לָעֹמֶק שֶׁנָּדַם.

These lines clearly address the same disturbing gap between aesthetic and allegorical nature that first emerges in "In the City of Killings." In both poems, the prophet extracts from the bowels of the earth the crime that has been literally covered up, an act equivalent to the painful evocation of the atrocity and its retrieval from the depths of oblivion. Nevertheless, the human addresser in Bialik's poem encounters the atrocity at its vanishing point, when its traces are still visible on the surface. Greenberg's prophetic dog, on the other hand, appears much later and disinters from the bowels of the earth the memory of a disaster that has already been long forgotten. This is the melancholic task of the lowly dog who always remains close to the ground:

What do I do down low?
I sniff and smell,
The embryo of the day in the fog
And the secret of what grows in the bush. (CW, 124)

מָה אֲנִי עוֹשֶׂה בַשָּׁפָל?
מֵרִיחַ אֲנִי וּמֵרִיחַ

לַעֲבֹר הַיּוֹם בָּעֲרָפֶל
וְלִסְוֹד-הַצּוֹמֵחַ בְּשִׁיחַ.

Like Bialik's prophetic poet, Greenberg's dog also knows the secret of the bush—namely, that it feeds on the blood of murdered Jews. The dog can thus read nature allegorically, as if it were a kind of hieroglyph, knowing that it always encapsulates, in transfigured form, a hidden record of the bloody past. Yet the dog's keen senses are not only related to a supersensory perception of past events; they are also linked to a form of clairvoyance, as the dog can smell the "embryo of the day" in the fog. This metaphor suggests that the present moment already contains, in a profane form, the seeds of future events in the same manner that a pregnant woman carries her unborn child. The future can be sensed at the present moment but not directly perceived (hence the dog's sniffing in the fog). Here, the crucial point is that the disinterment of a painful and forgotten past is mediated through the figure of the dog and associated with the prediction of catastrophic future events, for the dog is attuned to the cyclical rhythms of natural history, and can foretell with his keen senses the coming of spring, the season of pogroms and national catastrophes. The dog smells spilled blood from an impending catastrophe in much the same way that he can pick up the trail of blood that has been spilled two millennia ago, and he barks in warning. In other words, the prophetic wisdom of the dog consists in his ability to sense in the changing events of human history the cyclical recurrence of profane forces of natural history.

Greenberg himself, of course, is perfectly aware that his house dog belongs in a long line of "outcast prophetic dogs" that "bark at every distortion" (CW, 123). Greenberg indeed links the persona of the house dog to a genealogy that can be traced as far back as to Sabbatai Zevi and David Hareuveni, eccentric figures with messianic aspirations who were at first respected and hailed as messiahs, but were eventually cast out and despised. For Greenberg these men articulated a desacralized prophetic stance that laid bare the need for a homeland to which Jews could return and in which they could live in security and dignity. In these terms, Greenberg formulates the crucial distinction between "house dogs" and the diasporic "stray dogs." The distinction is elaborated in one of the first poems in the book, titled "Be-ma'amakim" (In the Depths):

Time is very deep. And in Spain there is no trace of the scaffold that
was erected.
There is no smell of the living Hebrew flesh that was burned at the
stake.
And no blackened-blood stains the asphalts.
And no outdoors dog there lingers and senses
With a deep sniff:
The amount of spilled Jewish blood. (CW, 53)

הַזְּמַן עָמֹק מְאֹד. וּבִסְפָרַד אֵין זֵכֶר לַגַּרְדּוֹם שֶׁהוּקָם.
אֵין רֵיחַ לִשְׂרֵפַת הַבָּשָׂר הָעִבְרִי הַחַי עַל הַמּוֹקֵד
וְאֵין כֶּתֶם דָּם-אֲשֶׁר-הִשְׁחִיר עַל פְּנֵי הָאַסְפַלְטִים.
וְאַף כֶּלֶב בַּחוּץ שָׁם אֵינוֹ מִתְמַהְמֵהַּ וְחָשׁ
בַּהֲרָחָה עֲמֻקָּה:
אֶת כִּבְרַת תִּשְׁפֹּכֶת הַדָּמִים הַיְּהוּדִים.

The diasporic street dog—not unlike Heine's Jewish dog or Bialik's poetic addresser in "Igeret ktana"—is too preoccupied with his own self-preservation to linger and smell the Jewish blood that has been spilled throughout the millennia. Living in a godforsaken world, he seeks no retribution and possesses no sense of historical justice. The house dog, on the other hand, plays an instrumental role in the preservation of the trail of "murder's blood," a blood that would ultimately legitimate the redemption of the Jewish people in history.

AN ILLUSTRATION of the prophetic role of the dog, merged with an autobiographical account of the poet's wanderings in the Diaspora, opens the book *House Dog*. The first poem, "Messiah," essentially affirms the persistence of a nonmessianic reality. This theological point of departure serves as background for the actions of the poet in the poems that follow, which describe his search for the messiah in Rome and his failed attempts at locating the grave of Simon Bar Giora, who serves as the primary role model for a rebellious and militaristic Jewish leadership envisioned by Greenberg. Bar Giora was the leader of the Zealots in Judea who waged war against the Roman Empire in the first century, but after the Jewish rebellion was quenched by Titus, Bar Giora was exiled to Rome and executed by being thrown off a rock. By attempting to disinter the grave of Bar Giora from the bowels of the earth, the poet fulfills the role of a prophetic dog who sees what "the spade of man has not dug," hoping to reclaim the legacy of the ancient Hebrew Zealots for the present age. Significantly, this comes to be expressed in the reference to the Arch of Titus, which is not enjoyed by the poet as an aesthetic artifact but is instead seen as a monument to the shameful defeat that initiated two thousand years of Jewish exile. Thus, under the asphalts of modern Rome, a vision of ancient Rome suddenly comes to life:

> Here a holiday was celebrated; high singing, lights; lechery reveling
>   in blood and joy of destruction;
> A thick shower of flowers upon the blowing of horns,
> And in my Jerusalem—from the upper to the lower city,
> On the slopes, high and low—
> My dead were laid, vanquished under the blaze of the sword like the
>   snow under the blaze of fire. (CW, 50)

> פֹּה הָיָה יוֹם חַג; רִנָּה גְבֹהָה, מְאוֹרוֹת; זִמָּה הוֹלֶלֶת בְּדָם וְגִיל הֶרֶס;
> מְטַר פְּרָחִים עָבֶה עֲלֵי תְּרוּעַת חֲצוֹצְרוֹת;
> וּבִירוּשָׁלַיִם שֶׁלִּי—מִן הָעִיר הָעֶלְיוֹנָה וְעַד הַתַּחְתּוֹנָה,
> בְּמַעֲלוֹת, בְּמוֹרָדוֹת—
> הֻצְּעוּ חַלְלֵי מַגֵּרִים כַּשֶּׁלֶג בְּלַהַט הַחֶרֶב כְּלַהַט הָאֵשׁ.

This vision is revealed to the poet in "the depth of time," and he goes on to affirm that "time is very deep and there is no echo to the Roman holiday even in the Arch of Titus!" (CW, 50). However, the poet as a prophetic dog is attentive to the depths that grew silent, and consequently he feels the urge to reclaim Jewish sovereignty in Eretz Israel. In this consists the messianic quality of the poet's vision: in the restoration of Jewish sovereignty in the Jewish ancestral homeland. Throughout the ages a few notable persons have attempted to reclaim the legacy of Bar Giora, namely, Sabbatai Zevi and David Hareuveni, who failed. Bar Giora himself fiercely fought the Romans and defended Jerusalem but was eventually put to death like a dog:

> Just so, like an outdoors dog, they decapitated him
> And threw him to the pit from the scaffold (CW, 51)

סְתָם, כְּמוֹ כֶּלֶב בַּחוּץ, עֲרָפוּהוּ
וְהִשְׁלִיכוּהוּ לַבּוֹר מִגְּרָדוֹם

The phrase *kelev bahutz* (stray dog; but literally "outdoors dog"), implicitly contrasted here with *kelev baiyt* (house dog), is associated with the ignominious death by decapitation (*arifa*): the same death to which Bialik's Kishinev pogrom victims were subjected. To die like an "outdoors dog" or a diasporic street dog, then, means to die a death that is *shechita* in the Bialikean sense. Because this death is *shechita*, "no trace is left of the lord of Jerusalem" (CW, 51). Similarly, "no one among the people knows the graves of Sabbatai Zevi and Hareuveni" (CW, 52). The bodies of these messiahs, just like the bodies of Bialik's pogrom victims, have been claimed by profane nature. And precisely here lies Greenberg's answer to the difficult symbolic status of the pogrom victims in Hebrew poetry after Bialik's "In the City of Killings." Nowhere does Greenberg challenge the Bialikean view that Jewish victims of atrocities throughout the ages have died a profane, meaningless death. And as in Bialik's poem, nature is implicitly conceived as a totality in which all elements undergo a continuous process of displacement and metamorphosis. Indeed, it is precisely the prospect of reincarnation of the messiah through metamorphosis (*gilgul*) that sustains the hope of his future return, bestowing an eternal meaning on those who died a profane death in pogroms and persecutions:

> But the reincarnation-of-messiah is the "dybbuk" of the people,
> That always cries in our blood—
> That softly lies on our tables. That sings in the voices of our newborn.
> That rests like a soft woolen fleece, on which all the tears shall fall,
> And bestows the majesty of an eternal kingdom upon our dead under
>   the cross—(CW, 52)

אַךְ גִּלְגּוּלוֹ-שֶׁל- מָשִׁיחַ הוּא הַ"דִּבּוּק" שֶׁבָּעָם,
הַבּוֹכֶה תָּמִיד בְּדָמֵינוּ——
שׁוֹרֶה רַךְ עַל שֻׁלְחָנֵנוּ. רַן בְּקוֹל תִּינוֹקוֹתֵינוּ.
נָח כְּגִזַּת צֶמֶר רַכָּה, בָּהּ תִּפֹּלְנָה כָּל הַדְּמָעוֹת,
וּמַשְׁרֶה הוֹד מְמַלְכוּת-עַד עַל פְּנֵי מֵתֵינוּ תַּחַת צְלָב——

Paradoxically, the same cyclical natural-historical process that obliterated all traces of the deaths of the victims and deprived them of human meaning guarantees the reappearance of the messiah in historical time and the future redemption of the Jewish people. The deaths of the victims, while undoubtedly profane in nature, nevertheless play a part in the general scheme of messianic redemption. Greenberg develops this solution not in opposition to the Bialikean vision of the pogrom as a bracketed zone of natural history, but as its genealogical continuation. In *House Dog* Greenberg not only expands the meaning of the problematic terms in which the pogrom victims were described in "In the City of Killings," but also establishes a direct continuity with Bialik's poem as a prophecy fulfilled.

However, one important discrepancy between Bialik's and Greenberg's poems should be noted. Whereas in "In the City of Killings" the obliteration of "murder's blood" would inspire a struggle for a historical existence as opposed to a diasporic life and a dog's death, in Greenberg's poem the house dog's evocation of murder's blood ultimately serves as a political weapon whereby diasporic existence is denigrated. Greenberg relies on the opposition between *kelev baiyt* ("house dog") and *kelev bahutz* ("outdoors dog") to base his claim that the misguided Zionist labor leadership is establishing a new Jewish Diaspora in mandatory Palestine instead of a sovereign Jewish state. In the "Addendum to my Book *House Dog*," he points to the main cause of the spiritual degradation of Zionist labor leadership in that the Zionist leaders "do not know that their diasporic cunning is not a genuine wisdom of the homeland.... The peddler's cunning, a diasporic Jewish peddling, that carries with it a psychology from place to place.... This inborn peddling of the mind and the soul, that even the fire of Zionism, after the great pogroms, did not consume, has found here, in the battlefront of the pioneers, the space and the right objective conditions—to establish its hold and flaunt its sovereignty" (CW, 38–39).

Greenberg's poetic remedy to the crisis of Zionist leadership is the establishment of "The Strongmen Alliance" (*Brit ha-biryonim*), which assumed a brief political manifestation during the early 1930s as a quasi-fascist faction of the Zionist Revisionist Movement (Greenberg was, of course, one of the Alliance's founding members). In *House Dog* the notion of "The Strongmen Alliance" appears as a violent response to the shortcomings of Zionist labor leadership, which is called "Sodom of the homeland, a new Sodom!" The poet accordingly suggests to "set fire to Sodom and topple its stones" (CW, 97). From within the framework of "The Strongmen Alliance," the poet is able to violently enforce the separation between the colonizing aspirations of the Zionist pioneers and their misguided Zionist leadership. The brutish and militaristic figure of the poet-strongman is yet another elaboration on the figure of the house dog, which now appears in the form of a beast baring its teeth in the face of mortal danger. The link between the brutal strongman and the dog is established in *House Dog* in stanzas such as the following: "I am still young and hot-blooded as a thug [*biryon*], / And I could have become a foreign poet: / drunk, hooligan, excellent, Don Juan. / If only I had been a lawful son of a nation and a homeland" (CW, 105). In this case the lowly outcast does not hesitate to make use of his raw animal faculties, because he realizes that being a dog frees him from the dictates of any national law or government. The only law that applies to the dog is the brutal struggle for survival in a state of exception. Thus he is determined to assume the role of an aggressor rather than that of the traditional victim. Ultimately, the metamorphosis of the poet to a dog and from a dog to a strongman is only a part of a complex series of transformations that take place throughout the book. In the penultimate poem, the lowly dog turns out to have been only a temporary phase out of which the messiah-king will emerge: "and I too shall emerge out of the dog skin / to hail the homeland: *a star shall rise*" (CW, 126; emphasis in original).[26] Whereas the prophetic addresser in Bialik's "In the City of Killings" has consigned the infrahuman to oblivion in the name of the fulfillment of a historical ideal, in Greenberg's *House Dog* a persona of a lowly dog is assumed only in order to ultimately surpass the human condition. But as Greenberg has discovered in his poetry, the road to the *Übermensch* inevitably passes through the realm of the infrahuman.

4 AT HOME IN A DISTORTED LIFE
The Dog as a Constellation in the Work of Franz Kafka

FRANZ KAFKA'S AVERSION to Hebrew literature in general, and to Bialik's poem "In the City of Killings" in particular, has been thoroughly documented in a recent scholarly work by Dan Miron.[1] Kafka was introduced to Bialik's poem on at least one occasion, when his acquaintance from the Yiddish theater, Yitshok Levy, recited the Yiddish version of "In the City of Killings" in 1911. With the exception of one sarcastic comment on Bialik in his diary, Kafka refrained from ever mentioning him again, along with most other contemporaneous writers of the Hebrew renaissance. Nevertheless, one of Kafka's most famous works, *Der Prozeß* (*The Trial*, 1915), suggests subtle points of convergence and continuity with Bialik's pogrom poems. Like the victims in "On the Slaughter" and "In the City of Killings," Josef K. dies "like a dog." The impression that Josef K.'s death is a *shechita* in the Bialikean sense is further reinforced by the choice of the instrument of killing: a butcher's knife (*Fleischermesser*). And, as in Bialik's pogrom poem, the killing takes place in an unregistered area of the law, as a bracketed act of violence that remains outside the purview of history and human memory.

Unaware of this uncanny resemblance to Bialik's pogrom poetry, Eric Santner has observed that the law at work in Kafka's writings is a law in a state of exception: "In Kafka, the dimension of the "unrevealed"— a dimension condensed in the objects that seize the allegorical imagination—pertains not to man's destiny in the openness of Being but to the status of law in its (now dispersed, now chronic) state of exception."[2] This definition, in a way, expands on Walter Benjamin's assessment of the status of the law as a "cloudy spot" in the work of Kafka.[3] Referring to the parable "Before the Law," Benjamin has argued that the law in Kafka's parables remains inaccessible, forming a zone of emptiness or absence: "do we have the doctrine which Kafka's parables interpret and which K.'s postures and the gestures of his animals clarify? It does not exist; all we can say is that here and there we have an allusion to it."⁴ This fundamental emptiness of the law is not the hallmark of the "full power" (*plenitudo potestatis*) or the pleroma of sovereignty, but rather of the kenomatic state of the law in a state of exception.⁵ Thus, one could read Kafka's "Before the Law"—as Santner does—as a parable of the law in a state of exception. Significantly, Benjamin himself does not take this step. Instead, he interprets the absence of the law in Kafka as a mark of a constitutive forgetfulness.

The absence of the law and its operation in a state of emergency in Kafka inevitably recall Benjamin's *Trauerspiel* essay, which depicted the workings of society and politics in the total disappearance of eschatology, that is, in the absence of revelation.⁶ Following Carl Schmitt, Benjamin claimed that in the Baroque, a new concept of sovereignty emerged that was no longer bound to or based on a revealed religious doctrine: "The ruler is designated from the outset as the holder of dictatorial power if war, revolt, or other catastrophes should lead to a state of emergency."⁷ Thus, the social and political order in the Baroque was paradoxically established on the absence of a law, an absence around which life and work came to be organized in society. Only in this context can we interpret Benjamin's cryptic remark that the question of the organization of life and work in human society "increasingly occupied Kafka as it became impenetrable to him."⁸ Everyday life in Kafka's world, just as in Bialik's post-pogrom reality, is established on the suppression of something that remains out of time and out of memory:

> What has been forgotten—and this insight affords us yet another avenue of access to Kafka's work—is never something purely individual. Everything forgotten mingles with what has been of the prehistoric world, forms countless, uncertain, changing compounds, yielding a constant flow of new, strange products. Oblivion is the container from which the inexhaustible intermediate world in Kafka's stories presses toward the light. "Here the very fullness of the world is considered as the only reality." ... To Kafka, the world of his ancestors was as unfathomable as the world of realities was important for him, and we may be sure that, like the totem poles of primitive peoples, the world of ancestors took him down to the animals. Incidentally, Kafka is not the only writer for whom animals

are the receptacles of the forgotten. In Tieck's profound story "Fair Eckbert," the forgotten name of a little dog, Strohmi, stands for a mysterious guilt. One can understand, then, that Kafka did not tire of picking up the forgotten from animals. They are not the goal, to be sure, but one cannot do without them.[9]

Here, the prehistoric world, which Benjamin conceived of as a mythical, primeval world (*Vorwelt*) along the lines of Bachofen's "hetaeric stage,"[10] is identified with the animal and the natural as the condition that lies outside justice, morality, and memory. Yet one need not posit a "hetaeric stage" in order to address the status of the forgotten in Kafka, as this association is allegorical in character and its exact meaning remains, for the most part, tentative and obscure. More importantly, at stake is the relation that the forgotten—as a zone of bracketed temporality—assumes with respect to the present condition of the protagonists in Kafka's work. Although animality and the obscurity of the forgotten are intrinsically linked in Kafka's work, as will become apparent, the forgotten makes itself felt in the present by virtue of an underlying allegorical modality.

A few emblematic examples will help clarify this point. For instance, when Josef K. is arrested, he looks at the guards and wonders: "What kind of people were they? What were they talking about? Which department did they belong to? After all, K. had rights, the country was at peace, the laws had not been suspended" (T, 7).[11] This last observation, which problematizes any simple identification of the law in Kafka with a state of exception, could hardly be deemed ingenuous. Is K. really pondering whether the country was in a state of emergency, or is he merely stating the obvious? Similarly, as K. confronts the guards in Frau Grubach's living room, it is mentioned that the room "looked almost exactly the same as it had been the previous evening" (T, 6). A similarly formulated commonplace observation assumes a more conspicuous character when, in "Die Verwandlung" ("The Metamorphosis," 1915) Gregor Samsa awakes one morning as a giant beetle and observes that despite his transformation, "his room, a proper, human being's room, rather too small, lay peacefully between its four familiar walls."[12] In *The Trial* and "The Metamorphosis," everyday reality is reaffirmed in its most banal aspects—the room remains the same, the country is at peace—against a monstrous transformation that has taken place, a transformation that emanates from the realm of the forgotten. "It was not a dream,"[13] Gregor Samsa realized. Indeed, it was allegory.

In Kafka's work, allegory mediates between what Santner calls "the dimension of the 'unrevealed'" or the forgotten, and the material fullness of the world. By means of allegory, the forgotten comes to assume concrete dimensions, condensing into everyday objects. To be sure, this does not imply a bridging of the abyss between "significance" and "physical nature" on which the allegorical is predicated, since the figural meaning remains undisclosed. In Kafka's work, the *allos* of allegory, the referent, is made present, yet we are not given a key to its "significance." Theodor Adorno was thinking along these lines when he wrote that "nowhere in Kafka does there glimmer the aura of the infinite idea; nowhere does the horizon open. Each sentence is literal and each signifies. The two moments are not merged, as the symbol would have it, but yawn apart and out of the abyss between them blinds the glaring ray of fascination."[14] This fundamental undisclosedness of meaning in the work of Kafka, which is not to be confused with a lack of meaning, is the hallmark of an allegorical modality. In light of these observations, I wish to offer a slight but not insignificant corrective to Santner's analysis of the operation of the law in Kafka's work. The "dimension of the 'unrevealed'" cannot be said to be predicated on a state of exception any more than it can be convincingly shown to be based on a primeval "hetaeric stage." Although such interpretations are useful in conceptualizing the literary and philosophical stakes involved in Kafka's work, ultimately the allegorical modality itself takes precedence over any of its concrete manifestations as well as over any conceptual apparatus in which it may be subsequently embedded. With regard to the obscure and the forgotten, any speculation regarding what it encapsulates must remain tentative and uncertain, and cannot be used to establish a solid claim pertaining to the purpose and significance of Kafka's work.

THE IMMERSION in the undisclosedness of meaning finds its most powerful emblematic expression in Kafka's work at the end of *The Trial*, in the final scene of Josef K.'s execution. Like the death of Bialik's pogrom victims, it is clear that K.'s death will be consigned to oblivion as the execution is conducted at night in an old, abandoned quarry at the outskirts of the city, without witnesses. But more importantly, K.'s death, too, is stripped of an overarching symbolic meaning as he dies without knowing the nature of his crime, and without receiving an opportunity to properly defend his case before a court. Up until his very last moments, K. still hopes for a horizon of meaning to open, as he suddenly perceives in the distance an enigmatic figure surrounded by light that shines in the darkness, recalling traditional motifs of divine redemption:

> His eye fell on the top storey of the house beside the quarry. Like a flash of light, the two casements of a window parted and a human figure, faint and thin from the distance and height, leant far out in one swift movement then stretched its arms out even farther. Who was it? A friend? A kind person? Someone who felt for him? Someone who wanted to help? Was it just one? Or all of them? Was help still possible? Were there still objections he'd forgotten? (T, 164; P, 312)

The distant figure in the window with its strange gesticulations merely serves to underscore the futility of K.'s situation. It is not that these gestures are necessarily meaningless, but that their meaning is withheld. There simply is no way of knowing whether they are directed at Josef K., done randomly, or perhaps even directed at his executioners. In the end, K. dies like a dog without discovering the truth of his situation. The undignified conditions under which he dies might explain, at least in part, the shame he felt in his moment of death: " 'Like a dog!' he said. It seemed as if his shame would outlive him." [" 'Wie ein Hund!' sagte er, es war, als sollte die Scham ihn überleben."] (T, 165, translation modified; P, 312) What is at stake, then, in this shame? What exactly was Josef K. ashamed of, and why does shame come to replace rage (such as we find in Bialik) as a viable reaction to a gratuitous death? As a point of departure for the consideration of shame in *The Trial*, I would like to refer to a 1935 essay titled *On Escape*, in which Emmanuel Levinas analyzes shame as a condition in which the uncontrollable urge to flee from oneself is countered by an equal impossibility of evasion:

> What appears in shame is thus precisely the fact of being riveted to oneself, the radical impossibility of fleeing oneself to hide oneself, the unalterably binding presence of the I to itself. Nakedness is

shameful when it is the sheer visibility of our being, of its ultimate intimacy. And the nakedness of our body is not that of a material thing, antithesis of spirit, but the nakedness of our total being in all its fullness and solidity, of its most brutal expression of which we could not fail to take note ... It is therefore our intimacy, that is, our presence to ourselves, that is shameful. It reveals not our nothingness but rather the totality of our existence.[15]

In a gloss on Levinas's text, Giorgio Agamben has clarified the relevance of this analysis of shame to Kafka's *Trial*:

> To be ashamed means to be consigned to something that cannot be assumed. But what cannot be assumed is not something external. Rather, it originates in our own intimacy; it is what is most intimate in us (for example, our own physiological life). Here the "I" is thus overcome by its own passivity, its ownmost sensibility; yet this expropriation and desubjectification is also an extreme and irreducible presence of the "I" to itself. It is as if our consciousness collapsed and, seeking to flee in all directions, were simultaneously summoned by an irrefutable order to be present at its own defacement, at the expropriation of what is most its own. In shame, the subject thus has no other content than its own desubjectification; it becomes witness to its own disorder, its own oblivion as a subject. This double movement, which is both subjectification and desubjectification, is shame.[16]

The crucial point that Agamben makes here is that in shame the rational human being, the subject, is inescapably confronted with the simple fact of his own physiological life—that is, with bare life as such. Shame thus attests to the unbridgeable "fracture between the living being and the speaking being, the inhuman and the human."[17] This "fracture," indeed, is nothing other than the locus of the infrahuman, the site of an unresolvable tension between figure and experience. Josef K.'s shame, which emerges in the transition from man to dog, is therefore not a protest against the degrading death to which he is subjected. On the contrary, his shame implies "the radical impossibility of fleeing" his own bare life. To put it differently, K.'s shame lays bare the gap between Josef K. the senior bank clerk, the defendant who is trying to make sense of his situation, and the dog who is killed (or perhaps more precisely, slaughtered) without knowing why he is put to death.

Significantly, K.'s death scene is not the only instance in which the threshold between human and dog is crossed in *The Trial*. The work contains two more explicit references to dogs, both of which are associated with a degradation of the human being and with a resulting sense of shame. The first instance takes place in the lumber room, where K. walks in on an unusual scene of corporal punishment. Surprised to hear groans coming from behind a closed door that leads to a lumber room at his bank office, K. opens the door and discovers three men bending under the low ceiling. One of them, identified only as a thrasher [*Prügler*], was clearly in charge and was "dressed in a kind of dark leather outfit which left his arms and much of his chest completely bare" (T, 58). The two other men turn out to be the guards who handled K.'s arrest, and were now being punished because K. complained about them during his appearance in court for having eaten his breakfast and taken some of his underwear. The guards immediately turn to K., pleading him to intercede on their behalf. One of them, Franz, stripped down to his trousers, kneels and in a pathetic outburst begs K. to intervene, lays the blame on his colleague and confesses: "my poor fiancée's waiting outside the bank to see what happens. I'm so miserably ashamed" [ich schäme mich ja so erbärmlich] (T, 60, translation modified; P, 113). At this point the thrasher loses patience and begins to strike Franz, who lets out

> [a] scream, one unchanging, uninterrupted scream that didn't sound as if it came from a human being, but from some tortured instrument, the whole corridor echoed with it, the whole building must have heard it. (T, 60)

When the office attendants arrive and inquire if everything is all right, K. replies that the noise came from "a dog howling in the courtyard [es schreit nur ein Hund auf dem Hof]" (T, 61; P, 114). K.'s reply is telling, since the original verb in German, *schreit*, does not connote a dog's howling but rather indicates human screaming. The idiosyncratic use of the verb *schreien* is here implicitly associated with an indeterminate state between humanity and animality.

As in the execution of Josef K., shame is invoked in the lumber room scene in the context of corporal punishment, but here the infliction of punishment is not entirely devoid of sexual overtones, specifically of a sadomasochistic nature. In the series of actions through which the guards (and Franz in particular) are dehumanized—bending, stripping, kneeling, begging, thrashing, and screaming—the infliction of corporal punishment, though dreaded, is suggestive of a latent libidinal dimension. This is also the case in the second scene that involves a dog, namely, the scene in which Block, the corn merchant, debases himself before Huld the lawyer.

When K. informs his lawyer that he would no longer require his services, Huld attempts to change K.'s mind by demonstrating "how other defendants are treated" (T, 136). Huld then orders Leni, his nurse, to summon Block to his room. Block's initial hesitation upon entering the room already betrays his lowly, undignified position:

> Block came as soon as he was called, but stood outside the door, as if wondering whether he should come in. He raised his eyebrows and inclined his head, seemingly listening for the lawyer's command to be repeated ... Block saw that at least no one was sending him away, so he came in on tiptoe, a tense expression on his face, hands clutched tightly behind his back ... Once the lawyer had started speaking, Block didn't look at the bed anymore but stared at some corner or other instead and just listened, as if the sight of the speaker were too dazzling for him to bear. (T, 136)

Still hesitant, Block asks the lawyer if he would like him to leave. The lawyer snaps at him, ordering him to stay, but his words seem to have a jarring effect on Block. "You would have thought that, instead of fulfilling Block's wish, the lawyer had threatened to have him thrashed [*Prügeln*], for now Block really did start to tremble" (T, 137; P, 260). The word *Prügeln*, of course, evokes the original context of punishment in the lumber room. In this case, however, the sadism is not physical but mental. In what follows, the lawyer, together with Leni, engage in a well-rehearsed role-play in which they subject Block to a form of elaborate humiliation. At first, the lawyer tells Block that he has news for him regarding his case, but then he takes a long pause, during which Block stoops low "as if he were about to kneel" (T, 137), an act for which he is scolded by K. But it is Block who is "punished" (*gestraft*) for K.'s intervention, for he then has to declare allegiance to the lawyer (although in reality he employs five other lawyers and is negotiating with a sixth). Block then kneels down beside the lawyer's bed; Leni joins them on the edge of the bed. Block is delighted, and motions for Leni to intercede on his behalf with the lawyer. Leni instructs Block to kiss the lawyer's hand, which he quickly does. The lawyer is somewhat appeased and inquires of Leni (rather than Block) about Block's behavior, as if he were a school child. Before replying, Leni looks down at Block who raises his hands to her, pleading for a favorable report. With that, K. realizes that Block's behavior, even though it may have been motivated by his own selfish needs, could never be justified in the eyes of a "fellow human being" [nichts konnte ihn in den Augen eines Mitmenschen rechtfertigen] (T, 139; P, 264).

> Such a person was no longer a client, he was the lawyer's dog. If the lawyer had ordered him to crawl under the bed, as if going into a kennel, and bark, he would have done so with pleasure. (T, 139)

> Das war kein Klient mehr, das war der Hund des Advokaten. Hätte ihm dieser befohlen, unter das Bett wie in eine Hundehütte zu kriechen und von dort aus zu bellen, er hätte es mit Lust getan. (P, 265)

At stake in this passage, as in the other dog scenes in *The Trial*, is shame—or more precisely, a lack thereof. Block's behavior can never be justified in the eyes of a fellow human being simply because it is utterly shameless. Even though Block himself does not seem to feel shame, the one observing him (namely, Josef K.) "almost felt degraded by [his behavior]" (Er entwürdigte fast den Zuseher) (T, 139; P, 264). Shame thus exposes the gap between Block the client, "an old businessman with a long beard" (T, 139), and Block, the lawyer's dog. In the same way, Franz's shame reveals the incompatibility between the guard whose fiancée supposedly awaits him outside the bank, and the "tortured instrument" under the thrashing rod. Indeed, in these moments shame is carried beyond itself, and is ultimately transformed into a principle of perverse enjoyment. In their moments of shame, both Franz and Block abdicate their autonomy as human beings by physically and mentally submitting to their respective masters. According to Agamben, such desubjectification occurs because "the masochist is able to enjoy what exceeds him only on the condition of finding outside himself a point in which he can assume his own passivity and his own unassumable pleasure. This external point is the sadistic subject, the master."[18] In a sadomasochistic relationship pleasure is transmitted through discipline and punishment, and shame occurs when punishment and enjoyment can no longer be distinguished from one another.

In view of the previous dog scenes, the shameful death of Josef K. in the final scene appears in a somewhat different light. In line with the previous scenes in which shame was consistently associated with a sadomasochistic principle that marked the transformation of punishment into pleasure, K.'s shame in the final scene could also be read as a highly ambivalent moment that encapsulates his subjection to the authority of the court as an instance of libidinal gratification. This aspect of perverse gratification might explain, for example, K.'s perplexing indignation at the sight of the two executioners that have been sent out for him: " 'They send old, second-rate actors for me,' K. said to himself, looking round to confirm that. 'They're trying to get rid of me on the cheap' " (T, 161). This complaint can only make sense once we take into account the theatricality of a well-rehearsed dialogue that underlies sadomasochistic humiliation, such as the dialogue conducted by Huld and Leni in the scene of Block's humiliation, and possibly also in Franz's pathetic plea for K.'s intervention just before he undergoes corporal punishment. In other words, K. complains that the people sent by the court were too "clean" and not intimidating enough, and resembled petty bureaucrats rather than, perhaps, sadistic masters. Nevertheless, K. resolves to go ahead with the process:

> Am I now going to show that I have not learnt anything from a trial that has lasted a year? Am I going to depart as a slow-witted person? Are people going to be able to say that at the beginning of the trial I wanted to end it, and now, at the end, I want to start it all over again? I don't want people to say that. I'm grateful that I've been given these two half-mute, uncomprehending men to accompany me on my way and it's been left to me to tell myself everything that is needful. (T, 163)

This passage confirms the observation made by Reiner Stach, that although the reader is told in *The Trial* that the court is "attracted" by K.'s guilt, it appears essentially powerless.[19] It is rather K. himself who sets events in motion. Thus, the executioners appear exactly when K. expects them, not before or after. When K. offers resistance they cannot move him, and the execution can take place only once he has resigned himself to die. Significantly, K.'s capitulation occurs only after he sees a woman (Fräulein Bürstner). We are explicitly told that he follows her "not because he wanted to catch up with her, not because he wanted to see her for as long as possible, but solely so as not to forget the admonition [*Mahnung*] she represented for him" (T, 162). Fräulein Bürstner, or someone that resembles her, strengthens K.'s resolve to die like a dog because she reminds him of what he will have to face if he shows resistance. K. seems to choose the dubious pleasure of a degrading death over the prospect of intimacy with a woman. His capitulation is not moral, but rather libidinal in nature.

The link between degradation, humiliation, and aberrant forms of sexuality in *The Trial* is suggested not only in the aforementioned dog scenes but in other passages as well. For example, after K. loses the struggle with the law student over the court usher's wife (who quite willingly plays the passive role of a trophy), he imagines in his frustration a scene in which the student is sexually humiliated by the prostitute that he sees on a regular basis:

> In his mind's eye he pictured a scene in which this wretched student, this puffed-up child with his bandy legs and his beard, was made to look as ridiculous as possible, on his knees beside Elsa's bed, hands clasped, begging for mercy. (T, 47)

Here, then, the question arises as to whether Josef K. can really be seen as a victim of the court or if the court itself is merely an extension of K.'s aberrant, submissive sexuality. The answer is, of course, not unequivocal. Despite the initial impression that K. is subjected to a fundamentally arbitrary legal process, upon closer inspection it appears that he willingly collaborates with the representatives of the court. K. in fact assists the incompetent executioners in finding the right position for himself to die: "Despite all the efforts [the executioners] made, and despite all the cooperation K. showed, his posture remained very strained and unconvincing" (T, 164). Once again, the context in which K. would orchestrate his own death, and in which it would make sense for his posture to be "unconvincing," is that of a sadomasochistic role-play. To be sure, this is a very poorly executed role-play. The executioners appear reluctant to perform their duty, and by passing the knife between each other, K. is led to understand that he is expected to take the initiative and plunge the knife into himself. But K. refuses to do so.

Here he exercises the only freedom left to him under the circumstances—the freedom to die like a dog, a death that is neither murder nor suicide. K. insists on *shechita*, devoid of symbolic meaning. Like Greenberg's fallen messiahs and Bialik's pogrom victims, his death too shall be forgotten. In fact, *The Trial* already incorporates the loss of K.'s memory in the form of his truncated surname and dearth of personal traits. K.'s essential anonymity is no puzzle or mystery, nor is it a mark of a deficient personality. It is instead an outcome of the oblivion associated with *shechita*. To put it in other words, Josef K. is quite simply a person whose individual traits have been wiped off, and in this specific sense he is dehumanized. His distorted form—like the distorted forms of such characters as Gregor Samsa, the cat-lamb, and Odradek—is the form that things assume in oblivion, as Benjamin observed.[20] As a result, K. no longer appears as a whole person, but solely as a "case" of the court, and this is to be seen as a direct outcome of his shameful death as a dog.

THE OBLIVION TO WHICH Josef K. willingly consigns himself is thus linked to the infrahuman as a locus of shame—the "fracture between the living being and the speaking being"—that emerges as a fulfillment of an ambiguous libidinal desire. In this context, we cannot fail to recall Margot Norris's claim regarding Kafka's work, namely, that "if suffering is seen as a means whose end is not the Law or the Ideal but pleasure, then Law and Ideal become mere pretexts, fraudulent rationales in a pornological fantasy."[21] Norris argues that in a sadomasochistic relationship the sadist employs the law subversively, by showing that the forms of rationality in the service of the law are implicated not with the idea of justice, but with sexuality, that is, with a desire to punish sadistically. Any subsequent rationalization of the law would only constitute an attempt to legitimize wanton punishment and to sublimate sexual desire.[22] Thus, Kafka's pornological narrative of the law possesses a redeeming cultural value: "Kafka wishes to recover pain—untranscended, mute, animal pain stripped of *alatheia* and *telos*—from its cultural falsifications."[23] The problem with this line of argumentation is that it neglects to address the kenomatic aspects of the law in Kafka's work. In *The Trial*, the law is not simply a form of "tyranny" to which the individual is subjected but is instead a zone of absence or emptiness. Therefore, the law does not "need" sexuality in order to expose its fraudulence and absurdity. Its emptiness provides the decisive evidence to its groundlessness without denying the binding validity it exerts. The aberrant sexuality with which this groundless law is associated is not a subversive element, as Norris believes, but is instead integral to the very operation of the law in a state of exception.

In light of these considerations, it becomes evident that the most pressing issue facing the individual in Kafka's world is the question of freedom. For the law, precisely by virtue of its absence, encompasses every aspect of human life, including the most private and shameful. And in relation to this problem that Deleuze and Guattari have posited the notion of "becoming-animal" as a potential remedy to the all-encompassing purview of the law: "To the inhumanness of the 'diabolical powers,' there is the answer of a becoming-animal: to become a beetle, to become a dog, to become an ape, 'head over heels and away,' rather than lowering one's head and remaining a bureaucrat, inspector, judge, or judged."[24] At stake is not the question of how to become free in relation to the law, but how to find a way out of the law's sphere of influence where none could be found before: "As Kafka himself says, the problem isn't that of liberty but of escape."[25] For Deleuze and Guattari, becoming-animal is a way to escape institutional authority, not by rebelling against it and thereby affirming one's human dignity, but by acknowledging that the system of coercion—be it political, paternal, or libidinal—could only work if one strives to become a subject, its subject. In becoming-animal, one relinquishes the subject-position, and thereby one is able to disrupt the designation to which authority refers itself (in *The Trial*, the accused; in "The Metamorphosis," the dutiful son; and in "A Report to an Academy," the ape). Becoming-animal thus appears as a radical transgression that undermines the power of institutions and the biopolitical authority that they hold over those subjected to their influence.

In these terms, it is possible to understand Gregor Samsa's metamorphosis as an escape from submission to the father as his son, disrupting an oedipal economy of desire and its negation in the form of filial duty. The web of family and work relations in which Gregor is ensnared, and in which he functions in the interchangeable servile position of a son and an employee, is disrupted at the moment that he turns into a giant bug. Becoming-animal here is an escape, not in the sense that it grants Gregor "freedom." On the contrary, it opens up a set of entirely different problems that lead ultimately to his death. But his metamorphosis does disrupt his role in capitalist economy and, more fundamentally, it disrupts the oedipal economy in which he is forced into a productive role that is at the same time a submissive filial role. In the same way, Josef K. disrupts the authority of the court by dying like a dog, that is, by dying a meaningless death in which the question of his guilt is rendered irrelevant.

In this context, it would be interesting to compare Josef K. to the figure of the condemned man in the short story "In der Strafkolonie" ("In the Penal Colony," 1919), which was written concurrently with *The Trial*. Here, too, the condemned man seems to have been turned into a dog through the operation of the law in a state of exception:

> The only figures present, apart from the officer and the traveler, were the condemned man, a dull-witted, wide-mouthed being with unkempt hair and a wild expression, and one soldier, who was holding the heavy chain attached to the small chains which fettered the condemned man by his ankles and wrists as well as by his neck, and which were also linked to one another by connecting chains. However, the condemned man looked so submissive and dog-like that it seemed as if one could let him run free on the hillsides, and would only have to whistle at the start of the execution for him to come.[26]

Even though he appears to be servile as a domesticated dog, and kept in heavy chains, the condemned man provides an emblematic example of "becoming-animal" as a way to escape institutional control. In contrast to Josef K., the prisoner has relinquished all agency and any pretense at making sense of his situation. Deprived of language and understanding, he is happily immersed in the undisclosedness of meaning of a dog-like existence. Paradoxically, this is precisely the condition that the elaborate torture and execution device is designed to undo. By inscribing the crime on the skin of the condemned, the apparatus "redeems" them from a state of not-knowing. At the moment of death, the condemned would learn the truth of their crime and understand it, thereby enacting a subtle rehumanization. The inscription of guilt on the skin of the prisoners thus emerges as the ultimate form of punishment and subjection because it does not allow the prisoner to escape the purview of the law. In dying a "human" death, the dimension of lived experience—in which escape could be potentially realized—is ultimately contained and sublated to a totalizing figural scheme.

In presenting and describing this mechanism for the inscription of guilt, Kafka was evidently more skeptical than Deleuze and Guattari regarding the redemptive potential of "becoming-animal," and its capacity to disrupt biopolitical forms of coercion. Indeed, the dog (and other animals) remains too vulnerable and creaturely, far too implicated in forms of libidinal, familial, and legal subjection, to unequivocally serve as a topos of emancipation in Kafka's work. Instead, I would like to suggest that the dog forms a constellation in Kafka's work—a constellation in which different, often contradictory, themes converge. By alluding to what falls outside the boundaries of the human subject, and relating to false, accidental, or heteronomous notions from which the rational subject seeks to extricate itself, the figure of the dog implies a potential disruption of institutional biopolitical power. However, the dog also signals in Kafka's writings a form of captivation to primordial guilt and aberrant sexuality from which the law seems to draw its undisputable power. In other words, it is precisely because the law occupies the locus of the forgotten, as Benjamin claimed, that it lays claim to the life of the individual. Its heteronomous institutional power is not external to the self but is embedded deep within its recesses. In these terms the image of the dog surfaces in Kafka's letters to Felice Bauer, in which he often expresses doubts regarding their marriage and presented obstacles that would come between them as a couple, as in the following letter from April 1, 1913:

> My one fear—surely nothing worse can either be said or listened to—is that I shall never be able to possess you. At best I would be confined, like an unthinkingly faithful dog, to kissing your casually proffered hand, which would not be a sign of love, but of the despair of the animal condemned to silence and eternal separation. I would sit beside you and, as has happened, feel the breath and life of your body at my side, yet in reality be further from you than now, here in my room. I would never be able to attract your attention, and it would be lost to me altogether when you look out of the window, or

lay your head in your hands. You and I would ride past the entire world, hand in hand, seemingly united, and none of it would be true. In short, though you might lean toward me far enough for you to be in danger, I would be excluded from you forever.[27]

The figure of the "unthinkingly faithful dog" is posited here not as a complement to normal sexuality, but rather as a symbol of its failure, suggesting that Kafka's anxiety over intimacy with women may have been triggered by fear of impotence. The inability to sexually possess a woman confines Kafka to a lowly, submissive kissing of her hand, not unlike Block who kisses the lawyer's hand. The kissing of the hand appears here as an unsatisfactory compensation for the inability to engage in normative sexual conduct, and is clearly the product of shame. Kafka's deep anxiety of intimacy is nevertheless not devoid of hints of perverse enjoyment. Thus, he imagines Felice "casually proffering" her hand for him to kiss (Deine zerstreut mir überlassene Hand zu küssen), a slight yet significant gesture that interpellates her into a sadomasochistic role-play. The kiss of the casually proffered hand marks a point of contact in which each party assumes its role with respect to the other, that is, a mistress and her dog, thus signaling an act of subjectification in the double sense of the word: an act that simultaneously spells both self-loss and self-possession. At work here is the same ambiguous logic that impels *The Trial*: the semiconscious desire for self-affirmation through humiliation and submission that ultimately leads to self-annihilation.

This relationship between dog and mistress, predicated on the silent "despair" (*Verzweiflung*) of an animal condemned to "eternal separation," is intimately associated with the emergence of primordial guilt that marks the presence of the forgotten in Kafka's work. The forgotten enters the sphere of conscious human life through the loss of symbolic agency, that is, when the individual experiences his own subjection to obscure processes that lie beyond his understanding and control. In the passage above, Kafka himself—along with the other pathetic, dog-like figures that populate his stories—is "sentenced" or "condemned" (*verurteilt*) to such a fate. To be condemned in this sense means to be set apart from ordinary human life after failing to fulfill a role in society, in the family, or in a relationship with a woman, to the degree that one ultimately loses touch with one's own humanity. In Kafka's work, the condemned men gradually (or suddenly) cease to be soldiers, guards, bank clerks, merchants, sons, or lovers as they become increasingly involved in questions of guilt and punishment. Eventually, the preoccupation with guilt and punishment becomes so encompassing that these men can no longer lead a human life, but only a bare life, naturalized to the point of equivalence with a life of a dog.

The distinctive preoccupation with fate and guilt marks a form of captivation in an undisclosedness of meaning that recalls, in certain respects, Martin Heidegger's discussion of "poverty in world" (*Weltarmut*). Originally, Heidegger used this term to describe the relation of an animal to its environment in contrast to man's relation to his environment, which he defined as "world-forming" (*weltbildend*). According to Heidegger, "the animal as such does not stand within a potentiality for revelation of beings. Neither its so-called environment nor the animal itself are revealed as beings."[28] In other words, the animal inhabits an environment that remains inaccessible to it. But this does not necessarily mean that the relation of the animal to its environment is to be conceived in purely negative terms.

> But if behaviour is not a relation to beings, does this mean that it is a relation to nothing? Not at all. Yet if it is not a relation to nothing, it must always be a relation to something, which surely must itself be and actually is. Certainly, but the question is whether behaviour is not precisely a kind of relation to … in which *that to which* the behaviour relates in the manner of not attending to it is *open* [offen] *in a certain way* for the animal. But this certainly does not mean *disconcealed* [offenbar] *as a being*.[29]

In a commentary on this passage from Heidegger, Agamben outlines the general form of the animal's involvement with the world:

> The ontological status of the animal environment can at this point be defined: it is *offen* (open) but not *offenbar* (disconcealed; lit. openable). For the animal, beings are open but not accessible; that is to say, they are open in an inaccessibility and an opacity—that is, in some way, in a nonrelation. This *openness without disconcealment* distinguishes the animal's poverty in world from the world-forming which characterizes man.[30]

These reflections shed light on the essential condition in which Kafka's protagonists find themselves with respect to the law. When attempting to enter the law, or to make sense of it, they come up against something that obstinately refuses itself. The structure of their experience with the law thus shows an opening to a closedness, similar to the animal's "poverty in world"—a continuous immersion in something unrevealed. Usually, this dimension of nonrevelation—that I have called the allegorical modality in Kafka's work—extends beyond the protagonists' perspective to include the perspective of the reader as well. However, in at least one case this opaque perspective yields itself to a relatively stable form of interpretation: in Kafka's late fragmentary work "Forschungen eines Hundes" ("Investigations of a Dog"). Kafka wrote the "Investigations" in the fall of 1922, just as he stopped working on *The Castle*. Whereas *The Trial* depicted the perspective of a human protagonist turned into a dog through his involvement with an obscure law, in "Investigations of a Dog" a similar perspective is attained through the unwitting involvement of a dog with the human world. To begin with, the dog's investigations are prompted by a disturbing discovery that, in some cases, the behavior of dogs is incommensurate with the common dog law, the law of the pack.

> There are to my knowledge no other creatures who live their lives as widely dispersed as we dogs lead ours ... Our kind, which wants to bond together ... we more than any lead lives separated from one another, pursuing strange occupations which our fellow dogs often cannot understand, clinging to rules which are not the law of the pack, and indeed are meant rather to go against it. What difficult things these are, things one would prefer not to touch on—I can understand this point of view, I can understand it better than I do my own—and yet they are things that utterly possess me.[31]

It is tempting to read passages like these, as Benjamin Harshav does, as "a veiled allegory on the Jewish condition."[32] The reader might easily be led to conclude that with sentences such as "there are to my knowledge no other creatures who live their lives as widely dispersed as we dogs lead ours," dog habits are not being discussed, but rather Jewish habits. And, of course, other elements in the story support that observation, such as the "aerial dogs" (*Lufthunde*) that recall the *Luftmenschen*—Jews who, like Isrolik in

Di kliatshe, are detached from the solid ground of reality and cannot find a place for themselves in both Jewish and gentile societies. Other examples might include the "music dogs" who conjure music out of thin air as a reference to Kafka's encounter with the eastern European Jewish actors in the Yiddish theater,[33] or the food that comes flying through the air as a parody of the biblical motif of manna descending from the sky in the wilderness,[34] and so on.

Without entirely disqualifying such allusions to Jewish themes, recent studies have shown that the many details that remain unexplained in "Investigations of a Dog" cohere once the reader dispenses altogether with allegorical interpretations. As Reiner Stach has remarked, "astonishingly, the text remains readable even when you assume there are no other layers to unearth, that this is simply one dog living among other dogs."[35] Taken literally, the world of dogs is distinguished by the complete absence of human existence from the dogs' perspective. The dogs perceive themselves as the only rational beings in the world, and, one might say, the epitome of earthly creation.

> For what is there besides dogs? Who else is there to call upon in the whole wide, empty world? All knowledge, the totality of all questions and all answers, is held in dogs.
>
> Denn was gibt es außer den Hunden? Wenn kann man sonst anrufen in der weiten, leeren Welt? Alles Wissen, die Gesamtheit aller Fragen und aller Antworten ist in den Hunden enthalten.[36]

This canine parody of the anthropocentric idea, apart from its blatant irony, conveys the essential poverty of the dog's world, a "wide, empty world" in which things remain for the most part in a state of nonrevelation. Yet this does not mean that the dog world stands in no relation to the human world. On the contrary, the human world manifests itself in the perspective of the inquisitive dog as an aggregate of disturbing and inexplicable phenomena to which the dog can find no satisfying explanation. Thus, as Rainer Nägele observed, "this inexistence of the human world in the perception of the dogs is at the same time the kernel and the reason for all the riddles that the investigating dog would like to decipher."[37] In this sense, the dog's "poverty in world" is not essentially different from the perspective of Josef

K., who embarks on a search for the truth of an obscure law that he does not understand. The dog's first encounter with such uncanny phenomena begins in childhood, with the experience of the music dogs.

> I had run a long way through the dark, with a vague sense of great things to come ... up and down, blind and deaf to everything, led by nothing but this indefinite longing. I stopped short suddenly, with the feeling that this was the right place for me, I looked up, and it was bright day, just a bit misty. I greeted the morning with little noises of bewilderment when—as if I had conjured them up—there emerged from some sort of darkness, creating a terrifying clamour such as I had never heard before, seven dogs, out into the light. If I hadn't clearly seen that these were dogs and that the clamour was coming with them, although I couldn't tell how they produced it—I might have run off straight away, but as it was, I stayed.[38]

Like the enigmatic figure that appears before the execution of Josef K., this passage depicts an occurrence that involves a source of illumination breaking through a surrounding darkness—"seven dogs, out into the light" (sieben Hunde ans Licht). But in contrast to the enigmatic occurrence in *The Trial*, in "Investigations of a Dog" the reader is provided with a possible key for interpreting this otherwise obscure phenomenon. Once the reader dispenses with allegorical interpretations, it may be possible to conclude that what the dog experiences as an unfathomable occurrence, bearing implicit theological resonances, is nothing more than the spectacle of seven circus-dogs performing a dance on stage. When appropriated in this way under a human perspective, many of the other enigmatic details in the story are revealed as mundane occurrences. Thus, for example, the seven dogs are not conjuring the music from thin air but rather are responding to manmade music; the enigmatic *Lufthunde* are highbred poodles carried by human hands; and the mysterious phenomenon of food that comes from above, which the dogs study as part of a "canine science," is merely the common feeding practice of domesticated animals.

In order to better grasp Kafka's technique of obfuscation, it might be useful to briefly compare the "Investigations" to another literary work narrated from the perspective of an animal, namely, Leo Tolstoy's famous story "Strider" (also known by its Russian name, *Kholstomer*). This story, completed in 1886, is written from the perspective of a horse. As Victor Shklovsky has shown, in "Kholstomer" Tolstoy adopted a technique of defamiliarization in which a familiar action or object appear in a changed form while retaining its original reference. Shklovsky points out that "Tolstoy makes the familiar seem strange by not naming the familiar object. He describes an object as if he were seeing it for the first time."[39] In "Kholstomer" Tolstoy employs this technique of defamiliarization in order to expose the irrational aspects of human behavior:

> I understood full well what he said about flogging and Christianity, but I didn't have the least idea what the words *mine, my foal* meant. I realized they implied some sort of connection between myself and my keeper. At that time I couldn't understand what that connection was in fact. It wasn't until much later, when I had been separated from the other horses, that I came to understand. But then I found it impossible to understand how and why I could be called a man's property. The words *my horse*, referring to me, a living creature, struck me as strange, just as if someone had said *my* earth, *my* air, *my* water.
>
> Yet those words made an enormous impression on me. I thought about them the whole time and only after long experience of people did I finally come to understand the meaning they attached to these odd words. Their meaning is as follows: people are guided in life not by actions but by words. They enjoy not so much the chance to do or not to do something as the chance to apply to objects certain words of predetermined meaning. Among the words to which they attach the greatest importance are *my* and *my own*, which they apply to all kinds of different creatures and objects—even to land, people, horses. They have agreed among themselves that only one person has the right to apply *my* to any one object. And according to the rules of the game (agreed upon beforehand), the person who can apply the word *my* to the greatest number of objects is considered the happiest. Why that is so I have no idea, but that's how it is.[40]

In the defamiliarizing perspective of the horse, words are encountered outside of their familiar context, and are consequently experienced in their artfulness or artificiality. Nevertheless, the reader never loses sight of the object's essential embeddedness in a human world. The horse may wonder about the meaning of the word "property," but he clearly grasps the essential function of property as a constitutive element in human social hierarchy. Moreover, this defamiliarizing perspective that exposes the artificiality of words is not consistently employed throughout the story. In certain cases, this perspective is suspended; for example, when it comes to the names of people and places, or with regard to the horse's relationship to his master—those correlations are tacitly experienced as natural.

When we compare Tolstoy's story to Kafka's "Investigations of a Dog," the difference in the perspectives of the animal narrators becomes readily apparent. Whereas the perspective of Tolstoy's horse *reveals* a dimension external to the habitual perception of objects, Kafka's text performs the opposite operation: it *obscures* the everyday object and distorts it beyond recognition. This distortion is an outcome of the absence of a human context in which the object is embedded. Thus, for example, in the above-quoted scene in which the narrator encounters the "music dogs," there is no indication where it takes place or who is involved. It is even likely that the source of illumination that the dog perceives as daylight is nothing more than circus stage lights. The dog's "poverty in world" entails an obstruction of any dimension of human meaning, and even fabricated objects associated with the human world are naturalized in the dog's perspective. Thus, rows of circus chairs are encountered as a "tangle of wood," cigarette smoke appears as "mist," and so on. Familiar objects seem to lose their "objecthood" as they are assimilated into the dog's perspective. And herein lies the essential dichotomy in the perspectives of the animal narrators: while Kholstomer's perspective *enriches* the human world by uncovering a hidden dimension in familiar words and objects, the perspective of Kafka's dog *impoverishes* the world, transforming the known and familiar into something muddled, opaque, and enigmatic.

Human intervention assumes a singular importance in the impoverished world of Kafka's dog, which is informed by rules and norms that govern and regulate social behavior. Paradoxically, these rules are predicated on the fundamental absence of the human world from the perspective of the dog. Even though the human world is not directly encountered as such, its impact is nevertheless felt by the dogs, as they are compelled to act against their own nature, deviating from dog norms.

> Carried away by sheer music, I had not until now noticed how [the dogs] were behaving. They had truly cast aside all shame; the miserable creatures were doing what was both the most ludicrous and the most indecent of things: they were walking upright on their hind legs. Shame on them! They exposed themselves and showed off their nakedness for all to see: they were proud of themselves, and, when for a moment they listened to their better impulses and dropped their forelegs, they were positively shocked, as if it were a mistake, as if Nature were a mistake. They lifted their legs once more and their eyes seemed to beg for forgiveness that they had had to pause for an instant in their sinfulness.[41]

Here once again shame recurs as the locus of the infrahuman, as the dogs bear the unmistakable marks of human intervention by standing upright. In his essay on *The Trial*, Elias Canetti explained that standing upright "signifies the power of man over beast; but precisely in this most obvious attitude man is exposed, visible, vulnerable. For this power is also guilt."[42] In other words, the essence of the human does not inhere in a human shape or in a capacity for rational thought, but rather in this act of defiance against nature—standing upright—which is at the same time experienced as a locus of shame. The example of the standing dogs, who serve here as the "receptacles of the forgotten,"[43] demonstrates how a captivation in an undisclosedness of meaning comes to be unavoidably associated with shame and guilt. These dogs, along with Josef K., Gregor Samsa, the condemned man, and Block the corn merchant, find themselves at home in a distorted life, fulfilling a demand later formulated by Paul Celan for an art that involves a "stepping outside of what is human, a stepping into an uncanny realm that is turned toward the human."[44]

Needless to say, the investigating dog, like Josef K., will die in ignorance, oblivious to the truth that surrounds him. This ignorance in death is the identifying mark of *shechita*, in which human life intersects with animal life insofar as the possibility of attaining "significance" is foreclosed. Paradoxically, it is not the presumptuous "science of nourishment" that perpetuates the dog's state of ignorance, but rather the unquestioned assumption that dogs are the measure of all things in existence. Since dogs do not recognize the existence of anything beyond the boundaries of their own world, they have not learned to pray to God or to observe man, their master. It goes without saying that the dogs' illusory autonomy does not eliminate their fundamental dependence on forces unknown to them. They study the consequences of a human act, which Kholstomer exposed in its artificiality, as if it were a law of nature. The obfuscation of the familiar world in the dog's perspective is directly linked to this naturalization of the human implied in the dog's "caninocentrism."

The dog thus seems to occupy a central position in a "wide, empty world" that contains no trace of human activity. Based on an unfounded assumption of ontological superiority, the dog conducts his "investigations" in this opaque world, while relying solely on his own faculties or on established "scientific" ideas. In this sense there is a marked similarity between Kafka's dog and modern man, who also studies nature from a privileged position in a world from which God is absent. Whereas the religious or premodern worldview acknowledged the existence of forces that lay beyond the scope of human comprehension, the modern worldview acknowledges only the agency and rational capacity of humankind. Modern science has appropriated the anthropocentric premise in detachment from its original theological context. Man, who was given divine sanction to tyrannize earthly creation, appears in the modern context as the rationally autonomous master of profane "nature." Paradoxically, the implicit resemblance between dog and man in "Investigations of a Dog" implies that modern man in his so-called rational autonomy is rendered more creaturely, and in certain respects closer to a dog than traditional man ever was. Just as the dog, convinced of his rational autonomy, is blatantly oblivious to the way in which his life is controlled by mankind, so too Josef K. is oblivious to the workings of the obscure law that he futilely tries to reveal. In these cases, the difference between dog and man is merely relative, a difference in orders of magnitude. For both dog and modern man are oblivious to any intervention in the world outside their own, yet both consistently experience mysterious disturbances that call their rational autonomy into question.

These disturbances that recur in Kafka's stories, in which human life is found in close proximity to animal life, do not point to an enigmatic transcendental realm. Rather, they demonstrate that the anthropocentric idea in its modern incarnation is compatible with an extreme form of compliance and submission. Indeed, one could be "an unthinkingly faithful dog" while believing oneself to be an autonomous subject and the center of the universe. This paradoxical yet inherent compatibility between a secularized anthropocentrism and a condition of doggish submission suggests a radical inversion of prevalent notions of human agency. In Kafka's work, modern man, whose true representative is the dog, never questions his mastery of nature nor his rational autonomy. At the same time, he submits again and again to a law that remains obscure to him—just as the standing dogs blindly submit to the intervention of humans in their own world. Both man and dog occupy the same world, but the dog, being "poor in world," lives in a state of nonrevelation in relation to man. Ultimately, there simply is no way for either man or dog to discover the truth of the law to which they are compelled to submit, for in attempting to reveal this truth they run up against a silence that encapsulates the mystery of their existence. As Kafka's investigating dog puts it:

> You prowl round your fellow dog, your mouth is foaming with desire, you are flogging yourself with your own tail, you ask, you beg, you howl, you bite, and you get—you get what you would get anyway without all this effort: loving attention, warm caresses, respectful sniffs, rapt embraces, my howls and thine blending into one, everything is arranged to this end, finding forgetfulness in ecstasy, but the one thing you wanted above all to get at: an admission of knowledge—that is still refused. Your plea, silent or loud, even if you have tried to tempt them to the limit, is answered at best only by blank faces, wry glances, veiled and clouded eyes. It is not very different from the time when I was a child, when I called on the dog-musicians and they were silent. Now you could say: "You are complaining about your fellow dogs, at their silence over things that are crucial; you are maintaining that they know more than they are admitting, more than they want to accept as true in life, and this reserve, whose source and mystery of course they also withhold, poisons life, makes it unbearable to you, you must change it or leave it ..." [And] if the whole truth were to be more unbearable than

half-truth, if it should prove that the ones who kept their silence, the upholders of life, were in the right, if out of the slight hope we have now there were to come total hopelessness, utterance is still worth the attempt, for the life that is permitted you is one you do not want to live.[45]

This predicament is shared by Josef K., who similarly attempts to reveal the nature of the accusations made against him, and both protagonists are engaged in futile attempts to unravel the mystery that surrounds their existence. Both fail in their attempts, but nevertheless when K. chooses to die like a dog, something happens. The mystery of his life is not solved but is instead neutralized, held in abeyance. By choosing a doggish death, K. is released from the hold of the law, for it no longer matters whether he is guilty or not, or what is the nature of his crime. He is freed from the dictates of rationality. The totality of his experience with the law, which laid bare the abyss between significance and physical nature, figure and lived experience, is gathered at his moment of death in the utterance "like a dog," not in order to open its meaning to the human world or to the sphere of revelation, but instead to give it back to a realm of muteness and closedness, which Benjamin has identified as "the night of nature."[46] As in Bialik's pogrom poem, the notion of nature at stake here is contrasted with that of revealed history, and therefore, according to Benjamin, it "does not await the day, and thus does not await judgment day either." It is a model of nature that is "neither the staging ground of history nor a human domicile. The night redeemed."[47] K.'s death as a dog redeems this "night of nature"—the realm of silence, obscurity, and oblivion—not in the sense that his death is presented as a lesson that has been forgotten and is now to be appropriated and learned, but precisely in that his death is preserved in its meaninglessness and obscurity as something utterly unredeemable. By offering himself up to nature, K. is finally redeemed of his own mystery.

THESE REFLECTIONS THAT PERTAIN to fundamental aspects of the infrahuman in Kafka's work must be presented before the question of Jewish identity can be properly addressed. Clearly, Kafka's depictions of an indeterminate state between animal and man echo previous examples in Jewish literature found in the writings of Heine, Abramovitsh, and Bialik. Yet in

Kafka's work the infrahuman is detached from its explicit reference to the Jewish world, and projected onto a general scheme that addresses existence as such. That is not to say that Kafka's literary works do not contain various allusions to Jewish themes, but these allusions at best remain tentative and ambiguous, and therefore cannot be used to establish a solid claim regarding Jewish identity in Kafka's literary oeuvre. In fact, in Kafka's entire literary output only one short fragmentary piece explicitly addresses Jewish themes. The piece is called "In Unserer Synagoge" (translated to English as "The Animal in the Synagogue"), written in the summer of 1922. "The Animal in the Synagogue" tells the story of a marten-like creature that inhabits an old synagogue in Thamühl. The synagogue is described as a neglected place, about to fall into disuse. In one of the preliminary drafts of this story, the synagogue is described as

> [a] simple, unadorned, low building from the end of the previous century. Although the synagogue is small in size, it is entirely sufficient for the congregation, which is also small and diminishes in size from year to year.[48]

The sense of impending abandonment and desolation is affirmed in the final draft of the story, where we are told that "it is not impossible that before long the synagogue will have become a granary or something of the sort."[49] In other words, we are told that the synagogue in its capacity as a house of worship will soon fade from memory and sink into the oblivion of the "night of nature." This outcome, clearly detrimental for the Jewish community, will be beneficial for the animal, as it will finally get the peace and quiet that it lacks. Preferring to live withdrawn and in seclusion, the animal is extremely timid and comes out of its hiding place only when disturbed by the presence of people, which occurs whenever religious services are being held. Like the dog of the "Investigations," the animal in the synagogue is "poor in world" and is entirely oblivious to the significance of its abode as a house of God.

> The curtain of the Torah ark hangs from a shining brass rod, and this seems to attract the animal, it quite often creeps towards it, but when it is there it is always quiet, not even when it is right up close to the ark can it be said to be causing a disturbance, it seems to be

gazing at the congregation with its bright, unwinking, and perhaps lidless eyes, but it is certainly not looking at anybody, it is only facing the dangers by which it feels itself threatened.[50]

Since the story is told from the external perspective of a human narrator, we do not know exactly how the animal experiences the religious services from within the confines of its narrow world, but we do know that it finds these occurrences very disturbing. The paradoxical outcome of this situation is that the animal, even though it is driven by its own extraneous considerations, is compelled to attend the services as if it, too, were a member of the congregation. The link between the animal and the Jewish community is thus established by virtue of a disturbance in the natural rhythms of the animal's life. Such a disturbance is equivalent to the disturbances experienced by the investigating dog as he encounters the music dogs, by Gregor Samsa as he turns into a beetle, or by Josef K. as he is placed under arrest. Nevertheless, the animal in the synagogue is so oblivious to what takes place around it, so hopelessly absorbed in its impoverished world, that it does not realize it is in no danger at all. Despite the recurrence of religious services at regular intervals, to which the animal should have become accustomed, it is always newly provoked into a genuine state of terror. At this point, however, in stark contrast to the undisclosedness of meaning in which Kafka's protagonists are condemned to spend their lives, we are told that the animal's blindness to the human world may actually harbor a peculiar kind of insight.

> And yet there is this terror. Is it the memory of times long past or perhaps the premonition of times to come? Does this old animal perhaps know more than the three generations of those who are gathered together in the synagogue?[51]

The animal's terror of commotion may be explained in view of past attempts to drive it out of the synagogue. From the point of view of Jewish law, the animal is considered to be a vermin, and the majority of rabbis consulted on the matter recommended "the expulsion of the animal and a reconsecration of the house of God."[52] Here too, then, a creature has been condemned by a law that remained entirely obscure to it. But since the animal was extremely timid and cautious, the sentence could not be carried out. The peculiar insight of the animal may therefore have something to do with the wisdom of the persecuted Jewish dog—the repulsive creature that lives in a "state of nature" within the bounds of human society—who has learned to find shelter in the face of adversity. In this sense, there is a direct correlation between the animal's illicit presence at the synagogue and the Jew's outlaw existence within Christian society. But whereas Heine's Jewish dog could at least find refuge in the synagogue on the Sabbath, where he could regain his humanity if only for a short while, Kafka's animal remains exposed to persecution even within the confines of the synagogue. The animal feels itself to be nowhere safe, and no longer has recourse to humanity, apart from the practice of attending services and gazing blankly at the congregation with its "bright, unwinking, and perhaps lidless eyes."

What is the relation between the animal and the Jewish community with which it is associated? We may guess that in contrast to the animal's genuine sense of terror, which grows undiminished with the years, the Jewish congregation has been lulled into a false sense of security, even if only within the narrow confines of the synagogue. Only by preserving an authentic sense of terror born of an exposure to a law in a state of exception can true longevity be attained. And, indeed, the animal has survived for many generations, and all attempts to drive it out of the synagogue have failed. However, this extraordinary capacity to survive hardships has not come without a price. The animal lives an empty, lonely life and lacks any religious, cultural, or social affiliations. Its existence betokens a life devoid of "significance" for the sake of mere "physical" survival. In its tenacious adherence to a bare life, the creature will continue to inhabit the synagogue long after the building has been converted into a granary, long after all Jews have vanished from Thamühl. Then the animal, too, will finally be redeemed of the mystery that has plagued it for so long. The animal in the synagogue thus stands in the writings of Kafka as a singular hieroglyph in which the memory of Jewish life is not preserved, but redeemed in oblivion. Ultimately, it is left for the reader to decide if this enigmatic figure is a symbol of redemption or damnation.

5 AFTER THE HOLOCAUST
Responses to the Infrahuman in the Works of
S. Y. Agnon and Paul Celan

THE CHALLENGES THAT THE WORK of Kafka posed for subsequent literary and critical endeavors, in its detachment of the infrahuman from a specifically Jewish frame of reference, coincided with the attempt to rethink the essence of the human in the aftermath of the Holocaust. Adorno's "Notes on Kafka" (1953) is emblematic of this juncture in which Kafka's work was interpreted as a "trial run of a model of dehumanization,"[1] foreshadowing the horrors of Auschwitz but also exemplifying the detrimental effects of commodification, reification, and alienation to which the individual is subjected in industrial-capitalist society. In what follows I will examine the ways in which two prominent Jewish authors have appropriated Kafka's legacy in their writings, albeit in the service of two different projects. Both authors incorporated the infrahuman into their work in order to chart the prospects for an assessment of the humanity of the Jew, indeed of humanity in general, in the aftermath of historical catastrophe. In the novel *Temol Shilshom* (*Only Yesterday*, 1945), S. Y. Agnon invokes the figure of an investigating dog as an allegory for the prospective failure of Zionism, whereas Paul Celan in his "Meridian" speech (1960) names the Kafkaesque attentiveness to the creaturely as a form of poetic openness toward the "altogether Other."[2] Despite their different trajectories, the texts converge in a preoccupation with the relationship between the artificial and the creaturely, a relationship that bears directly on the changed role of literature after Auschwitz.

S. Y. AGNON'S HISTORICAL NOVEL, *Temol Shilshom*, tells the story of a young man, Isaac Kumer, who immigrated to Palestine during the first decade of the twentieth century. Kumer is part of the second *Aliya*, the second wave of Jewish immigration to Palestine—at the time an underdeveloped southern Syrian province under Ottoman rule. The Jewish settlers who took part in the second *Aliya* were secular idealist Zionists who came to work the soil and revive Hebrew language and labor in the Land of Israel. A fervent Zionist, Isaac also dreams of realizing such ideals. Coming from a poor Jewish family in eastern Galicia (a former part of Poland incorporated into the Austro-Hungarian Empire during the second half of the nineteenth century), he makes his way to Palestine by train and ship. However, upon reaching Palestine he soon discovers that agricultural work is impossible to come by, since the immigrants of the first *Aliya*, who had become land-owning farmers in new Jewish settlements, preferred cheap Arab labor over the more expensive and inexperienced Jewish labor. Brought to the brink of starvation by lack of work, Isaac is forced to abandon his dream of labor Zionism and instead takes up a job as a house painter. Living in Jaffa, he gives up his traditional way of life and develops an intimate relationship with Sonya, a Russian girl who later rejects him. Sonya's rejection prompts Isaac to move to Jerusalem, where he gradually becomes involved in the ultra-orthodox, anti-Zionist community of the old *Yishuv*.

The story of Kumer's immigration to Palestine, his dream of becoming a tiller of the soil, his failure to achieve his dream, his adaptation to the harsh realities of life in Palestine, the sense of shame resulting from his failure, and his subsequent attempt to join the Jewish orthodox community in Jerusalem serve as the background against which life in pre-mandatory Palestine unfolds in the novel in vivid detail. Through Kumer's encounters with the various inhabitants of the land, the reader is confronted with a rich and complex weave of opinions, beliefs, and behaviors that document the collective experiences of the generation of the second *Aliya*. Yet *Only Yesterday* is not just a historical novel, but a "master-novel" that, according to Boaz Arpaly, incorporates several models and fundamental aspects of the modern European novel.[3] Behind the novel's seemingly realistic façade lies a complex web of ambiguous meanings, subplots, and literary constructs in which the storyline is continuously unraveled and recast anew. Consequently, this literary work has drawn the attention of all major Hebrew literary critics, including Baruch Kurzweil, Dov Sadan, Dan Miron, Benjamin Harshav, Robert Alter, and Amos Oz, among others.

The most striking enigma offered in the novel, which has puzzled critics for decades, concerns the appearance of the dog Balak and his relation to

Isaac Kumer. Balak is a street dog on whose back Kumer inscribes the words "mad dog." Balak is then brutally chased away from his native Meah Shearim (the ultra-orthodox quarter in Jerusalem) by Jews who read the Hebrew inscription on his back. He roams about Jerusalem among non-Jews looking for shelter, but eventually contracts rabies, returns to Meah Shearim, and bites Isaac, who consequently dies a terrible death. Balak's appearance in the novel is striking because it fractures the historical, realistic continuity that has been established throughout the first two hundred pages, plunging the plot quite unexpectedly into the strange and foreign world of a dog, an allegorical realm that has been interpreted alternatively as emblematic of Zionism, or of Isaac's repressed sexuality, or of Jewish exile, or of a destructive demonic force, and so on.

Significantly, Balak is identified right from the outset as a "stray dog" or a "street dog" (*kelev hutzot*) in the fateful encounter with Isaac: "he [Isaac] chanced on a stray dog, with short ears, a sharp nose, a stub of a tail, and hair that looked maybe white or maybe brown or maybe yellow, one of those dogs who roamed around Jerusalem until the English entered the Land."[4] The reference to street dogs in the historical context of pre-mandatory Palestine is by no means self-evident. It alludes to the fact that prior to British rule there was no existing Society for the Prevention of Cruelty to Animals in Palestine. The British, who brought with them Western standards of animal welfare, founded the JSPCA (Jerusalem Society for Prevention of Cruelty to Animals), an organization that still exists today. Without an animal-protection society to guarantee a modicum of animal rights, Balak would have been entirely exposed to wanton cruelty. Thus, we are told that the case of Balak has drawn the attention of Western anthropologists, who claim that "the Jews of Palestine are to be condemned . . . they throw big stones at the dog and chase him furiously. . . . But this should be called to the attention of the SPCA [*tsa'ar ba'alei hayim*], if there is such a society in the Oriental lands, so that they may pay heed to this brutal custom" (OY, 490; translation modified). Living exposed and unprotected on the margins of society, Balak resembles Abramovitsh's kliatshe as an easy victim of persecution and abuse. However, the possibility that the figure of Balak may unequivocally serve as an allegory for diasporic Jewish life is ruled out in the text itself, which makes an explicit reference to Abramovitsh's *Di kliatshe*:

When the Jerusalem newspapers reached Jaffa, Jaffa thought that dog was a parable, like Mendele's horse and other stories of livestock and animals and birds which a person reads for pleasure, and if he's intelligent, he applies his intelligence to the moral. The people of Jaffa, who are all intelligent, applied their intelligence to that, but they didn't know who they were against. This one says, There's something to this; and that one says, We have to derive the implicit from the explicit. But what is explicit here no one explained. Meanwhile, opinions were divided, and there were as many opinions as there were inhabitants of the city. (OY, 485)

As the "intelligent" people of Jaffa read about Balak's exploits, they are tempted to ascribe them an allegorical meaning. But Balak's existence, as the above-quoted passage asserts, is ultimately irreducible, testifying to the unbridgeable gap between "significance" and "physical nature," the gap that serves as the locus of the infrahuman. The indeterminacy of meaning associated with the figure of the dog does not necessarily rule out in advance a variety of allegorical interpretations, but rather suspends them in the spatial dimension of the allegory. In this sense, the figure of Balak bears a distinctive structural resemblance to the figure of Kafka's dog in the "Investigations of a Dog." Indeed, in *Only Yesterday* Agnon seems to have adopted the narrative strategy that Kafka had developed in the "Investigations," which revolves on a dog's unwitting involvement in the human world. In the perspective of the dog, the human world appears as an aggregate of inexplicable phenomena to which he can find no satisfying explanation—hence the need for "investigations." The essential disruption in the life of Kafka's dog, which occurs with the experience of the "music dogs," is paralleled in *Only Yesterday* by the inscription of the words "mad dog" on Balak's back.

And when the dog came to Meah Shearim and jumped to his hole and wanted to sit quietly and rest from his suffering, all of Meah Shearim was shocked, and all those who walk on two legs, men, women, and children, started running in panic. The dog thought they were running to hear a sermon from the preacher. And since everyone ran, the dog thought that Rabbi Grunam May-Salvation-Arise was preaching, for his sermons were all the rage in Jerusalem . . .

He too, that is, the dog, began running, like dogs who, if they see human beings running, they immediately run after them. As soon as he ran he knew he was mistaken. There is no Reb Grunam here and no sermon, but there is something here that never had been before. He sniffed a little here and a little there and nothing came into his nose. He raised his voice and asked, Where are the feet going? And everyone who heard his voice and saw him and the writing on his back picked up his feet and fled, wailing, Crazy dog, crazy dog. When there are many voices screaming at once, they can't be heard, but a wail added to them is heard. That wail went from one end of Meah Shearim to the other, and the farther it went, the less it was understood. (OY, 288–89)

From this point on, the focus will be placed on Balak's repeated "investigations" aimed at deciphering the meaning of the written signs on his back. To him, these signs that carry such palpable consequences as brutal expulsion and exile appear as hieroglyphs. That is, Balak recognizes the basic signifying function of the marks, but the reference eludes him:

He thrust his head toward his back, as he was accustomed to do because of the fleas. And he saw strange signs. It came to him that those signs were the handiwork of the owner of the instrument . . . At that moment, all his suffering was naught compared to the search for truth. And once again he turned his head back to see what were those signs and what was that truth. But all his pains were in vain because he couldn't read. He was amazed and stunned, Everyone who sees me knows the truth about me, and I, who possess the truth itself, I don't know what it is. He shouted loud and long, Hav Hav Hav, this truth, what is it? . . . Truth has a covenant, that all who seek it seek the whole truth. Balak too. Since he paid heed to the truth he wasn't content with some of it and sought to know the whole truth. He stood before the legs of the principal and called out, Hav Hav Hav, give me the interpretation of things, give me the true truth. The janitor came out and saw the dog and what was written on his back. He picked up his feet and ran away. Said Balak, He knows the truth, he knows the truth, but what shall I do since he ran away with it. And Balak was still far from the truth, at any rate investigating the truth was a bit of consolation for his sorrow. (OY, 302–4; translation modified)

In a peculiar inversion of the opaqueness of the figure of the dog from a human perspective, the human world and its products appear equally enigmatic from the perspective of the dog. Denied access to the meaning of the signs that encapsulate the truth of his existence and the reason for his expulsion, Balak remains in a state of non-knowledge, constantly running up against a meaning that remains undisclosed. Just as in Kafka's work, in *Only Yesterday* this immersion in undisclosedness of meaning emerges as the hallmark of the infrahuman. For Balak, not knowing is experienced as an oppressive, at times even unbearable distress that can be temporarily alleviated only by the prospect of the investigations, which defer the discovery of truth to a later point in time. The distress associated with the state of not knowing finds expression in the dog's barks, which are phonetically written in Hebrew as "hav, hav, hav." But "*hav*" in Hebrew also means "give," and thus the dog's frantic barks become indistinguishable from an urgent request for the disclosure of meaning. The barks provide a literal manifestation for Deleuze and Guattari's designation of "an asignifying intensive utilization of language"[5] in which the meaningful word merges with the meaningless sound. The dog's request reads in Hebrew as follows: "hav, hav, hav, give [*hav*] me the interpretation of things, give [*hav*] me the truth."

The thirst for truth that goes unanswered and the lingering immersion in an undisclosedness of meaning eventually give rise to a pervasive melancholy affect that emerges from the unresolvable gap between meaning and letter, "significance" and "physical nature." The first indication of melancholia takes place when Balak intrudes on the young lovers sitting on the rocks next to the Bukharan Houses:

> This one fled here and that one fled there and the rocks once again stood like rocks of the wilderness with no person and no love. And the dog too stood like a stone with no love and no person. But amazement spread over his face and a question twitched in his mouth and hung on his tongue, What is this, wherever human beings look at him, there is either stoning or fleeing. His solitude struck him and he was sad. (OY, 291)

The stone, in its association here with "no love and no person," is emblematic of the telluric aspects of melancholia, which has long been identified, in accordance with a Pythagorean tradition, with the element of earth.[6] Benjamin has expounded on this association between melancholia and the coldness and dryness of stone in his *Trauerspiel* essay by observing that "in the inert mass there is a reference to the genuinely theological conception of the melancholic, which is to be found in one of the seven deadly sins. This is *acedia*, dullness of the heart, or sloth."[7] As an emblematic term, the stone represents the subjection of the melancholic to abject matter and to earthly influences that are entirely deaf "to the voice of revelation"[8] and acknowledge no higher law than the world of earthly things.

In this constellation, the figure of the dog, too, appears as a key association with a state of melancholia, as it comes to represent "sadness with regard to the essential spiritual good of man, that is, to the particular spiritual dignity that had been conferred on him by God."[9] Melancholia implies a collapse into the self, a fall into self-absorption in which the human being turns his back on God and the cosmic order so as to indulge in sinful contemplation of earthly goods. In this depraved state, the fundamental equivalence between human and animal existence is revealed. Melancholia, as Benjamin remarked, is "the most genuinely creaturely of the contemplative impulses, and it has always been noticed that its power need be no less in the gaze of a dog than in the attitude of a pensive genius."[10] Consequently, the dog was a popular emblem of melancholia, and was used to represent the melancholic attachment to the dimension of the earthly in Renaissance and Baroque art.[11]

In *Only Yesterday*, two other characters apart from Balak succumb to the effects of melancholia: Reb Fayesh and Isaac Kumer. Both, indeed, are animalized. Isaac contracts rabies and is thus turned into a dog, whereas Fayesh, who collapses after being frightened out of his wits by Balak in the dead of night, comes to resemble an animal in his debilitated state:

> Balak saw the downfall of that man and was stunned, What is the matter? Just a little while ago, he was walking around on two legs and now he's down on four. I'll go and smell him, maybe the creature isn't a human, or maybe he needs help and I'll be kind to him" (OY, 325–26).

Reduced to a miserable four-legged state, Fayesh no longer cares about the Torah and the Commandments. All that remains of him is pure bodily existence: "Nothing was left but this body sunk in pillows and blankets and sweating" (OY, 328). As they suffer from melancholia, Fayesh and Kumer are also identified with stones. Fayesh spends his days lying in bed "like a silent stone and has no control over his limbs, his hands and his tongue don't obey him, and the rest of his body also seems removed from the world" (OY, 326). Isaac, too, is compared to a stone toward the end of the novel, as he seeks a home in the ultra-orthodox community of Meah Shearim. He is described as a sad orphan, "a child solitary as a stone in the field" (OY, 581). In both cases, then, the melancholy state of solitude and detachment from the world is associated with animality and stone-like qualities.

In *Only Yesterday*, melancholia comes to play a role similar to that of shame in Kafka's stories, namely, as the emotional and psychological tonality intimately associated with the infrahuman. However, melancholia also encapsulates a latent threat, namely, that of subjection to demonic influences. The demonic makes its appearance in the novel on the first night after the inscription is made on Balak's back. Balak then has the following nightmare:

> Meah Shearim rose and stoned him with its shadows, until he was all covered by shadows, and from the shadows leaped the skeleton of a wolf, who then turned himself into a jackal and a fox and a kind of dog unlike any dog in this world. The dog's hairs stood on end, even those hairs that were stippled by the painter with two words that mustn't be mentioned. The skeleton's bones began rattling and saying, Don't be scared, for we are your father and you are our son. (OY, 292)

The terrifying apparitions of wild canines that trigger a primordial fear in Balak recur in a later dream in which a jackal appears with a head erect like an ostrich and "spectacles of flesh cover his eyes from below halfway up, and the spectacles gleam like a peacock's tail." There is also a fox whose eyes are "big and bulging, and they look purple and black ... And the mouths of the animals, oh, their mouths, herald evil" (OY, 614). In both dreams the appearance of wild canines is associated with deep-seated predatory urges, urges that dogs have suppressed as they became domesticated animals. In the dream, it is Balak's doggish nature that compels him to warn the neighborhood of the beasts approaching to devour the turkeys strutting on the street. But then Balak discovers that his throat is parched and he cannot bark, thus failing to fulfill his role as a dog. The parched throat serves as an indication of rabies, marking Balak's estrangement from the position that he occupies in the human world. Insofar as the infrahuman is designated, following Kafka's investigating dog, as a "stepping outside of what is human, a stepping into an uncanny realm that is turned toward the human,"[12] the onset of rabies in Balak marks the other possibility, that the expulsion from a state of humanity can lead to the domain of pure, savage bestiality. In this sense, the skeletal wolf's words "don't be scared, for we are your father and you are our son" should be taken as an invitation to unearth the primordial predatory urges that lie dormant within the dog.

Balak thus pursues his investigations not only to discover the truth of the signs inscribed on his back, but also as an attempt to avoid regression into a state of pure bestiality. Wandering among the different national and ethnic groups in Jerusalem, he eventually comes to adopt a materialist outlook on life:

> The earth is the same everywhere, said Balak, and there is no distinction between the people of this place and the people of that place. And if there is a difference, it is an external difference, for the end of every creation is flesh and bone, that is sustenance, whether they say a blessing over slaughter like the Jews, and say Who hath sanctified us with his commandments and commanded us to slaughter, or say a blessing like the Karaites, who say, Who allowed us to slaughter, or say a blessing like the Ishmaelites, who bless in the name of the merciful and compassionate Allah, or they slit the neck like all other nations, they all intend the same thing, sustenance. (OY, 499)

According to Balak's newly espoused materialism, cultural diversity among human beings appears merely as an accidental or arbitrary feature through which basic biological needs are satisfied in sublimated form. From this perspective, humans appear to be no different from dogs, except that they devised elaborate rituals by which they believe themselves to be superior to animals. Thus, Balak's materialism leads him to reject the anthropocentric notion of man's superiority over creation, and he eventually imagines an entire cosmogony tailor-made for dogs. In this alternative creation story, in the beginning there was a camel that ate many fields of prickly pears and died. All the animals gathered and fed on the contents of his belly and on his flesh. Thus, both the camel and the animals that fed on it thoughtlessly conformed to the essential purpose of their existence, sustenance. But the dog and the vulture nobly stood out among these animals, and guarded the camel's skin from the mice that came to nibble on it. From that skin the sky was formed. The flapping of the vulture's wings created the wind, and the pounding of the dog's tail created the surface of the earth, with valleys, mountains, and rifts. The dog shouted from the earth and the vulture shrieked in the air, frightening the sky and causing it to weep. From the sky's tears the land was filled with water, but the animals soon drank it all, and the world was on the brink of destruction. The dog then went to the vulture and convinced him to let him ride on his back up to the sky. The dog bit the firmament and it began weeping, releasing rain upon the land.

The role of the dog as earth's savior in this myth of creation is intimately linked to the occurrences depicted in the novel. To begin with, the drought that came upon the world in its state of creation is related to the prolonged and terrible drought that plagues Jerusalem in the last section of the novel. Balak invokes the myth of the Great Dog when he is overcome by thirst: "Balak stuck out his dry tongue and shouted hav, bring [*hav*] us a downpour, bring [*hav*] us a drop of water, I am going mad from thirst. He bared his teeth and looked at the firmament. Presumably he recalled the deed of his forefather, the Great Dog who, during a drought, poked a hole in the firmament and brought down rain" (OY, 616; translation modified). Here, the mythical story of the Great Dog has come to replace the traditional Jewish-anthropocentric association between the blowing of the Shofar and the outpouring of rain. In ascribing redemptive power to the bite of the dog, Balak's animal religion has estranged him from the human world. Ultimately, his failure to overcome the gap between letter and meaning compels him to renounce human agency altogether and ascribe absolute autonomy to dogs, even under the most blatant subjection to human mastery: "And thus he stood and questioned, Where do the sticks get their power to hit if not from the dog who attracts the stick to him. The proof of this is that, as long as the stick doesn't see the dog it doesn't hit him. And not only the stick, but also human feet, as long as they don't see the face of a dog they pass by or creep by" (OY, 623). Unlike Kafka's investigating dog, who assumed an ontological superiority of dogs in a "wide, empty world" devoid of human beings, Balak asserts the primacy of dogs in a world inhabited and governed by humans. His claim for canine superiority does not stem from ignorance and repression but from deliberate refusal.

Balak's extreme assertion of canine ontological superiority is counterposed not only to human dominion over creation, but also to the demonic bestiality of the wolf and the jackal, which does away with meaning altogether. Paradoxically, then, the bite with which Balak infects Isaac with rabies is not an expression of brute animality but of the dog's ultimate claim to truth:

> Said Balak . . . I'll bite him and the truth will leak out of his body. And Balak already saw the truth leaking from the blood of the painter like the bountiful rains, as when the Great Dog bit the firmament. (OY, 628)

Here, once again, the redemptive power of the bite finds its archetypal evocation in the Great Dog, not in order to quench a literal thirst for water, but a figurative "thirst" for truth. In Balak's profane religion the bite comes to assume the role of the singular, redemptive act through which the world will be brought to a state of messianic redemption, bridging the intolerable gap between figure and lived experience, between "significance" and "physical nature."

BEFORE BALAK ARRIVES at Meah Shearim to bite Isaac Kumer and extract the truth from him, he has one more encounter with a demonic figure that will prove to be decisive in the aftermath of the bite. At the outskirts of Jerusalem, in the dead of night at an old abandoned windmill, Balak encounters Lilith, an old night owl "who knew the world and knew everything that was done in every house, under every roof" (OY, 604). Although the word "Lilith" means "owl" in Hebrew, the name also refers to a female demon in Jewish mythology. In Hasidism, Lilith came to symbolize the root of all despondency—a force dialectically opposed to joy. Indeed, the high value placed in Hasidism on joy, song, and dance is due to conquering the despair and melancholia associated with Lilith.[13] Lilith's demonic provenance thus links her directly with Balak's melancholia as well as with the other apparitions that Balak encountered, the skeletal wolf and the jackal with the spectacles of flesh. Like them, Lilith appears at night when Balak is in a semiconscious state, and she too tries to convince him to turn his back on the human world and embrace a bestial existence.

Lilith attempts to discourage Balak from going to Meah Shearim to seek the truth of the inscription on his back by telling him a parable of the hyenas that came to Arzef the taxidermist and asked him to be stuffed because they wished to live forever. The appearance of Arzef in Lilith's tale is surprising because this character is first encountered in the novel in a wholly realistic context. He first appears when Isaac, after moving to Jerusalem from Jaffa, goes with his friends to Eyn Rogel and visits his house. Arzef is a native of Jerusalem, but he has left human society behind and "lives alone like the First Adam in the Garden of Eden, with no wife and no sons and no cares and no troubles, among all kinds of livestock and animals and birds and insects and reptiles and snakes and scorpions" (OY, 242). Like Balak, Arzef lives on the margins of the human world, inhabiting a creaturely realm, but as First Adam, the lord of all creatures. His mastery of creation is exemplified by his art, which embellishes nature and supposedly overcomes mortality, as he explains to the curious hyena who sees him stuffing a fox in Lilith's tale:

> As long as your flesh exists you're considered dead, for everyone wants to eat your flesh and break your bones, and if you are saved from the foes and you die in the hands of Heaven, your end is dust and vermin and worms, which is not the case if you threw away your flesh and tossed off your bones and put straw instead of flesh and bones, for then you live forever and exist for eternity, and moreover, they put you in a museum and everyone desires and yearns to see you. (OY, 606)

The hyena, naively fascinated by Arzef's powers, is eager to get rid of his flesh and be stuffed in order to gain immortality, and Arzef readily grants him his wish. After the hyena fails to return home, his brothers go looking for him. They eventually find him in Eyn Rogel, and are struck by the gleaming glass eyes of the stuffed animal. When they ask their brother what happened to him, Arzef, who hides behind the back of the stuffed hyena, tells them with the hyena's voice that he is now immortal, and an object of envy for all, repeating the explanation that he gave to their brother. Upon hearing this, the brothers become jealous and plead with Arzef to grant them immortality as well. Arzef agrees and grants them their request.

At the crux of this parable is the animals' profound misunderstanding of the art of taxidermy. The stuffed animal, with its embellished form and gleaming eyes, fascinates them, and Arzef cunningly presents taxidermy as a kind of redemption from natural history and from the sorrows that plague creaturely existence, but this is clearly a deception. The real ontological character of the stuffed animals is revealed earlier in the novel, when Arzef travels to Jaffa to send a pair of stuffed animals abroad and is bothered by the customs officials "who had trouble assessing how much customs duties to impose on [the stuffed animals], either the rate for live animals but they weren't alive, or the rate for inanimate objects but they did have skin and they did have bones" (OY, 458). Far from exalted immortal beings, the stuffed animals are degraded creatures, located somewhere between the animal and the inanimate object. Most important, such a demotion on the scale of creation reveals the fundamental consequence of art. Though the work of art may appear to save the creature from decay, it ultimately debases its corporeality, its very creatureliness. When art appears to overcome decay, it will do so only by rendering the object hollow and insubstantial, like Arzef's stuffed animals. The only immortality the artifact can ever attain is the false "immortality" of inanimate objects, characterized not by eternal life but by an inability to die.

Nevertheless, the authority that the work exudes by virtue of its aesthetic qualities belies its artificiality, and the fascinated spectator is drawn into the depth of the work, exemplified by the wish to "live forever and exist for eternity, and moreover, they put you in a museum and everyone desires and yearns to see you." The spectator, captivated and distracted by the false promise of art, forgets the essential deception involved in it. Such captivation is achieved because the art object essentially appears as something mysterious and opaque. Indeed, the sway of the artwork's mystery is so great that the animals renounce their own nature and willingly submit to the dominion of man. In this way man truly emerges as the lord of earthly creation: not by divine sanction, but through the deception inherent in the mastery of opaque and fascinating art.

The implications of this parable for Balak involve artifice and the artificial in their capacity as language, as written words. Like the hyenas that are fascinated by the enigmatic form of the stuffed animal, Balak is captivated by the opaqueness of the signs inscribed on his back. From the demonic perspective, the dog's desperate wish to uncover the truth of these signs is not born of his own volition, but is rather the consequence of the creaturely fascination with art and its false promise of a hidden meaning that lies behind the written sign. By going back to Meah Shearim in an attempt to decipher the hidden meaning of the signs, Balak is thus willingly (yet unwittingly) submitting to human dominion. Thus, Lilith's parable seems to imply that the signs inscribed on Balak's back are as hollow as Arzef's stuffed animals; they carry no meaning, and therefore in his investigations and in his journey to Meah Shearim, Balak merely perpetuates human dominion instead of breaking its hold. The real freedom, the parable implies, lies in obeying the call of the flesh, surrendering to predatory impulses, or as Lilith puts it: "instead of flesh what will you wish and instead of skin what will you desire?" (OY, 608). Lilith's solution to the dog's hopeless search for meaning is to revert to a primordial state of animality.

As he faces the prospect that the signs on his back may be no more than empty signifiers that do not lead to a hidden truth, Balak experiences an extreme bout of melancholy:

> Balak folded his paws and shut his eyes and lay and thought of the same thing all the scholars of all generations are toiling to discover, What are we and what is our life, and are all the sufferings and pains and insults and grief that come to us worthwhile for the sake of a little bit of ephemeral pleasure. Especially me, since I don't have even a bit of pleasure, but I do have many pains, and on top of every pain comes an even harder pain. Black bile overcame him and he wanted to die. (OY, 608)

Overcome by melancholy, Balak senses the intrinsic connection between his condition and demonic influence, speculating that the "black bile that clasped him like scabies and bubbled up all over his body came from them, from the demons in the windmill" (OY, 609). His aggravated state of melancholia is born of the real fear of "leaving the world and not grasping the truth" (OY, 626). Indeed, after Balak bites Isaac, this fear becomes a reality:

> After he dug himself a hole in the flesh of the painter and dripped the truth from it, the truth should have filled all his being, but in the end there is no truth and no nothing. And he is still as at the beginning, as if he hadn't done a thing. (OY, 630–31)

Balak's madness, culminating in the bite, is the endpoint of his desperate attempts to breach the veil of obscurity and attain truth and meaning. Once he realizes that truth is denied him, that he will die "like a dog," Balak reverts to the state of savage bestiality exemplified by the jackal and the wolf. This is the final outcome of Balak's melancholia and his despair, not only with the meaning of the signs on his back, but with meaning as such. Instead, he opts for the substantiality of flesh—human flesh—as a substitute for the meaning from which he is excluded. Balak's newly acquired taste for flesh is an inversion of the eagerness, which the hyenas demonstrated in Lilith's parable, to reject flesh and submit to artifice.

Despite its obscure allegorical format, Lilith's parable offers some penetrating insights into the relationship between art and creaturely life. Specifically, it addresses the attraction that the artificial holds for the creature as well as its detrimental effect on it. Art is fascinating not only because it is beautiful, but also because it offers redemption from the futility of natural-historical progression. The age-old creaturely complaint of the futile suffering of earthly life is answered by art's promise to "live forever and exist for eternity." But the redemption that art offers is illusory, and those who submit to art's authority and mystery are degraded in the process. The stuffed hyenas and Balak in his relentless investigations are victims of the misappropriation of art, that is, of the naïve attempt to possess and embody the meaning encapsulated in the artificial.

In *Only Yesterday*, animals are not the only victims of art's misappropriation. Isaac, too, is led astray by the Zionist idea of a sweeping transformation in Jewish mentality that will take place after settlement in the Land of Israel. The move to the new homeland was to redeem the Jew of his inherent doggishness and fashion a new man who would have natural and creative bonds with his community, his sexuality, and the land. Before embarking on his journey to Palestine, Isaac fantasized about such a sweeping transformation into manhood that would compensate for his personal shortcomings. We are told, for example, that "never in his life had Isaac paid any heed to girls. If his passion struck him, his heart carried him to the fields and vineyards of the Land of Israel" (OY, 24). In Isaac's imagination the fulfillment of masculinity is tied to the idea of tilling the soil, and Zionist ideology provided him with a compensation in which the attainment of manhood was deferred until his arrival to the Land of Israel. Isaac's story, however, proves to be the reversal of the common Zionist narrative. As long as he lived in the Diaspora he belonged in a community and adhered to a coherent worldview. Upon making the *Aliya*, Isaac's naïve dreams of tilling the soil, belonging in a community of pioneers, and becoming a man are shattered in the face of the harsh realities of pre-mandatory Palestine. As Michal Arbell writes, "since [Isaac] lost his place among the pioneers who till the soil, he cannot claim either Jaffa or Jerusalem as his own. The failure of the attempt to become an organic part of the pioneer society leaves him without affiliation, without a clear national-ideological identity, and without such a framework of affiliation Isaac probably cannot define himself in a stable and satisfactory manner as an individual."[14]

This failure to integrate socially and become a tiller of the soil is complemented by Isaac's inability to consummate a relationship with Sonya. Like Balak when he was cast out of Meah Shearim, Isaac is left with no affiliations, and his utter failure to realize his dreams leaves him in an undisclosedness of meaning. Helplessly confronted with an unattainable ideal of masculinity, Isaac experiences, through his commitment to Zionism, the gap between figure and lived experience. It is therefore no surprise that toward the end of the novel Isaac appears as a melancholic street dog, at least in the metaphorical sense. After Balak bites him, Isaac completes his transformation into a dog in the literal sense as well. The rabies that he contracts from Balak signifies an animalization that is nothing but the culmination of melancholia.[15] The disease removes Isaac, like Fayesh before him, from the world of human concerns and thrusts him deep into an allegorical modality in which he is rendered a "receptacle of the forgotten." In his rabid state Isaac is subjected to demonic influences, and he begins to experience the artifacts of the human world as enigmatic hieroglyphs. In one dream, for example, Isaac sees Arzef reading *The Fables of Foxes*, "and the book was strange for it wasn't made of letters but of voices" (OY, 631). Isaac tries to decipher the voices and sees that his own hand "strolls over to the book and writes hav hav" (OY, 632; translation modified), but Isaac's hand that wrote was completely detached from Isaac who observed the hand writing. In this dream the meaningful human word degenerates into a meaningless animal sound, depicting the loss of legibility associated with the infrahuman. Nevertheless, the written bark is not entirely devoid of meaning; as a form of an "asignifying intensive utilization of language," it exemplifies the extreme stage of Isaac's self-alienation. In his fascination with artifice, Isaac has become estranged from his self, a creaturely self that articulates an urgent, deep-seated need for a disclosure of meaning.

Ultimately, Isaac's failure to achieve human fulfillment is not presented in the novel as an inherent flaw in Zionism itself but as the result of its misappropriation. For Isaac naively believed the promises of poets, such as Bialik in "In the City of Killings," that Zionism could offer redemption from a flawed diasporic mentality. He failed to realize that adherence to the ideals of Zionism does not liberate the individual, but rather imposes upon him a set of harsh physical and material demands. Like Balak and his myth of the Great Dog, Isaac uses Zionism to construct a personal myth, a myth that helps him avoid rather than confront the demands of modern masculinity. Isaac's colleagues, such as Menachem and the pragmatic Rabinovitch, might have been initially drawn to Zionism for the same reasons, but they eventually learn to perceive these ideals as artificial, and in a long and arduous process of adaptation were able to secure a place for themselves in Palestine. Isaac, on the other hand, is unable to adapt to life in his new homeland because he cannot overcome the gap between the ideal and the real, between "significance" and "physical nature." After failing to achieve the ideal image of masculinity propagated by Zionism, he could do nothing but sink into depression. Isaac, the melancholic man, is thus not the antithesis of the Zionist pioneer (that would be the diasporic Jew) but is rather the symbol of his failure.

It was precisely this melancholic legacy that had to be resisted and suppressed in order for Zionism to fulfill its goals in the Land of Israel during the first decades of the twentieth century. By closely depicting the various factors that led to Isaac's downfall, the novel charts the internal challenges that Zionism faced in order to establish its project of individual and collective emancipation. Isaac, who failed to become pragmatic, had to die a doggish death, a death that is neither murder nor suicide but *shechita*. Like the pogrom victims in Bialik's "In the City of Killings," there is a correspondence between Isaac's death and natural occurrences. On the day that Isaac is buried we are told that the sky became cloudy and rain began to fall. This was the first rain after the long drought that plagued Jerusalem. The rain lasted for a week, and when it stopped "the earth was smiling with its plants and its flowers. And from one end of the Land to the other came shepherds and their flocks, and from the soaked earth rose the voice of the sheep, and they were answered by the birds of the skies. And a great rejoicing was in the world. Such rejoicing had never been seen" (OY, 641). The final pastoral scene in the wake of Isaac's death is not simply a natural occurrence, but a natural-historical one. It serves to symbolically obliterate the memory of Isaac's life and the circumstances of his death in order to commemorate "the elite of our salvation in Kinneret and Merhavia, in Eyn Ganim and in Um Juni, which is now Degania, you went out to your work in the fields and the gardens, the work our comrade Isaac wasn't blessed with" (OY, 642). Isaac's death is consigned to oblivion because the account of his life and death epitomize and expose some the inherent flaws and weaknesses of Zionism in the early days of the second *Aliya*. From the retrospective viewpoint in which *Only Yesterday* was written in 1945, Zionism had already established itself as a successful settlement project in Palestine, and the failures and meaningless deaths of its early adherents could now be safely unearthed and contemplated.

AGNON'S SOMBER ACCOUNT of the Zionist pioneering act as a suppression of creaturely melancholia marks a shift from the fervently idealistic tone that informed Zionist literature from Bialik to Greenberg. More importantly, however, it foreshadows the terms in which the dichotomy between history and nature will be staged in Jewish literature after the Holocaust. In this context, Anat Pick has argued that the Holocaust enters Jewish literature as a "cosmic upheaval" in which the "challenge of the *Muselmann* is not confined to the 'zone of the human,' but projected unto creation as a whole."[16] Or to put it in other words, the Holocaust lays bare the capacity for bodily vulnerability shared by both humans and animals. As we have seen, the theme of creaturely vulnerability appeared in Jewish literature long before the Holocaust in Abramovitsh's writings. However, in *Only Yesterday*, this theme was taken up and given a unique allegorical expression in Lilith's parable of the stuffed hyenas, epitomizing the bodily degradation to which animals were subjected as a result of human art.[17] Thus, Agnon remained true to the spirit of Kafka's work in which creaturely vulnerability was always framed within a spatialized allegorical modality. After the Holocaust, creaturely vulnerability would be displaced from the realm of allegory into a markedly historical referent, as in Isaac Bashevis Singer's famous line from "The Letter Writer": "in relation to [nonhuman animals], all people are Nazis; for the animals it is an eternal Treblinka."[18]

This paradoxical displacement of the allegorical into the realm of the historical marks the reduction of the infrahuman in post-Holocaust literature and critical thought to a mere openness to nonhuman lifeforms. By contrast, my analysis has shown that the figures of animals that populate the writings of such authors as Abramovitsh, Bialik, and Kafka emblematize a fundamental gap between figural expression and lived experience. As Benjamin wrote in his Kafka essay, "[animals] are not the goal, to be sure, but one cannot do without them."[19] Pick's reductive reading of the infrahuman as attentiveness to the suffering of animals, even though it is not entirely misguided, nevertheless distorts the crucial allegorical modality upon which the depiction of animals in Jewish literature is predicated. As we have seen, in allegory the temporality associated with the gap between "significance" and "physical nature" is experienced as a natural-historical progression: the bracketed time of the pogrom, of Isrolik's hallucinations, of Josef K.'s execution, and of Balak's encounter with Lilith. Everything that transpires within this bracketed zone remains outside the purview of history and memory and is pervaded by oblivion and forgetfulness. In turn, the forgotten, in its claim on the life of the individual, exerts the binding force of a law in a state of exception, maintaining its validity despite its absence. These three interrelated aspects of the infrahuman—natural history, forgetfulness, and the law in its kenomatic state of exception—have already been fully articulated in the pre-war writings of Kafka and Benjamin, and they subsequently reappear after the war in the work of another German-Jewish writer, Paul Celan. Celan's poetry bears a close affinity with Kafka and Benjamin—and for that matter, with Agnon as well—in its blatant refusal to reduce the allegorical to the purview of the historical. Here, one could think of no better example than his early poem "Todesfuge" ("Death Fugue," 1948):

Black milk of daybreak we drink it at evening
we drink it at midday and morning we drink it at night
we drink and we drink

Schwarze Milch der Frühe wir trinken sie abends
wir trinken sie mittags und morgens wir trinken sie nachts
wir trinken und trinken[20]

This poem, which addresses the formative experience of the concentration camp, invokes a distinctive allegorical modality that accounts for its so-called "surrealist" atmosphere. To begin with, the dimension of natural-historical progression is brought to the fore in the very first lines of the poem, which present, as John Felstiner intuited, a distorted account of the first days of creation.[21] Yet if these lines refer to the sequence of creation, it is creation without grace in which time progresses through repetition and not by means of development. The days are thus punctuated by acts of drinking that mark the passage of time—morning, midday, and night—but this is the empty time of natural history. In the concentration camp, historical time has come to a standstill, or rather, it has "merged into the setting."[22] This empty time is nevertheless not devoid of certain forms of activity, for example, shoveling and the playing of music. The German "whistles his Jews into rows has them shovel a grave in the ground / he commands us play up for the dance."[23] These and other senseless acts testify above all to the absence of a law or a governing principle in which such forms of behavior would find their ultimate justification. As in Kafka's world, in the concentration camp of Celan's "Todesfuge" the organization of life and work is based on the constitutive absence of the law.[24] Yet this absence nevertheless produces a binding effect, as everyone in the camp seems to know their place: the German "whistles his hounds to stay close / he whistles his Jews into rows."[25] In the reality of the camp, the forgotten makes itself manifest in this distorted and groundless order to which one is compelled to obey. Thus the poem bears witness to the unraveling of the human in the exposure to the law in a state of exception, and what emerges in its place is the creature, bare life.

In these terms, the literary representation of the Holocaust in Celan can be seen as an extension of the poetic modalities and philosophical notions found in the work of Benjamin and Kafka. Celan, in a way, inhabits their world and extends it further, poetically, into the concentration camp. Notably, Celan explicitly invokes the legacy of Benjamin and Kafka in a sustained reflection on the relationship between figure and lived experience, the artificial and the creaturely, in his "Meridian" speech. The speech was given on the occasion of receiving the Georg Büchner Prize in 1960, and is widely considered today to be one of the most significant statements on poetry after the Holocaust. Celan frames his speech by addressing what he calls "the problem of art":

> Art, ladies and gentlemen, with everything that belongs to it and will yet belong to it, is also a problem, and as you can see, a mutable, tough and long-lived, I want to say, an eternal problem. (M, 2)

For Celan, the term "art" (Kunst) refers to the realm of the artificial, to the "puppet-like, iambically five-footed," to an association with automatons, the mechanical, and the ability to "string word upon word" (M, 2; PCTM, 2). But Celan is not interested in the sphere of meaning opened up by means of art. For him, the crucial dimension in which art is experienced is undisclosedness of meaning:

> But whenever there is talk about art, there is also always someone present who ... doesn't really listen.
>
> More exactly: someone who hears and listens and looks ... and then doesn't know what the talk was all about. But who hears the speaker, "sees him speak," who perceives language and shape, and also—who could doubt this here, in writing of this order?— breath, that is, direction and destiny. (M, 3)

Celan draws the decisive portrayal of art from the realm of the infrahuman, that is, from the gap between "significance" and "physical nature." Although the individual who experiences art in this way remains excluded from art's meaning, he can nevertheless perceive "breath" (Atem), as well as "direction" (Richtung) and "destiny" (Schicksal). These terms mark a concern with the nonverbal elements in language: with the intervals between words and timbre of speech ("breath"); with the inevitability of death ("direction"); and, finally, with the specific route that physical life must take in order to satisfy art's prescriptions ("destiny"). Celan identifies such a peculiar perspective on art—which recalls Balak's preoccupation with the unintelligible signs on his back—with the figure of Lucile from Büchner's play *Danton's Death*. When Danton and the other leaders of the French Revolution mount the scaffold toward the end of the play, Lucile, the wife of Camille Desmoulins, goes mad and cries "Long live the King!" thereby guaranteeing her own death sentence. Celan emphasizes that Lucile's utterance stands in sharp contrast to the words spoken by the condemned group of revolutionaries on the scaffold, which are characterized by their excessive artificiality and theatrical quality:

> The passengers are there, all of them, Danton, Camille, the others. Here too they all have words, many artful words, and they make them stick, there is much talk—and here Büchner only needs to quote—talk of going-together-into-death, Fabre even maintains that he can die "doubly," they are all at their best—only a few voices, "a few"—nameless—"voices" find that "all of this is old hat and boring."
>
> ... when all around Camille pathos and sententiousness confirm the triumph of "puppet" and "string," then Lucile, one who is blind to art, the same Lucile for whom language is something person-like and tangible, is there, once again, with her sudden "Long live the king!" (M, 3)

Celan refers here to a preeminently historical situation. The condemned men—who could well be seen as the literary antithesis to the figure of Josef K.—recognize the historical "significance" of their execution, and they do not lack words and memorable declarations to fit the occasion. Caught up in the matrix of figural meaning, they seem to be oblivious to their own vulnerability or creatureliness. It is Lucile, who in her madness has been deprived of the capacity to appreciate the artificial, that perceives the fundamental futility of the situation. Lucile's "Long live the king!" is not a declaration of loyalty to the ancien régime any more than it is a statement meant to produce a dramatic effect. Rather, her utterance infuses human speech with the "breath" that emanates from the creaturely realm. That is to say, Lucile has appropriated human language, reproducing an utterance in order to shape a "direction" and a "destiny" for herself. As Philippe Lacoue-Labarthe observed, "by shouting 'Long live the King!' Lucile simply kills herself. Here, the word is suicidal ... As pure provocation, it signifies (the decision to die), but in a mode other than signification. It signifies without signifying: it is an act, an event."[26] My one reservation regarding Lacoue-Labarthe's formulation is that it is somewhat misleading to designate Lucile's utterance as an "event," since the artificial solidity of the historical event is precisely what this utterance seeks to unravel. Like Shylock's "I am not well," Lucile's "Long live the king!" bears witness to the unbridgeable gap between lived experience and figural expression. Celan calls it a "counterword" (Gegenwort), a "step," and "an act of freedom" (M, 3; PCTM, 3).

In what exactly does this "act of freedom" consist? To be sure, the emphasis is not placed on the decision to die per se, but rather on the manner in which one is to die. The crucial point is that like Josef K. or Isaac Kumer, Lucile dies like a dog, in obliviousness to historical "significance." Her utterance is an act of resistance to the sublation of life to a totalizing figural scheme. In turn, it also exposes the death of the condemned men as subject not to historical necessity, but to the futility of natural-historical progression. The historical "injustice" of the Revolution is thus revealed, through Lucile's counterword, as a traumatic exposure to a law in a state of exception. In this sense, Celan mentions that Lucile's utterance pays homage "to the majesty of the absurd as witness for the presence of the human" (M, 3). And significantly, Celan proceeds to call this form of utterance "poetry" (Dichtung) (M, 4; PCTM, 4).

In this short exposition on Büchner's *Danton's Death*, Celan demonstrates "the problem of art" to which he alluded at the beginning of his speech. To put it simply, the problem of art—an eternal problem—is poetry. Poetry becomes a problem for art, that is, for the attempt to claim historical significance for human life and death, because poetry exposes the artificiality of the attempt to merge figure and creature, "significance" and "physical nature." In this respect, the distinction between "art" and "poetry" in Celan's "Meridian" speech corresponds to the distinction between symbol and allegory in Benjamin's *Trauerspiel* essay.

Nevertheless, poetry, as Celan envisions it, is not entirely bereft of any relation to history. Poetry is nothing but the articulation of the creaturely as it is implicated in a constitutive historical experience. As an example, Celan cites the opening line of Büchner's *Lenz*—"On the 20th of January Lenz walked through the mountains," marking his way into madness and death. And Celan proceeds to frame the encounter between poetry and history as a question: "perhaps one can say that each poem has its own '20th of January' inscribed in it?" (M, 8). Celan alludes here, among other things, to the date of the infamous Wannsee Conference during which the "Final Solution" of the Jewish question was resolved, thus locating the poem on a fracture between figural representation and lived experience. In his speech notes he writes:

> These dates and moments, they cannot be read off the calendars and clocks, the "old war-horses and bystanders of history" miss them; only the victims of what appears from the perspective of that "bystander" as history, know something about it. (M, 58)

The poem, as a writing that emanates from the bracketed time of the catastrophe, must therefore proceed from a congenital condition of undisclosedness of meaning. The opacity and hermeticism of the poem affirm not the absolute autonomy of art (as in the poetry of Mallarmé), but the "angle of inclination of [the poet's] creatureliness" ["dem Neigungswinkel seiner Kreatürlichkeit"] (M, 9; PCTM, 9). The poem aims at establishing a set of correlations between the historical date, in its multivalency, and a creaturely "angle of inclination." Thus, the poem becomes emblematic of the experience of the victims of history, exemplifying—as Ulrich Baer put it—"the near impossibility of witnessing a historical trauma through which language seems to have lost the capacity for genuine address."[27] In its obscurity, the poem gives voice to a traumatic experience that

> can neither be considered subjective or empirically verifiable ... nor dismissed as mystical or transcendental because it does not leave the realm of the material. Its historical dimension derives partly from the blurring or the "wounding" of the distinction between an inside and an outside ... through which a traumatic memory controls a subject's life like an external stimulus, as if from the outside, although in reality it is lodged inside the subject.[28]

The poem that speaks the opaque language of trauma blurs the distinction between inside and outside, subject and object, and thus signals the resurgence of the allegorical modality in the realm of history. The poem aims to liberate the trauma from the purview of forgetfulness, from the demands of subjectivity as well as from the regimes of representation that govern historical existence. Simply put, poetry does not release the subject from its trauma, but the trauma from its subject. The poem approaches this goal not by excavating an original trauma that lies behind language and subjectivity, but by working on artificiality itself, by estranging what is in itself already estranged and artificial.

Celan illustrates this approach by introducing Büchner's notion of "medusoid" art. He emphasizes that Büchner's Lenz "has only disparaging words for 'Idealism' and its 'wooden puppets'" (M, 4). Lenz counters these constructions of the figural by paying attention to the "natural and the creaturely" [Natürliche und Kreatürliche] (M, 4; PCTM, 4). But for Büchner the depiction of the creaturely, of "physical nature," does not take place by means of mimetic art. Instead, when he sees two peasant girls sitting on a rock, he wishes that "one . . . were a Medusa's head in order to turn a group like this into stone, and call everybody over to have a look" (M, 5). Here, the attention to the "natural and the creaturely" is paradoxically achieved by means of an art that renders itself uncanny, that is, by an art that deliberately presents itself as artificial. By announcing its own artificiality, "medusoid" art exposes the deception involved in the attempt to merge figure and experience, as exemplified in Arzef's fascinating art of taxidermy that involved the debasement of the creaturely through the embellishment of form and figure. By contrast, "medusoid" art does not seek to overcome or transcend the creaturely, but to simply detach it from its dependence on the figural.

The poem, as language emanating from the creaturely or experiential dimension of human life, must therefore employ the artificial in its very artificiality in order to authentically address the creaturely. This is what Celan means when he mentions that "poetry has to tread the route of art" ["Dichtung, die doch den Weg der Kunst zu gehen hat"] (M, 6; PCTM, 6). Here, the poem is charged with extracting the profound expressions of the creaturely from the uncanniest manifestations of the artificial. And Celan provides another example from Büchner's *Lenz*: ". . . except sometimes it annoyed him that he could not walk on his head" (M, 7). Seemingly an early statement of autonomous art that impresses the reader with its cryptic obscurity, as a poetic expression it exemplifies the encounter of the creature with itself as a being possessing insufficient ground, because "he who walks on his head, has the sky beneath him as an abyss" (M, 7). Lenz's experience of his own fundamental otherness is thus rendered equivalent to Lucile's "Long live the king," marking the unravelling of subjectivity under conditions of insanity, silence, and death. Here, the creaturely emerges out of the strange, or more precisely, out of a constitutive allegorical modality.

The strangeness of "medusoid" art calls into question the modernist tradition that emphasized the role of poetry in expanding the domain of autonomous art. In response to the demand to "enlarge art," Celan proposes instead to "go with art into your innermost narrows. And set yourself free" ["geh mit der Kunst in deine allereigenste Enge. Und setze dich frei"] (M, 11; PCTM, 11). The freedom that Celan conceives of here is the freedom from totalizing figural schemes in which subjectivity is consolidated and the creaturely is suppressed. In its medusa-likeness, the poem unravels subjectivity by paying attention to the creaturely aspects of everything it addresses without disclosing the meaning of the whole. Attention to creaturely otherness therefore emerges as the most decisive aspect of poetic language, illuminating its innate darkness and obscurity. And in a famous passage, Celan identifies such a form of attention in the work of Benjamin and Kafka:

> The attention the poem tries to pay to everything it encounters, its sharper sense of detail, outline, structure, color, but also of the "tremors" and "hints," all this is not, I believe, the achievement of an eye competing with ever more precise instruments, but it is rather a concentration that remains mindful of all our dates.
>
> "Attention"—permit me to quote here a phrase by Malebranche, via Walter Benjamin's essay on Kafka—"Attention is the natural prayer of the soul." (M, 9)

In locating his own work within a literary trajectory that stretches from Büchner to Kafka and Benjamin, Celan affirms the decisive role of the attentiveness to the creaturely as a longstanding literary preoccupation. Yet Celan has gone further than his predecessors in articulating the poetic and ethical stakes of such attentiveness, and even more importantly, in explicitly identifying the infrahuman in its relation to a formative historical experience: the trauma of the victims. In this respect Celan's poetry is diametrically opposed to Zionist literature in which attentiveness serves to ultimately consign the creature to oblivion. Even in Agnon's novel, which presents a relatively sober account of the early failures of Zionism, the gratuitous obliteration of Isaac's death by means of natural occurrences implies a principle of natural-historical selection in which the weak are weeded out from the strong in the course of the adaptation to life in the Land of Israel. Those who fall away from the historical process return to nature without leaving a trace. In the poetry of Celan, by contrast, nature itself is exposed in its artificiality in order to allow the trauma to resurface from oblivion, and thereby effect a "breathturn" [Atemwende] in which authentic being is manifested. But this authentic mode of being, which is identical with the creature, owes nothing to a native land and lies "outside all enrootedness and all dwelling."[29] Under such conditions of statelessness a new poetry, which has outlived the human, must begin to establish itself.

POSTSCRIPT

IN HIS ESSAY on Kafka, Walter Benjamin has addressed the question of the possibility of redemption in a world thoroughly permeated by forces of oblivion and forgetfulness. The figure that for Benjamin suggested the possibility of overcoming forgetfulness was that of the horse Bucephalus in Kafka's story "The New Attorney." The story introduced the attorney Bucephalus, who in a previous life was Alexander the Great's horse, and who had retired to a peaceful life of studying and reading. Benjamin invokes Kafka's image of Bucephalus "in the quiet lamplight, his flanks unhampered by the thighs of a rider, free and far from the din of Alexander's battle, he reads and turns the pages of our old books."[1] To be sure, Bucephalus does not practice the law, nor does his studying constitute an attempt to transmit or even retain knowledge of the law. "Perhaps these studies had amounted to nothing," Benjamin writes in reference to another story by Kafka, "but they are very close to that nothing which alone makes it possible for something to be useful—that is, to the Tao."[2] Studying thus does not produce knowledge, but a kind of agitated awareness that keeps one awake in the darkness and obscurity of forgetfulness. It sheds light on the inherent condition of forgetting as an opening to redemption:

> This is what directs him to learning, where he may encounter fragments of his own existence, fragments that are still within the context of the role. He might catch hold of the lost *gestus* the way Peter Schlemihl caught hold of the shadow he had sold. He might understand himself, but what an enormous effort would be required![3]

And, employing imagery that foreshadows the subsequent figure of the angel of history from the *Theses on the Philosophy of History*, Benjamin goes on to compare the forces of forgetting to a storm, and the practice of learning to an attack against its pull: "It is a tempest that blows from the land of oblivion, and learning is a cavalry attack against it."[4] Certainly, then, studying appears here as a primarily Quixotean endeavor, a battle in which one is destined to lose. The futility of the attempt is also echoed in Benjamin's subsequent interpretation of the figure of Bucephalus. After asserting that "the law which is studied and not practiced any longer is the gate to justice,"[5] Benjamin immediately proceeds to undercut the redemptive potential implied in the act of learning:

> The gate to justice is learning. And yet Kafka does not dare attach to this learning the promises which tradition has attached to the study of the Torah. His assistants are sextons who have lost their house of prayer, his students are pupils who have lost the Holy Writ. Now there is nothing to support them on their "untrammeled, happy journey."[6]

Despite being doomed to failure in advance, studying nevertheless provides an "Umkehr," a point of inversion or reversal: "reversal is the direction of learning which transforms existence into writing."[7] And, as Beatrice Hanssen has remarked, "the term *Umkehr* first of all signaled the many displacements (*Entstellungen*) that typified Kafka's work, whether it be Alexander's horse Bucephalus turning into a man or the episode in which the servant Sancho Panza conquered his master."[8] But perhaps most important—and this Hanssen neglects to mention—the topos of inversion appears in its full force at an earlier point in Benjamin's essay on Kafka, in his evocation of the figure of "The Little Hunchback" (Das bucklicht Männlein):

> This little man is at home in distorted life; he will disappear with the coming of the Messiah, of whom a great rabbi once said that he did not wish to change the world by force, but would only make a slight adjustment in it.[9]

In these terms, Benjamin conceives of messianic inversion as the release of all creatures from their distorted forms—the distorted forms that they have assumed in oblivion.[10] Significantly, only at this point Benjamin introduces the famous passage on Kafka's attentiveness to the creaturely:

> Even if Kafka did not pray—and this we do not know—he still possessed in the highest degree what Malebranche called "the natural prayer of the soul": attentiveness. And in this attentiveness he included all living creatures, as saints include them in their prayers.[11]

The agitated awareness that Benjamin referred to, the product of learning, the "nothing which alone makes it possible for something to be useful" and in which existence is transformed into writing, is nothing other than this attentiveness to the creaturely. Attentiveness is a willingness to remember that is devoid of any specific content—a receptivity to messianic redemption. The crucial point here is not whether this form of attentiveness can ultimately guarantee redemption, as that remains unclear. What matters is that with the attentiveness to the creaturely one struggles to regain an irretrievable lived experience. And in this attempt to recall the forgotten, the difference between human and animal no longer seems to matter: "Whether it is a man or a horse is no longer important, if only the burden is removed from the back."[12] In the Ovidian world of the forgotten to which attentiveness applies itself, the infrahuman finds one of its most profound poetic-philosophical articulations.

In view of the context in which Benjamin's notion of attentiveness was originally embedded, it is easy to see its subsequent appeal for Celan, the Holocaust survivor. For Celan, attentiveness to the creaturely is of the utmost importance because it constitutes an attempt to overcome forgetting, to provide testimony. The subsequent simplifications and reductive readings of Benjamin's notion as mere "attentiveness to the bodily and the embodied"[13] in Pick; or as a form of openness toward the nonhuman in Hanssen;[14] or even Levinas's famous ethical reading of attentiveness as "the first meaning of that insomnia that is conscience—rectitude of responsibility before any appearance of forms, images, or things"[15]—provide only a partial, and at best incomplete, account. For Celan, attentiveness to the creaturely, in its application to the realm of the forgotten, is precisely the link between lived experience and the figural historical expression in which it is embedded. Thus, attentiveness can be seen as a form of receptivity implicated in the struggle to overcome the artificial dimension of language that has taken hold in the aftermath of the Holocaust. In this constellation, the "breathturn," the encounter with the creaturely "Other" within oneself, emerges as the "slight adjustment" that would take place with the coming of the Messiah.

NOTES

INTRODUCTION

1. Andrew Benjamin, *Of Jews and Animals* (Edinburgh: Edinburgh University Press, 2010), 4; see also 16, fn. 2.

2. Daniel Boyarin, *A Radical Jew: Paul and the Politics of Identity* (Berkeley: University of California Press, 1997), 31.

3. John Chrysostom, *Homilies against the Jews*, trans. Wayne Meeks and Robert Wilken in *Jews and Christians in Antioch in the First Four Centuries of the Common Era* (Missoula, MT: Scholars Press for the Society of Biblical Literature, 1978), I.II.1–2.

4. Kenneth Stow, *Jewish Dogs: An Image and Its Interpreters* (Stanford, CA: Stanford University Press, 2006).

5. Leonid Livak, *The Jewish Persona in the European Imagination: A Case of Russian Literature* (Stanford, CA: Stanford University Press, 2010), 74–75.

6. Ibid., 74.

7. Thomas Hobbes, *On the Citizen* (Cambridge: Cambridge University Press, 1998), 3–4.

8. Giorgio Agamben, *Homo Sacer: Sovereign Power and Bare Life*, trans. Daniel Heller-Roazen (Stanford, CA: Stanford University Press, 1998), 28.

9. Ibid., 105.

10. Jacques Derrida, " 'Eating Well,' or The Calculation of the Subject," in *Points: Interviews, 1974–1994*, ed. Elisabeth Weber, trans. Peggy Kamuf, et al. (Stanford, CA: Stanford University Press, 1995), 255–87. See also Beatrice Hanssen, *Walter Benjamin's Other History: Of Stones, Animals, Human Beings, and Angels* (Berkeley: University of California Press, 1998), 105.

11. William Shakespeare, *The Merchant of Venice* in: *The Complete Works of Shakespeare, 4th Edition*, ed. David Bevington (Reading: Addison-Wesley Educational Publishers, 1997).

12. A. Erler, "Friedlosigkeit und Werwolfglaube," in *Paideuma*, vol. 1, H. 7 (Sept., 1940): 303–17. According to Wilhelm Eduard Wilda, the origin of this

practice can be found in early Germanic law. In his doctrine of *Friedlosigkeit* elaborated in 1842, Wilda claimed that early Germanic law was characterized above all by a concept of a general peace (*Volksfrieden*), in which the breaking of a law was thought to have been an aberration from the norm, and was met with a punishment of banishment from the community. Those expelled from the community became *friedlos*, peaceless, and this condition amounted to civil death, removing any semblance of communal protection. See also Agamben, *Homo Sacer*, 104–5.

13. Indeed, as Derrida shows, the figure of the werewolf preoccupied Western thinkers such as Plautus, Hobbes, Rousseau, and Schmitt precisely in the sense that it represented an indeterminate position between humanity and animality that implied an exclusion from the political community. See Jacques Derrida, *The Beast and the Sovereign*, vol. 1, trans. Geoffrey Bennington (Chicago: University of Chicago Press, 2009), 63–96.

14. Agamben, *Homo Sacer*, 109.

15. Julia R. Lupton, *Citizens-Saints: Shakespeare and Political Theology* (Chicago: University of Chicago Press, 2005), 96.

16. Heinrich Heine, "Shylock (Jessica)," in *Jewish Stories and Hebrew Melodies*, trans. F. Ewen (New York: Markus Wiener Publishing, 1987), 83.

17. Heinrich Heine, "Princess Sabbath" in *The Complete Poems of Heinrich Heine: A Modern English Version*, trans. Hal Draper (Cambridge, MA: Suhrkamp, 1982), 651; translation modified.

18. Mendele Moykher Sforim, *Dos Vinshfingerl* (Kiev: Kooperativer Farlag, 1927), 112–13.

19. Hayim Nachman Bialik, *Shirim*, (Tel Aviv: Dvir, 1976), 39.

20. Eric L. Santner, *On Creaturely Life: Rilke, Benjamin, Sebald* (Chicago: University of Chicago Press, 2006), 12.

21. Lupton, *Citizens-Saints*, 96.

22. Ibid.

23. Carl Schmitt, *Political Theology: Four Chapters on the Concept of Sovereignty*, trans. George Schwab (Chicago: University of Chicago Press, 2005), 5.

24. See Giorgio Agamben, *State of Exception*, trans. Kevin Attell (Chicago: University of Chicago Press, 2006), 5–6.

25. Schmitt, *Political Theology*, 6–7.

26. Agamben, *State of Exception*, 6.

27. This distinction is drawn from Agamben's *Homo Sacer*, 1, where he excavates the ancient Greek designation of *zoë* as a term that refers to "the simple

fact of living common to all living beings (animals, men, or gods)" as opposed to *bios*, which indicates "the form or way of living proper to an individual or a group." See also Lupton, *Citizens-Saints*, 98.

28. See note 1, above.

29. Lupton, *Citizens-Saints*, 99.

30. Following Simone Weil, Pick addresses the beauty of vulnerable things as a point of departure for a "radical aesthetics and an equally radical ethics" that undermine the anthropocentric boundaries between human and animal. This attempt rests on the universal appeal of a vague theological notion: "If fragility and finitude possess a special kind of beauty, this conception of beauty is already inherently ethical. It implies a sort of sacred recognition of life's value as material and temporal." See Anat Pick, *Creaturely Poetics: Animality and Vulnerability in Literature and Film* (New York: Columbia University Press, 2011), 3.

31. As Pick writes, "the creaturely is not simply a synonym for the material and corporeal. It carries within it (as inflection, as horizon) an opening unto a religious vocabulary of creation and created, and so attempts a rapprochement between the material and the sacred." Ibid., 17.

32. For a general discussion on the opposition of symbol and allegory as modes of aesthetic representation see Hans-Georg Gadamer, *Truth and Method*, trans. Joel Weinsheimer and Donald G. Marshall (New York: Continuum, 1989), 61–70.

33. Walter Benjamin, *The Origin of German Tragic Drama*, trans. John Osborne (New York: Verso, 1998), 166. Subsequent references to this work will be made in the text.

34. Walter Benjamin, "Trauerspiel and Tragedy," in *Selected Writings, Volume 1: 1913–1926*, trans. Rodney Livingstone (Cambridge, MA: Harvard University Press, 1996), 56.

35. Max Pensky, *Melancholy Dialectics: Walter Benjamin and the Play of Mourning* (Amherst: University of Massachusetts Press, 1993), 114.

36. According to Benjamin, the spatialization of the historical involves "the transposition of originally temporal data into figurative spatial inauthenticity [*Uneigentlichkeit*] and simultaneity." *The Origin of German Tragic Drama*, 81; translation modified. For the German original, see *Gesammelte Schriften*, vol. 1, ed. R. Tiedemann and H. Schweppenhäuser (Frankfurt am Main: Suhrkamp Verlag, 1977), 271. The crucial word *Uneigentlichkeit* (omitted from the English translation) implies that the historical object literally appears as "not itself" in its "spatial" or aesthetic manifestation.

37. In this respect, my approach diverges from Margot Norris's reading of such animals, which for her are "finally the masks of the human animals who create them." See Margot Norris, *Beasts of the Modern Imagination: Darwin, Nietzsche, Kafka, Ernst, & Lawrence* (Baltimore: Johns Hopkins University Press, 1985), 1.

38. Mendele Moykher Sforim, "The Mare," in *Yenne Velt: The Great Works of Jewish Fantasy and Occult*, vol. 2, ed. and trans. J. Neugroschel (New York: Stone Hill Publishing Company, 1976), 213.

39. Jacob Taubes has pointed to the strong parallels between the Pauline and the Benjaminian notions of the creaturely: "Benjamin . . . has a Pauline notion of creation: he sees the labor pains of creation, the futility of creation. All of this is of course to be found in Romans 8: the groaning of the creature . . . that is the idea of creation as decay, since it is without hope." Jacob Taubes, *The Political Theology of Paul*, trans. Dana Hollander (Stanford, CA: Stanford University Press, 2004), 72.

40. Santner, *On Creaturely Life*, 126–27.

41. For the link between allegory and a postlapsarian state in Benjamin's thought, see Richard Wolin, *Walter Benjamin: An Aesthetic of Redemption* (New York: Columbia University Press, 1982), 68.

42. Walter Benjamin, "Franz Kafka: On the Tenth Anniversary of his Death," in *Illuminations*, trans. Harry Zohn (New York: Schocken, 1968), 134. Heidegger, too, seems to have reached a similar conclusion when he wrote that "in the end we do not first require the Christian faith in order to understand something of the saying of St. Paul (Romans 8:19) concerning . . . the yearning expectation of creatures and of creation, the paths of which, as the Book of Ezra 4:7,12 says, have become narrow, doleful, and weary in this aeon." See *The Fundamental Concepts of Metaphysics: World, Finitude, Solitude*, trans. William McNeill and Nicholas Walker (Bloomington: Indiana University Press, 1995), 272–73.

43. Walter Benjamin, "The Storyteller," in *Selected Writings*, vol. 3, 1935–1938, ed. H. Eiland and M. Jennings, trans. Harry Zohn (Cambridge, MA: Harvard University Press, 2002), 158; translation modified.

CHAPTER 1

1. This was attested, for example, by Karl Gutzkow, Heine's contemporary and a leading German Christian liberal, who wrote about the prevalence of the

negative image of the Polish Jew in the university fraternity system. According to Sander Gilman, "the image of the Polish Jew—crippled, vindictive, boastful—had become the standard fare of German political anti-Semitism, an anti-Semitism lodged in institutions such as the universities." See Sander L. Gilman, *Jewish Self-Hatred: Anti-Semitism and the Hidden Language of the Jews* (Baltimore: Johns Hopkins University Press, 1986), 172.

2. Ibid., 2.
3. Quoted in Gilman, *Jewish Self-Hatred*, 169.
4. See S. S. Prawer, *Heine's Jewish Comedy: A Study of His Portraits of Jews and Judaism* (Oxford: Clarendon Press, 1983), 61–62.
5. Gilman, *Jewish Self-Hatred*, 165.
6. Ibid.
7. Ibid.
8. For a discussion on the reception of Heine in modern Hebrew literature, see Na'ama Rokem, *Prosaic Conditions: Heinrich Heine and the Spaces of Zionist Literature* (Evanston, IL: Northwestern University Press, 2013).
9. In this early essay, Heine already makes a distinction between Christian and Greek mentalities: "in ancient times, that is with the Greeks and Romans, sensuality prevailed. [. . .] But . . . when mankind began to feel that there was something still better than sensual intoxication, when the uneffusive blissful idea of Christianity—love—began to permeate the minds: then mankind wanted this secret thrill, this endless longing and at the same time to utter and sing about this lust." Heinrich Heine, *Historisch-kritische Gesamtausgabe der Werke*, ed. M. Winfuhr et al., vol. 10 (Hamburg: Hoffman und Campe, 1973–1997), 194–95.
10. Heinrich Heine, "The Gods of Greece," in *The Complete Poems*, trans. Hal Draper (Cambridge: Suhrkamp/Insel, 1982), 153.
11. For a detailed account of the influence of Saint-Simonism on Heine's concept of Hellenism see Robert Holub, *Heinrich Heine's Reception of German Grecophilia* (Heidelberg: Carl Winter Verlag, 1981), 111–49.
12. Heinrich Heine, *Ludwig Börne: A Memorial*, trans. J. Sammons (New York: Camden House, 2006), 9–10.
13. Lloyd S. Kramer, *Threshold of a New World: Intellectuals and the Exile Experience in Paris, 1830–1848* (Ithaca, NY: Cornell University Press, 1988), 110.
14. Holub, *Heine's Reception of German Grecophilia*, 144.
15. English translation quoted in S. S. Prawer, *Heine's Jewish Comedy* (Oxford: Oxford University Press, 1983), 531. The German original appears in

Heinrich Heine, *Prinzessin Sabbat: Über Juden und Judentum*, ed. Paul Peters (Bodenheim: Philo Verlag, 1997), 511.

16. E. H. Jellinek, "Heine's Illness: The Case for Multiple Sclerosis," in *Journal of The Royal Society of Medicine*, vol. 83 (August, 1990), 517.

17. Quoted in Jellinek, *Heine's Illness*, 517. The original references in his letters in German to his developing illness can be found at http://www.heinrich-heine-denkmal.de/krankheit.shtml

18. The original letter (in French) can be found online at http://www.hhp.uni-trier.de/Projekte/HHP/Projekte/HHP/searchengine/briefe?briefnr=HSA22,1184&letterid=W22B1184&lineref=A249_13&mode=2&textpattern=caroline%20jaubert&firsttid=0&widthgiven=30

19. Macdonald Critchley, "Four Illustrious Neuroluectics," in *Australian Journal of Forensic Sciences*, vol. 4, no. 3, 1972, 99–106.

20. Jellinek, "Heine's Illness," 516–19.

21. Yigal Lossin, *Heine: Ha-haiym ha-kfulim* (Jerusalem: Shocken, 2000), 396–99.

22. Heine, Letter to Julius Campe, June 7, 1848, in *Heinrich Heine's Life Told in his Own Words*, 339.

23. Quoted in Jellinek, "Heine's Illness," 517.

24. Heine, Afterword to *Romanzero*, in *Heinrich Heine's Life Told in his Own Words*, trans. A. Dexter (New York: Henry Holt & Co., 1893), 344.

25. Ibid., 346; translation modified.

26. Heinrich Heine, *The Confessions*, in H. Ellis (ed.), *The Prose Writings of Heinrich Heine* (New York: Arno Press, 1973), 304–5; translation modified. Heinrich Heine, *Geständnisse*, in *Heinrich Heine: Werke und Briefe in zehn Bänden*, vol. 7 (Berlin und Weimar, 1972), 128–30; translation modified.

27. Karl Marx, *Critique of Hegel's "Philosophy of Right,"* trans. A. Jolin and J. O'Malley (Cambridge: Cambridge University Press, 1970), 131; Karl Marx, Friedrich Engels, *Werke*, vol. 1 (Berlin: Karl Dietz Verlag, 1976), 378.

28. Heinrich Heine, *Ludwig Börne*, 95.

29. Ritchie Robertson, *Heine* (London: Halban, 2005), 85.

30. Novalis, *Hymns to the Night and Spiritual Songs*, trans. G. MacDonald, ed. C. Appleby (Maidstone, UK: Crescent Moon, 2010), 13; translation modified.

31. Willi Goetschel, "Nightingales Instead of Owls: Heine's Joyous Philosophy," in Roger F. Cook (ed.), *A Companion to the Works of Heinrich Heine* (Rochester, NY: Camden House, 2002), 139–69.

32. Novalis, *Hymns to the Night*, 12; translation modified. See Novalis, *Schriften. Die Werke Friedrich von Hardenbergs*, vol. 1 (Darmstadt: Wissenschaftlische 1960), 134.
33. Ibid., 13.
34. Ibid., 13.
35. Ibid., 24.
36. Ibid., 9.
37. Quoted in Prawer, *Heine's Jewish Comedy*, 61–62.
38. Charles Baudelaire, *Œuvres Complètes, Edition Plèiade* (Paris: Gallimard, 1975), 869. The Pléiade edition lists the initial date of publication of this poem as June 1850.
39. Baudelaire, *Œuvres Complètes*, 21; trans. William Aggeler, *The Flowers of Evil* (Fresno, CA: Academy Library Guild, 1954).
40. Martha C. Nussbaum, *Hiding from Humanity: Disgust, Shame, and the Law* (Princeton, NJ: Princeton University Press, 2004), 126–27.
41. Michel Foucault, *History of Madness*, trans. J. Murphy and J. Khalfa (London: Routledge, 2006), 143–45.
42. Ibid., 145.
43. Ibid.
44. The translation is taken from Gilman, *Jewish Self Hatred*, 175.
45. Ibid.

CHAPTER 2

1. See, for example, Ruth Wisse's assessment of *Di kliatshe* in *The Modern Jewish Canon* (New York: Free Press, 2000), 330–36. A similar claim is also made in Susanne Klingenstein's exhaustive *Mendele der Buchhändler* (Wiesbaden: Harrassowitz Verlag, 2014), 241.
2. Dan Miron, "Pirkei mavo le-susati le-Abramovitsh bimlot me-ah shanim le-hofa'at ha-yetsira," *Ha-doar* 51 (New York, 1972), 606–7.
3. Wisse, *Modern Jewish Canon*, 336.
4. Miron, "Pirkei mavo le-susati," 606.
5. Sholem Aleichem, "Fir zenen mir gezesn," in *Ale verk*, vol. 10 (Buenos Ayres: Ikuf Farlag, 1955), 324–25.
6. Klingenstein, *Mendele der Buchhändler*, 242.
7. Mendele Moykher Sforim, "The Mare," in *Yenne Velt: The Great Works of Jewish Fantasy and Occult*, ed. and trans. J. Neugroschel, vol. 2 (New York: Stone

Hill Publishing Company, 1976), 209; translation modified. Subsequent references to this work will be made with the letter "M."

8. Amy Nelson, "The Body of the Beast, Animal Protection and Anticruelty Legislation in Imperial Russia," in *Other Animals, Beyond the Human in Russian Culture and History*, eds. J. Costlow and A. Nelson (Pittsburgh: University of Pittsburgh Press, 2010), 96–97.

9. Ibid., 97.

10. Ibid., 104.

11. Ultimately the enforcement of animal protection laws in imperial Russia existed more on paper than in practice, because police were often reluctant to take orders from civilians. After 1873, the RSPA's charter no longer specified that police were obligated to assist RSPA members. See ibid., 106–7.

12. Benjamin Nathans, *Beyond the Pale, The Jewish Encounter with Late Imperial Russia* (Berkeley: University of California Press, 2004), 61–63.

13. Steven Zipperstein, *The Jews of Odessa* (Stanford, CA: Stanford University Press, 1986), 106–7.

14. Stacey Meryl Willis interprets the shift in the representation of the Russian government as a benevolent force and an ally of Haskala in *Di takse* to a diabolical power in *Di kliatsche* as the result of Abramovitsh's disillusionment with the typical maskilic belief in the "tsar liberator" and the Russian government as a force of enlightenment and change. See Stacey Meryl Willis, "Irrational Discourse: Authority and the Ambivalent Maskil in S. Y. Abramovitsh's 'Di Takse' and 'Di Kliatsche,'" *Monatshefte*, vol. 90, no. 2 (Summer, 1998), 198–207.

15. Zipperstein, *The Jews of Odessa*, 116.

16. Nelson, "The Body of the Beast," 103.

17. This passage originally appeared in a feuilleton titled "Cruelty to Animals" (*Tza'ar Ba'alei Chaim*) during Frishman's tenure as assistant editor of the Hebrew journal "Ha-yom," based in Saint Petersburg. It is included in a collection of his essays titled "Otiot Porchot" (*Flying Letters*), available online (in Hebrew) at http://www.benyehuda.org/frischmann/otiot_063.html

18. Gidi Nevo, "Kama hirhurim al ha-teva be-yetsirato shel abramovitsh al pi 'sefer ha-behemot' ve-misefer hazichronot'" (in Hebrew), in Shulamit Elitzur and David Vinfeld (eds.), *Mehkarei Yerushalayim be-sifrut 'ivrit*, vol. 18 (Jerusalem: Magnes Press, 2001), 171.

19. Gershon Shaked has pointed to recurring instances in Abramovitsh's writings in which the images of birds are allegorically linked to the wanderings

of exiles. See Gershon Shaked, *Bein tsehok le-demah: Iyunim be-yetsirato shel Mendele Mokher Sefarim* (Ramat-Gan: Massada, 1965), 49.

20. David G. Roskies, *Against the Apocalypse: Responses to Catastrophe in Modern Jewish Culture*, (Syracuse, NY: Syracuse University Press, 1999), 62.

21. Benjamin, *Origin of German Tragic Drama*, 92.

22. The impact that *Di kliatshe* exerted on contemporaneous readers is attested by notable Jewish writers such as Samuel Wermel, Avrom Reyzen, Akim Volynsky, and Y. L. Peretz, who referred to the *Di kliatshe* as the first proper literary work in the Yiddish language. By the 1890s it had been translated to Polish and Russian and subsequently appeared also in a Hebrew version written by Abramovitsh himself. See Klingenstein, *Mendele der Buchhändler*, 280–82.

23. Yankev Dinezon (1856–1919) was a Yiddish writer and educator who gained popularity through the publication of sentimental novels depicting Jewish middle-class life in the turn of the century Russia.

24. Yankev Dinezon, *Zikhroynes un bilder: shtetl, kinderyorn, shrayber* (Warsaw: Farlag Akhiseyfer, 1928), 189. See also Klingenstein, *Mendele der Buchhändler*, 283.

25. Alyssa Quint, " 'Yiddish Literature for the Masses'? A Reconsideration of Who Read What in Jewish Eastern Europe," *AJS Review*, vol. 29, no. 1 (April, 2005), 82–83. Quint aims her argument specifically against Dan Miron, who uncritically assumes that *Di kliatshe* was read by the Jewish masses as well as by the intelligentsia. See Miron, "Pirkei mavo le-susati," 606.

26. See chapter 2, note 3, above.

27. Max Vasmer, *Russisches Etymologisches Wörterbuch*, vol. 1 (Heidelberg: Carl Winter Universitätsverlag, 1953), 577–78.

28. In his description of the mare in *Crime and Punishment*, Dostoevsky was probably influenced by Nikolai Nekrasov's poem "Before Evening" from the cycle *About the Weather* (1859) that features a beaten horse. Dostoevsky explicitly refers to Nekrasov's poem in *The Brothers Karamazov* (1880) in the context of cruelty to animals. See Fyodor Dostoevsky, *The Brothers Karamazov*, trans. David McDuff (London: Penguin, 2003), 314–315. Significantly, in his poem Nekrasov uses the term *loshad'-kaleka* (crippled mare) rather than *kliacha* when referring to the horse. See Caryl Emerson, *The Cambridge Introduction to Russian Literature* (Cambridge: Cambridge University Press, 2008), 155.

29. Fyodor Dostoevsky, *Crime and Punishment*, trans. Constance Garnett (New York: Cosimo, 2008), 53.

30. Ibid., 54.
31. Ibid., 55.
32. Ibid., 57.
33. Leo Tolstoy, "Strider: The Story of a Horse," in *Master and Man and Other Stories*, trans. Ronald Wilks and Paul Foote (London: Penguin Classics, 2005), 67–108. Victor Shklovsky famously pointed to the denaturalization of the notion of property through the horse's perspective as the hallmark of Tolstoy's literary technique of defamiliarization. See Victor Shklovsky, "Art as Technique," in *Russian Formalist Criticism: Four Essays*, trans. Lee T. Lemon and Marion J. Reis (Lincoln: University of Nebraska Press, 1965), 13.
34. Joseph Frank, *Dostoevsky: The Miraculous Years 1865–1871* (Princeton, NJ: Princeton University Press, 1995), 103–7.
35. Brian Bonhomme, "Russian Compassion: The Russian society for The Protection of Animals—Founding and Contexts, 1865–1875," *Canadian Journal of History* vol. 45, no. 2 (Autumn 2010), 273.
36. Fyodor Dostoevsky, *A Writer's Diary: Volume 1, 1873–1876*, trans. K. Lantz (Evanston, IL: Northwestern University Press, 1993), 327–28.
37. Joseph Frank, *Dostoevsky: The Seeds of Revolt 1821–1849* (Princeton, NJ: Princeton University Press, 1976), 71.
38. Ibid., 71–72.
39. Ibid., 72.
40. Sholem Aleichem, "Fir zenen mir gezesn," 324–25.
41. Mikhail Krutikov, "Berdichev in Russian-Jewish Literary Imagination: from Israel Aksenfeld to Friedrich Gorenshteyn," in *The Shtetl Image and Reality: Papers of the Second Mendel Friedman International Conference on Yiddish* (Oxford: Legenda, 2000), 95.
42. Dan Miron, *The Image of The Shtetl and Other Studies of Modern Jewish Literary Imagination* (Syracuse, NY: Syracuse University Press, 2000), 110–12.
43. Willis, "Irrational Discourse," 200.
44. Mendele Moykher Sforim, *Fishke der Krumer* (Zhitomir: Shadov, 1869), 3–4.
45. Ibid., 8.
46. Mendele Moykher Sforim, *Fishke der Krumer* 1888 (Moscow: Melukhefarlag, 1940), 17.
47. S. Y. Abramovitsh, *Tales of Mendele the Book Peddler: Fishke the Lame and Benjamin the Third*, trans. Ted Gorelick (New York: Schocken, 1996), 21.
48. Shaked, *Bein tsehok le-demah*, 13–21.

49. See Introduction, fn. 43.

50. For a concise list of the prohibitions involved in the principle of tsaʻar baʻalei hayim, see Abraham P. Bloch, *A Book of Jewish Ethical Concepts: Biblical and Postbiblical* (New York: Ktav, 1984), 79–83.

51. Yael Shemesh, "Khemla klapei baʻalei hayim be-sifrut hazal uvaparshanut ha-masortit," in *Studies in Bible and Exegesis*, ed. Shmuel Vargon, Amos Frisch, and Moshe Rahimi, vol. 8 (Ramat-Gan: Bar-Ilan University Press, 2008), 677–99.

52. Moses Maimonides, *Guide of the Perplexed*, trans. Shlomo Pines (Chicago: University of Chicago Press, 1963), 599.

53. Nachmanides, *Commentary on the Torah*, vol. 3—Leviticus, trans. C. Chavel (New York: Shilo Publishing House, 1974), 239.

54. Fishel Lachower, *Rishonim ve-Aharonim: masot u-maʼmarim*, vol. 1 (Tel Aviv: Dvir, 1934), 84.

55. This piece was originally published in Yiddish in 1902 and, like many other works by Abramovitsh, was readapted to Hebrew by him in 1912. Both Yiddish and Hebrew versions are similar but are not exact copies. Abramovitsh utilized his command of both languages to provide a unique style in each language in which the work was written.

56. The quote is taken from the Hebrew version of *The Book of Cattle*. See Mendele Mocher Sfarim, *Kol Kitve* (Tel-Aviv: Dvir, 1958), 357. Compare with the Yiddish version in Mendele Moykher Sforim *Ale Verk fun Mendele Moykher Sforim*, vol. 1 (Warsaw: Farlag "Mendele," 1928), 50–51.

57. See in particular Mendele, *Kol Kitve*, 368–69.

58. See Introduction, note 27, above.

59. Pick, *Creaturely Poetics*, 7.

60. Ibid., 4.

61. Benjamin, "Franz Kafka," 140.

CHAPTER 3

1. Shlomo Lambroza, "The Pogroms of 1903–1906," in John Klier and Shlomo Lambroza (eds.), *Pogroms: Anti-Jewish Violence in Modern Russian History* (Cambridge: Cambridge University Press, 1992), 200.

2. See Fishel Lachower, " 'Be-ʻir ha-haregah'—shira u-metsiʻut," in Uzi Shavit and Ziva Shamir (eds.), *Be-mevoʻei ir ha-haregah: mivʻhar maʻamarim al shiro shel Bialik* (Tel Aviv: Hakibbutz Hameuchad, 1994), 9–10.

3. I have deviated from the standard (and inaccurate) translation of "Be-'ir ha-haregah" as "In the City of Slaughter" for two reasons. First, to differentiate this poem from "Al ha-shechita" in which the Hebrew word for "slaughter" (shechita) does explicitly appear; and second, in order to prevent confusion, as the term "slaughter" emerges as an important distinction in Bialik's pogrom poems.

4. Dan Miron, "Mi-'be-'ir ha-haregah' va-hal'ah: hir'hurim al ha-po'ema shel Bialik bi-melot me'ah shanah le-ho'fa'ata," in Dan Miron (ed.), *Be-'ir ha-haregah, bikur me'uhar : bi-melot me'ah shanah la-po'emah shel Bialik* (Tel Aviv: Resling, 2005), 119.

5. Shmuel Versas, "Be'in tohakha le-apologetica: 'Be-'ir ha-haregah' u-misaviv la" in *Be-mevo'ei ir ha-haregah*, 52–53.

6. See Michael Gluzman's essay " 'Hoser ko'ach—ha-machala ha-mevisha be-yoter': Bialik ve-ha-pogrom be- Kishinev," in *Be-'ir ha-haregah, bikur me'uhar*, 13–35.

7. David G. Roskies, *Against the Apocalypse*, 86–87.

8. Alan Mintz, *Hurban: Responses to Catastrophe in Hebrew Literature* (New York: Columbia University Press, 1984), 3.

9. Hannan Hever, "Korbanot ha-tzionut: al be-'ir ha-haregah me'et H. N. Bialik" in *Be-'ir ha-haregah, bikur me'uhar*, 62–63.

10. Mintz refers to Bialik's extensive use of metonymical figures in the above-quoted lines, noting that "metonymy is a technique of annoyance. . . . [It] frustrates by deflecting us from the thing itself and allowing us access only to its residuum, its atmosphere, its paraphernalia." See Mintz, *Hurban*, 146.

11. Fishel Lachower was the first to point to a connection between this epithet and the book of Ezekiel in his book on Bialik, published in 1944; See Lachower, " 'Be-'ir ha-haregah'—shira u-metsi'ut," 12. Following Lachower, literary critics such as Hillel Barzel and Shmuel Tertner also emphasized the importance of prophets such as Jonah and Jeremiah as models for the formation of Bialik's prophetic persona in "In the City of Killings." See Hillel Barzel, "Ge'ula derekh to'hakha: idealism ve-harisatam be-'Be-'ir ha-haregah,' " in *Be-mevo'ei ir ha-haregah*, 77–80; and Shmuel Tertner, " 'Be-'ir ha-haregah ve-ha-genre shel ha-monolog ha-dramati," in Ibid., 128–30.

12. Eyal Chowers, *The Political Philosophy of Zionism: Trading Jewish Words for a Hebraic Land* (Cambridge: Cambridge University Press, 2012), 150.

13. H. N. Bialik, "Surely the People is Grass," in *Selected Poems of Hayyim Nahman Bialik*, trans. Nina Salaman (New York, Bloch Publishing House, 1965), 67–68; translation modified.

14. Miron, "Mi-'be-'ir ha-haregah' va-hal'ah," 103–4.

15. Roskies, *Against the Apocalypse*, 89.

16. Dan Miron, *H. N. Bialik and the Prophetic Mode in Modern Hebrew Literature* (Syracuse, NY: Syracuse University Press, 2000), 12–13.

17. Paul de Man, "The Rhetoric of Temporality," in *Blindness and Insight: Essays in the Rhetoric of Contemporary Criticism* (Minneapolis: University of Minnesota Press, 1983), 187–208.

18. Yishuv is the body of Jewish residents in Palestine prior to the establishment of the State of Israel.

19. Uri Zvi Greenberg, "Levai lesifri kelev bayit," in *Kol Ktavav*, vol. 2 (Jerusalem: Mossad Bialik, 1991), 37. This volume will henceforth be abbreviated to "CW."

20. See Miron, *The Prophetic Mode*, 28–33; Hannan Hever, *Paytanim u-biryonim: tsmihat ha-shir ha-politi ha-ivri be-eretz Israel* (Jerusalem: Mossad Bialik, 1994), 243–48.

21. Translation of these lines is by Harold Schimmel. Quoted in Miron, *The Prophetic Mode*, 36.

22. Hever, *Paytanim u-biryonim*, 250.

23. Ibid., 253.

24. Gilles Deleuze and Félix Guattari, *Kafka, Toward a Minor Literature*, trans. Dana Polan (Minneapolis: University of Minnesota Press, 1987), 22.

25. Miron, *The Prophetic Mode*, 37.

26. For the political-messianic implications of the biblical allusion to Numbers 24:17 encapsulated in the phrase "a star shall rise," see Hever, *Paytanim u-biryonim*, 253.

CHAPTER 4

1. Dan Miron, *From Continuity to Contiguity: Toward a New Jewish Literary Thinking* (Stanford, CA: Stanford University Press, 2010), 323–30.

2. Santner, *On Creaturely Life*, 22.

3. Benjamin, "Franz Kafka," 122.

4. Ibid.

5. See Introduction, note 26, above.
6. Benjamin, *The Origin of German Drama*, 66.
7. Ibid., 65.
8. Benjamin, "Franz Kafka," 123.
9. Ibid., 131–32.
10. Ibid., 130.
11. Subsequent references to the English translation of Kafka's *The Trial*, trans. Mike Mitchell (Oxford: Oxford University Press, 2009) will be abbreviated with the letter "T." References to the German edition of *Der Proceß, Kritische Ausgabe*, ed. Jost Schillemeit (Frankfurt am Main: Fischer Verlag, 2002) will be abbreviated with the letter "P."
12. Franz Kafka, *The Metamorphosis and Other Stories*, trans. Joyce Crick (Oxford: Oxford University Press, 2009), 30.
13. Ibid.
14. Theodor W. Adorno, "Notes on Kafka," in *Prisms*, trans. Samuel and Shierry Weber (Cambridge, MA: MIT Press, 1984), 246.
15. Emmanuel Levinas, *On Escape*, trans. Bettina Bergo (Stanford, CA: Stanford University Press, 2003), 64–65.
16. Giorgio Agamben, *Remnants of Auschwitz: The Witness and the Archive*, trans. Daniel Heller-Roazen (New York: Zone Books, 1999), 105–6.
17. Ibid., 134.
18. Ibid., 108.
19. Reiner Stach, *Kafka: The Decisive Years*, trans. Shelley Frisch (Orlando, FL: Harcourt, 2005), 476.
20. Benjamin, "Franz Kafka," 133.
21. Margot Norris, "Sadism and Masochism in 'In the Penal Colony' and 'A Hunger Artist,'" in Mark Anderson (ed.), *Reading Kafka: Prague, Politics, and the Fin de Siècle* (New York: Schocken, 1989), 170.
22. Norris, *Beasts of the Modern Imagination*, 101–17.
23. Ibid., 104.
24. Deleuze and Guattari, *Kafka, Toward a Minor Literature*, 12.
25. Ibid., 10.
26. Franz Kafka, "In the Penal Colony," in *The Metamorphosis and Other Stories*, 79.
27. Franz Kafka, *Letters to Felice*, trans. James Stern and Elisabeth Duckworth (New York: Schocken Books, 1973), 338; Franz Kafka, *Briefe an Felice*

und andere Korrespondenz aus der Verlobungzeit (Frankfurt am Main: Fischer Verlag, 2009), 351–52.

28. Martin Heidegger, *The Fundamental Concepts of Metaphysics: World, Finitude, Solitude,* trans. William McNeill and Nicholas Walker (Bloomington: Indiana University Press, 1995), 248; translation modified.

29. Ibid., 253. Emphases in the original; translation modified. The word *offenbar* (which means manifest or evident) is mistranslated as "disconcealed" in the English rendition of Agamben's *The Open,* which quotes this passage from Heidegger. I have retained this mistranslation, since it functions as an important term in Agamben's subsequent gloss on Heidegger.

30. Giorgio Agamben, *The Open: Man and Animal,* trans. Kevin Attell (Stanford, CA: Stanford University Press, 2004), 55. Emphasis in the original.

31. Franz Kafka, "Investigations of a Dog," in *A Hunger Artist and Other Stories,* trans. Joyce Crick (Oxford: Oxford University Press, 2012), 122; Franz Kafka, "Forschungen eines Hundes," *Kritische Ausgabe, Nachgelassene Schriften und Fragmente II,* ed. Jost Schillemeit (Frankfurt am Main: Fischer Verlag, 2002), 426.

32. Benjamin Harshav, *The Meaning of Yiddish* (Berkeley: University of California Press, 1990), 115.

33. David Suchoff, *Kafka's Jewish Languages: The Hidden Openness of Tradition* (Philadelphia: University of Pennsylvania Press, 2012), 57–58.

34. Iris Bruce, *Kafka and Cultural Zionism: Dates in Palestine* (Madison: University of Wisconsin Press, 2007), 191.

35. Reiner Stach, *Kafka: The Years of Insight,* trans. Shelley Frisch (Princeton, NJ: Princeton University Press, 2013), 489. Ritchie Robertson has arrived at a similar conclusion in his seminal work on Kafka, published in 1985. See *Kafka: Judaism, Politics, and Literature* (Oxford: Oxford University Press, 1985), 273–79.

36. Kafka, "Investigations of a Dog," 130; Kafka, "Forschungen eines Hundes," 441.

37. Rainer Nägele, "I Don't Want to Know that I Know: The Inversion of Socratic Ignorance in the Knowledge of Dogs," in *Philosophy and Kafka,* ed. Brendan Moran and Carlo Salzani (Lanham, MD: Lexington Books, 2013), 22.

38. Kafka, "Investigations," 123; "Forschungen," 427.

39. Shklovsky, "Art as Technique," 13.

40. Tolstoy, "Strider: The Story of a Horse," 86.

41. Kafka, "Investigations," 125–56; "Forschungen," 431–32.

42. Elias Canetti, *Kafka's Other Trial; The Letters to Felice*, trans. Christopher Middleton (New York: Schocken Books, 1974), 88.

43. See chapter 4, note 9, above.

44. "ein Hinaustreten aus dem Menschlichen, ein Sichhinausbegeben in einen dem Menschlichen zugewandten und unheimlichen Bereich"—see Paul Celan, "Der Meridian," ed. Bemhard Boschenstein and Heino Schmull, in collaboration with Michael Schwarzkopf and Christiane Wittkop, in *Werke*, Tübingen edition (Frankfurt am Main: Suhrkamp, 1999), 5. The English translation is taken from Paul Celan, *The Meridian: Final Version—Drafts—Materials*, trans. Pierre Joris (Stanford, CA: Stanford University Press, 2010), 5; translation modified.

45. Kafka, "Investigations of a Dog," 130–31; Kafka, "Forschungen eines Hundes," 441–42.

46. Walter Benjamin, *The Correspondence of Walter Benjamin: 1910–1940*, trans. Manfred R. Jacobson and Evelyn M. Jacobson (Chicago: University of Chicago Press, 1994), 224.

47. Ibid.; translation modified.

48. Franz Kafka, "In Unserer Synagoge," in *Kritische Ausgabe, Nachgelassene Schriften und Fragmente II*, 405. Translation is mine.

49. Franz Kafka, "The Animal in the Synagogue," in *Parables and Paradoxes in German and English*, trans. Nahum Glatzer (New York, Schocken, 1961), 51; translation modified.

50. Ibid., 55.

51. Ibid., 57.

52. Ibid.

CHAPTER 5

1. Adorno, "Notes on Kafka," 255.

2. Paul Celan, "Der Meridian," ed. Bemhard Boschenstein and Heino Schmull, in collaboration with Michael Schwarzkopf and Christiane Wittkop, in *Werke*, Tübingen edition (Frankfurt am Main: Suhrkamp, 1999), 8. The "Meridian" speech will be cited in the text in this edition as "PCTM," followed by the page number. The English translation of Celan's "Meridian" speech is taken from Paul Celan, *The Meridian: Final Version—Drafts—Materials*, trans.

Pierre Joris (Stanford, CA: Stanford University Press, 2010). This edition will be parenthetically quoted as "M," followed by page number.

3. Boaz Arpaly, *Rav-roman: hamisha ma'amarim al Temol Shilshom le-S. Y. Agnon* (Tel Aviv: Hakibbutz Hameuchad, 1998).

4. S. Y. Agnon, *Only Yesterday*, trans. Barbara Harshav (Princeton, NJ: Princeton University Press, 2000), 286. Subsequent references to the novel will be abbreviated as "OY."

5. Deleuze and Guattari, *Kafka, Toward a Minor Literature*, 22. In contrast to Greenberg, who refers to barking as a gesture marking the expressive limits of human despair, Agnon appropriates the bark literally as a sound that blends seamlessly with human language. See chapter 3 note 23, above.

6. The stone has recurred as an emblem of melancholia in modern Hebrew literature in the poems of David Fogel. For an analysis of melancholia in Fogel's poetry, see my article, "The Love of a Dog: Melancholia in David Vogel's *Before the Dark Gate*," *Jewish Studies Quarterly*, vol. 23 (2016), no. 2, 168–90.

7. Benjamin, *Origin of German Tragic Drama*, 155.

8. Ibid., 152.

9. Giorgio Agamben, *Stanzas: Word and Phantasm in Western Culture*, trans. Ronald L. Martinez (Minneapolis: University of Minneapolis Press, 1993), 5.

10. Benjamin, *Origin of German Tragic Drama*, 146.

11. Raymond Klibansky, Erwin Panofsky, and Fritz Saxl, *Saturn and Melancholy* (New York: Basic Books, 1964), 322–33.

12. See chapter 4, note 44, above.

13. Yehuda Liebes, *Studies in Jewish Myth and Messianism*, trans. Batya Stein (Albany: State University of New York Press, 1993), 139.

14. Michal Arbell, *Katuv al oro shel ha-kelev: al tfisat ha-yetsira etzel S. Y. Agnon* (Jerusalem: Keter Publishing, 2006), 216.

15. In the *Trauerspiel* essay, Benjamin explicitly links melancholia and rabies: "If the spleen, an organ believed to be particularly delicate, should deteriorate, then the dog is said to lose its vitality and become rabid. In this respect it symbolizes the darker aspect of the melancholy complexion." *Origin of German Tragic Drama*, 152.

16. Pick, *Creaturely Poetics*, 50.

17. Here it is also important to recall Agnon's vegetarianism as another element comprising the ethical foundation that Pick has termed "creaturely fellowship." See *Creaturely Poetics*, 50.

18. Isaac Bashevis Singer, "The Letter Writer," in *The Séance and Other Stories* (New York: Penguin, 1974), 234.

19. See chapter 4, note 9, above.

20. Paul Celan, "Deathfugue," in *Selected Poems and Prose of Paul Celan*, trans. John Felstiner (New York: Norton, 2001), 30–31.

21. John Felstiner, *Paul Celan: Poet, Survivor, Jew* (New Haven, CT: Yale University Press, 1995), 34–35.

22. See chapter 2, note 21, above.

23. Celan, "Todesfuge," 31.

24. See chapter 4, note 8, above.

25. Celan, "Todesfuge," 31.

26. Philippe Lacoue-Labarthe, "Catastrophe," in Aris Fioretos (ed.), *Word Traces: Readings of Paul Celan*, trans. Andrea Tarnowski (Baltimore: Johns Hopkins University Press, 1994), 137.

27. Ulrich Baer, *Remnants of Song: Trauma and the Experience of Modernity in Charles Baudelaire and Paul Celan* (Stanford, CA: Stanford University Press, 2000), 198. Baer's description of trauma is clearly informed by Dori Laub's account of testimony and trauma in Holocaust survivors as an "event without a witness": "The historical reality of the Holocaust became ... a reality which extinguished philosophically the very possibility of address, the possibility of appealing, or of turning to, another. But when one cannot turn to a 'you' one canot say 'thou' even to oneself. The Holocaust created in this a world in which one *could not bear witness to oneself.*" Dori Laub, "An Event Without a Witness: Truth, Testimony and Survival" in *Testimony: Crises of Witnessing in Literature, Psychoanalysis, and History* (New York: Routledge, 1992), 82.

28. Baer, *Remnants of Song*, 278.

29. Emmanuel Levinas, "Paul Celan: From Being to the Other," in *Proper Names*, trans. Michael B. Smith (Stanford, CA: Stanford University Press, 1996), 44.

POSTSCRIPT

1. Benjamin, "Franz Kafka," 138–39.
2. Ibid., 136.
3. Ibid., 137–38.
4. Ibid., 138.

5. Ibid., 139.
6. Ibid.
7. Ibid., 138.
8. Hanssen, *Walter Benjamin's Other History*, 148.
9. Benjamin, "Franz Kafka," 134.
10. See chapter 4, note 20, above.
11. Benjamin, "Franz Kafka," 134.
12. Ibid., 140.
13. Pick, *Creaturely Poetics*, 5.
14. Hanssen, *Walter Benjamin's Other History*, 156–58.
15. Levinas, "Paul Celan," 43.

BIBLIOGRAPHY

Abramovitsh, Sholem Yankev. *Ale Verk fun Mendele Moykher Sforim*, vol. 1 (Warsaw: farlag "Mendele," 1928).
———. *Ale Verk fun Mendele Moykher Sforim*, vol. 5 (Warsaw: farlag "Mendele," 1928).
———. *Dos Vinshfingerl* (Kiev: Kooperativer farlag, 1927).
———. *Fishke der Krumer* (Zhitomir: Shadov, 1869).
———. *Fishke der Krumer* 1888 (Moscow: Melukhe-farlag, 1940).
———. *Kol kitve* (Tel-Aviv: Dvir, 1958).
———. *Tales of Mendele the Book Peddler: Fishke the Lame and Benjamin the Third*, trans. Ted Gorelick (New York: Schocken, 1996).
———. "The Mare," in *Yenne Velt: The Great Works of Jewish Fantasy and Occult*, vol. 2, ed. and trans. J. Neugroschel (New York: Stone Hill Publishing Company, 1976).
Adorno, Theodor W. "Notes on Kafka," in *Prisms*, trans. Samuel and Shierry Weber (Cambridge, MA: MIT Press, 1984),
Agamben, Giorgio. *Homo Sacer: Sovereign Power and Bare Life*, trans. Daniel Heller-Roazen (Stanford, CA: Stanford University Press, 1998).
———. *Remnants of Auschwitz: The Witness and the Archive*, trans. Daniel Heller-Roazen (New York: Zone Books, 1999).
———. *Stanzas: Word and Phantasm in Western Culture*, trans. Ronald L. Martinez (Minneapolis: University of Minneapolis Press, 1993).
———. *State of Exception*, trans. Kevin Attell (Chicago: University of Chicago Press, 2006).
———. *The Open: Man and Animal*, trans. Kevin Attell (Stanford, CA: Stanford University Press, 2004).
Agnon, Shmuel Yosef. *Only Yesterday*, trans. Barbara Harshav (Princeton, NJ: Princeton University Press, 2000).
Aleichem, Sholem. *Ale Verk*, vol. 10 (Buenos Ayres: Ikuf farlag, 1955).

Arbell, Michal. *Katuv al oro shel ha-kelev: al tfisat ha-yetsira etzel S. Y. Agnon* (Jerusalem: Keter Publishing, 2006).

Arpaly, Boaz. *Rav-roman: hamisha ma'amarim al Temol Shilshom le-S. Y. Agnon* (Tel Aviv: Hakibbutz Hameuchad, 1998).

Baer, Ulrich. *Remnants of Song: Trauma and the Experience of Modernity in Charles Baudelaire and Paul Celan* (Stanford, CA: Stanford University Press, 2000).

Bashevis Singer, Isaac. *The Séance and Other Stories* (New York: Penguin, 1974).

Baudelaire, Charles. *Œuvres Complètes, Edition Plèiade* (Paris: Gallimard, 1975),

———. *Paris Spleen, 1869*, trans. L. Varese (New York: New Directions, 1947).

———. *The Flowers of Evil*, trans. William Aggeler (Fresno: Academy Library Guild, 1954).

Barzel, Hillel. "Ge'ula derekh to'hakha: idealism ve-harisatam be-'Be-'ir ha-haregah,' " in *Be-mevo'ei ir ha-haregah: miv'har ma'amarim al shiro shel Bialik*, ed. U. Shavit and Z. Shamir (Tel Aviv: Hakibbutz Hameuchad, 1994).

Benjamin, Andrew. *Of Jews and Animals* (Edinburgh, UK: Edinburgh University Press, 2010).

Benjamin, Walter. *Gesammelte Schriften*, vol. 1, ed. R. Tiedemann and H. Schweppenhäuser (Frankfurt am Main: Suhrkamp Verlag, 1977).

———. *Gesammelte Schriften*, vol. 2, ed. R. Tiedemann and H. Schweppenhäuser (Frankfurt am Main: Suhrkamp Verlag, 1977).

———. *Illuminations*, trans. Harry Zohn (New York: Schocken, 1968).

———. *Selected Writings, Volume 1: 1913–1926*, ed. Howard Eiland, Michael Jennings, and Gary Smith (Cambridge, MA: Harvard University Press, 1996).

———. *Selected Writings, Volume 3, 1935–1938*, ed. Howard Eiland and Michael Jennings (Cambridge, MA: Harvard University Press, 2002).

———. *The Correspondence of Walter Benjamin: 1910–1940*, trans. Manfred R. Jacobson and Evelyn M. Jacobson (Chicago: University of Chicago Press, 1994).

———. *The Origin of German Tragic Drama*, trans. John Osborne (London: Verso, 1998).

Bialik, Chaim Nachman. *Shirim* (Tel Aviv: Dvir, 1976).

———. *Selected Poems of Hayyim Nahman Bialik*, trans. Nina Salaman, (New York, Bloch Publishing House, 1965).

Bloch, Abraham P. *A Book of Jewish Ethical Concepts: Biblical and Postbiblical* (New York: Ktav, 1984).

Bonhomme, Brian. "Russian Compassion: The Russian Society for the Protection of Animals— Founding and Contexts, 1865–1875," *Canadian Journal of History* vol. 45 no. 2 (autumn 2010).

Boyarin, Daniel. *A Radical Jew: Paul and the Politics of Identity* (Berkeley: University of California Press, 1997).

Brod, Max. *Franz Kafka: A Biography*, trans. G. Humphreys Roberts and Richard Winston (New York: Schocken, 1960).

Bruce, Iris. *Kafka and Cultural Zionism: Dates in Palestine* (Madison: The University of Wisconsin Press, 2007).

Canetti, Elias. *Kafka's Other Trial; The Letters to Felice*, trans. Christopher Middleton (New York: Schocken, 1974).

Celan, Paul. "Der Meridian," in *Werke*, Tübingen edition, ed. Bemhard Boschenstein and Heino Schmull, in collaboration with Michael Schwarzkopf and Christiane Wittkop (Frankfurt am Main: Suhrkamp, 1999).

———. *Selected Poems and Prose of Paul Celan*, trans. John Felstiner (New York: Norton, 2001).

———. *The Meridian: Final Version—Drafts—Materials*, trans. Pierre Joris (Stanford, CA: Stanford University Press, 2010).

Chowers, Eyal. *The Political Philosophy of Zionism: Trading Jewish Words for a Hebraic Land* (Cambridge: Cambridge University Press, 2012).

Chrysostom, John. "Homilies against the Jews," in *Jews and Christians in Antioch in the First Four Centuries of the Common Era*, trans. Wayne Meeks and Robert Wilken (Missoula, MT: Scholars Press for the Society of Biblical Literature, 1978).

Critchley, Macdonald. "Four Illustrious Neuroluectics," *Australian Journal of Forensic Sciences* 4, no. 3 (1972).

Derrida, Jacques. *Points: Interviews, 1974–1994*, ed. Elisabeth Weber, trans. Peggy Kamuf, et al. (Stanford, CA: Stanford University Press, 1995).

———. *The Beast and the Sovereign*, vol. 1, trans. Geoffrey Bennington (Chicago: University of Chicago Press, 2009).

Deleuze, Gilles, and Félix Guattari. *Kafka: Toward a Minor Literature*, trans. Dana Polan (Minneapolis: University of Minneapolis Press, 1986).

de Man, Paul. *Blindness and Insight: Essays in the Rhetoric of Contemporary Criticism* (Minneapolis: University of Minnesota Press, 1983).

Dinezon, Yankev. *Zikhroynes un bilder: shtetl, kinderyorn, shrayber* (Warsaw: farlag Akhiseyfer, 1928).
Dostoevsky, Fyodor. *Crime and Punishment*, trans. Constance Garnett (New York: Cosimo, 2008).
———. *The Brothers Karamazov*, trans. David McDuff (London: Penguin, 2003).
———. *A Writer's Diary: Volume 1, 1873–1876*, trans. K. Lantz (Evanston, IL: Northwestern University Press, 1993).
Emerson, Caryl. *The Cambridge Introduction to Russian Literature* (Cambridge: Cambridge University Press, 2008)
Erler, A. *Friedlosigkeit und Werwolfglaube*, in *Paideuma* 1, no. 7 (Sept. 1940).
Felstiner, John. *Paul Celan: Poet, Survivor, Jew* (New Haven, CT: Yale University Press, 1995).
Foucault, Michel. *History of Madness*, trans. J. Murphy and J. Khalfa (London: Routledge, 2006).
Frank, Joseph. *Dostoevsky: The Miraculous Years 1865–1871* (Princeton, NJ: Princeton University Press, 1995).
———. *Dostoevsky: The Seeds of Revolt 1821–1849* (Princeton, NJ: Princeton University Press, 1976).
Frishman, David. "Flying Letters." www.benyehuda.org/frischmann/otiot_063.html
Gadamer, Hans-Georg. *Truth and Method*, trans. Joel Weinsheimer and Donald G. Marshall (New York: Continuum, 1989).
Gilman, Sander. *Jewish Self-Hatred: Anti-Semitism and the Hidden Language of the Jews* (Baltimore: Johns Hopkins University Press, 1986).
Gluzman, Michael. " 'Hoser ko'ach—ha-machala ha-mevisha be-yoter': Bialik ve-ha-pogrom be- Kishinev," in *Be-'ir ha-haregah, biḳur me'uḥar : bi-melot me'ah shanah la-po'emah shel Bialiḳ In the City of Killings:*, ed. Dan Miron (Tel Aviv: Resling, 2005).
Goetschel, Willi. "Nightingales Instead of Owls: Heine's Joyous Philosophy," in *A Companion to the Works of Heinrich Heine*, ed. Roger F. Cook (Rochester, NY: Camden House, 2002).
Greenberg, Uri Zvi. *Kol Ktavav*, vol. 2 (Jerusalem: Mossad Bialik, 1991).
Hanssen, Beatrice. *Walter Benjamin's Other History: Of Stones, Animals, Human Beings, and Angels* (Berkeley: University of California Press, 1998).
Harshav, Benjamin. *The Meaning of Yiddish* (Berkeley: University of California Press, 1990).

Heidegger, Martin. *The Fundamental Concepts of Metaphysics: World, Finitude, Solitude*, trans. William McNeill and Nicholas Walker (Bloomington: Indiana University Press, 1995).

Heine, Heinrich. *Heinrich Heine's Life Told in his Own Words*, trans. A. Dexter (New York: Henry Holt & Co., 1893).

———. *Historisch-kritische Gesamtausgabe der Werke*, vol. 10, ed. M. Winfuhr, et al.(Hamburg: Hoffman und Campe, 1973–1997).

———. *Jewish Stories and Hebrew Melodies*, trans. F. Ewen (New York: Wiener, 1987).

———. *Ludwig Börne: A Memorial*, trans. J. Sammons (New York: Camden House, 2006).

———. *Prinzessin Sabbat: Über Juden und Judentum*, ed. Paul Peters (Bodenheim: Philo Verlag, 1997).

———. *The Complete Poems*, trans. Hal Draper, (Cambridge: Suhrkamp/Insel, 1982).

———. *The Prose Writings of Heinrich Heine* (New York: Arno Press, 1973).

———. *Werke und Briefe in zehn Bänden*, vol. 5 (Berlin and Weimar, 1972).

———. *Werke und Briefe in zehn Bänden*, vol. 7 (Berlin und Weimar, 1972).

Hever, Hannan. *Paytanim u-biryonim: tsmihat ha-shir ha-politi ha-ivri be-eretz Israel* (Jerusalem: Mossad Bialik, 1994).

———. "Korbanot ha-tzionut: al be-'ir ha-haregah me'et H. N. Bialik" in *Be-'ir ha-haregah, bikur me'uhar : bi-melot me'ah shanah la-po'emah shel Bialik*, ed. D. Miron (Tel Aviv: Resling, 2005).

Hobbes, Thomas. *On the Citizen* (Cambridge: Cambridge University Press, 1998).

Holub, Robert. *Heinrich Heine's Reception of German Grecophilia* (Heidelberg: Carl Winter Verlag, 1981).

Jellinek, E. H. "Heine's Illness: The Case for Multiple Sclerosis," *Journal of the Royal Society of Medicine* 83 (August 1990).

Kafka, Franz. *A Hunger Artist and Other Stories*, trans. Joyce Crick (Oxford: Oxford University Press, 2012).

———. *Briefe an Felice und andere Korrespondenz aus der Verlobungzeit* (Frankfurt am Main: Fischer Verlag, 2009).

———. *Kritische Ausgabe, Der Proceß*, ed. Jost Schillemeit (Frankfurt am Main: Fischer Verlag, 2002).

———. *Kritische Ausgabe, Drucke zu Lebzeiten*, ed. Jost Schillemeit (Frankfurt am Main: Fischer Verlag, 2002).

———. *Kritische Ausgabe, Nachgelassene Schriften und Fragmente II*, ed. Jost Schillemeit (Frankfurt am Main: Fischer Verlag, 2002).

———. *Parables and Paradoxes in German and English*, trans. Nahum Glatzer (New York: Schocken, 1961).

———. *Letters to Felice*, trans. James Stern and Elisabeth Duckworth (New York: Schocken, 1973).

———. *The Complete Stories*, trans. Willa and Edwin Muir (New York: Schocken, 1971).

———. *The Metamorphosis and Other Stories*, trans. Joyce Crick (New York: Oxford University Press, 2009).

———. *The Trial*, trans. Mike Mitchell (Oxford: Oxford University Press, 2009).

Klibansky, Raymond, et al. *Saturn and Melancholy* (New York: Basic Books, 1964).

Klingenstein, Susanne. *Mendele der Buchhändler* (Wiesbaden: Harrassowitz Verlag, 2014).

Kramer, Lloyd S. *Threshold of a New World: Intellectuals and the Exile Experience in Paris, 1830–1848* (Ithaca, NY: Cornell University Press, 1988).

Krutikov, Mikhail. "Berdichev in Russian-Jewish Literary Imagination: from Israel Aksenfeld to Friedrich Gorenshteyn," in *The Shtetl Image and Reality: Papers of the Second Mendel Friedman International Conference on Yiddish*, ed. Krutikov Mikhail (Oxford: Legenda, 2000).

Lachower, Fishel" 'Be-'ir ha-haregah'—shira u-metsi'ut," in *Be-mevo'ei ir ha-haregah: miv'har ma'amarim al shiro shel Bialik*, ed. U. Shavit and Z. Shamir (Tel Aviv: Hakibbutz Hameuchad, 1994).

——— *Rishonim ve-Aharonim: masot u-ma'marim*, vol. 1 (Tel Aviv: Dvir, 1934).

Lacoue-Labarthe, Philippe. "Catastrophe," in *Word Traces: Readings of Paul Celan*, ed. Aris Fioretos, trans. Andrea Tarnowski (Baltimore: Johns Hopkins University Press, 1994).

Lambroza, Shlomo. "The Pogroms of 1903–1906," in *Pogroms: Anti-Jewish Violence in Modern Russian History*, ed. John Klier and Shlomo Lambroza (Cambridge: Cambridge University Press, 1992).

Laub, Dori. "An Event Without a Witness: Truth, Testimony and Survival" in *Testimony: Crises of Witnessing in Literature, Psychoanalysis, and History* (New York: Routledge, 1992).

Levinas, Emmanuel. *Proper Names*, trans. Michael B. Smith (Stanford, CA: Stanford University Press, 1996).

——— *On Escape*, trans. Bettina Bergo (Stanford, CA: Stanford University Press, 2003).

Liebes, Yehuda. *Studies in Jewish Myth and Messianism*, trans. Batya Stein (Albany: State University of New York Press, 1993).

Livak, Leonid. *The Jewish Persona in the European Imagination: A Case of Russian Literature* (Stanford, CA: Stanford University Press, 2010).

Lossin, Yigal *Heine: Ha-haiym ha-kfulim* (Jerusalem: Shocken, 2000).

Lupton, Julia R. *Citizens-Saints: Shakespeare and Political Theology* (Chicago: University of Chicago Press, 2005).

Maimonides, Moses. *Guide of the Perplexed*, trans. Shlomo Pines (Chicago: University of Chicago Press, 1963).

Marx, Karl. *Critique of Hegel's "Philosophy of Right,"* trans. A. Jolin and J. O'Malley (Cambridge: Cambridge University Press, 1970).

Marx, Karl, and Friedrich Engels. *Werke*, vol. 1 (Berlin: Karl Dietz Verlag, 1976).

Meryl Willis, Stacey. "Irrational Discourse: Authority and the Ambivalent Maskil in Sh. Y. Abramovitsh's 'Di Takse' and 'Di Kliatsche,'" *Monatshefte* 90, no. 2 (summer 1998).

Mintz, Alan. *Hurban: Responses to Catastrophe in Hebrew Literature* (New York: Columbia University Press, 1984).

Miron, Dan. ""Mi-'be-'ir ha-haregah' va-hal'ah: hir'hurim al ha-po'ema shel Bialik bi-melot me'ah shanah le-ho'fa'ata," in *Be-'ir ha-haregah, biḳur me'uḥar : bi-melot me'ah shanah la-po'emah shel Bialiḳ*, ed. Dan Miron (Tel Aviv: Resling, 2005).

———. *From Continuity to Contiguity: Toward a New Jewish Literary Thinking* (Stanford, CA: Stanford University Press, 2010).

———. *H. N. Bialik and the Prophetic Mode in Modern Hebrew Literature* (Syracuse, NY: Syracuse University Press, 2000).

———. "Pirkei mavo le-susati le-Abramovitsh bimlot me-ah shanim le-hofa'at ha-yetsira," *Hadoar* 51 (New York, 1972).

———. *The Image of The Shtetl and Other Studies of Modern Jewish Literary Imagination* (Syracuse, NY: Syracuse University Press, 2000).

Nachmanides, *Commentary on the Torah*, vol. 3, trans. C. Chavel (New York: Shilo Publishing House, 1974).

Nägele, Rainer. "I Don't Want to Know That I Know: The Inversion of Socratic Ignorance in the Knowledge of Dogs," in *Philosophy and Kafka*, ed. Brendan Moran and Carlo Salzani (Lanham, MD: Lexington Books, 2013).

Nathans, Benjamin. *Beyond the Pale: The Jewish Encounter with Late Imperial Russia* (Berkeley: University of California Press, 2004).

Nelson, Amy. "The Body of the Beast: Animal Protection and Anticruelty Legislation in Imperial Russia," in *Other Animals, Beyond the Human in Russian Culture and History*, ed. J. Costlow and A. Nelson (Pittsburgh, PA: University of Pittsburgh Press, 2010).

Nevo, Gidi. "Kama hirhurim al ha-teva be-yetsirato shel abramovitsh al pi 'sefer ha-behemot' ve-misefer hazichronot,'" in *Mehkarei Yerushalayim be-sifrut 'ivrit*, vol. 18, ed. Shulamit Elitzur and David Vinfeld (Jerusalem: Magnes Press, 2001).

Norris, Margot. *Beasts of the Modern Imagination: Darwin, Nietzsche, Kafka, Ernst, & Lawrence* (Baltimore: Johns Hopkins University Press, 1985).

———. "Sadism and Masochism in 'In the Penal Colony' and 'A Hunger Artist,'" in *Reading Kafka: Prague, Politics, and the Fin de Siècle*, ed. Mark Anderson (New York: Schocken, 1989).

Novalis. *Hymns to the Night and Spiritual Songs*, ed. C. Appleby, trans. G. MacDonald (Maidstone, UK: Crescent Moon, 2010).

———. *Schriften. Die Werke Friedrich von Hardenbergs*, vol. 1 (Darmstadt: Wissenschaftlische, 1960).

Nussbaum, Martha C. *Hiding from Humanity: Disgust, Shame, and the Law* (Princeton, NJ: Princeton University Press, 2004).

Pensky, Max. *Melancholy Dialectics: Walter Benjamin and the Play of Mourning* (Amherst: University of Massachusetts Press, 1993).

Pick, Anat. *Creaturely Poetics: Animality and Vulnerability in Literature and Film* (New York: Columbia University Press, 2011).

Pines, Noam. "The Love of a Dog: Melancholia in David Vogel's *Before the Dark Gate*," *Jewish Studies Quarterly* 23, no. 2 (2016).

Prawer, S. S. *Heine's Jewish Comedy: A Study of His Portraits of Jews and Judaism* (Oxford: Oxford University Press, 1983).

Quint, Alyssa. "'Yiddish Literature for the Masses'? A Reconsideration of Who Read What in Jewish Eastern Europe," *AJS Review* 29, no. 1 (April 2005).

Robertson, Ritchie. *Kafka: Judaism, Politics, and Literature* (New York: Oxford University Press, 1985).

———. *Heine* (London: Halban, 2005).

Rokem, Na'ama. *Prosaic Conditions: Heinrich Heine and the Spaces of Zionist Literature* (Evanston, IL: Northwestern University Press, 2013).

Roskies, David G. *Against the Apocalypse: Responses to Catastrophe in Modern Jewish Culture* (Syracuse, NY: Syracuse University Press, 1999).

Santner, Eric. *On Creaturely Life: Rilke, Benjamin, Sebald* (Chicago: Chicago University Press, 2006).

Schmitt, Carl. *Political Theology: Four Chapters on the Concept of Sovereignty*, trans. George Schwab (Chicago: University of Chicago Press, 2005).

Shaked, Gershon. *Bein tsehok le-demah: Iyunim be-yetsirato shel Mendele Mokher Sefarim* (Ramat-Gan: Massada, 1965).

Shakespeare, William. *The Merchant of Venice* in: *The Complete Works of Shakespeare, 4th Edition*, ed. David Bevington (Reading: Addison-Wesley Educational Publishers, 1997).

Shemesh, Yael. "Khemla klapei ba'alei hayim be-sifrut hazal uvaparshanut ha-masortit," in *Studies in Bible and Exegesis*, vol. 8, ed. Shmuel Vargon, Amos Frisch, and Moshe Rahimi (Ramat-Gen: Bar-Ilan University Press, 2008).

Shklovsky, Victor. "Art as Technique," in *Russian Formalist Criticism: Four Essays*, trans. Lee T. Lemon and Marion J. Reis (Lincoln: University of Nebraska Press, 1965).

Stach, Reiner. *Kafka: The Decisive Years*, trans. Shelley Frisch (Orlando, FL: Harcourt, 2005).

——— *Kafka: The Years of Insight*, trans. Shelley Frisch (Princeton, NJ: Princeton University Press, 2013).

Stow, Kenneth. *Jewish Dogs: An Image and Its Interpreters* (Stanford, CA: Stanford University Press, 2006).

Suchoff, David. *Kafka's Jewish Languages: The Hidden Openness of Tradition* (Philadelphia: University of Pennsylvania Press, 2012).

Taubes, Jacob. *The Political Theology of Paul*, trans. Dana Hollander (Stanford, CA: Stanford University Press, 2004).

Tertner, Shmuel. " 'Be-'ir ha-haregah ve-ha-genre shel ha-monolog ha-dramati," in *Be-mevo'ei ir ha-haregah: miv'har ma'amarim al shiro shel Bialik*, ed. U. Shavit and Z. Shamir (Tel Aviv: Hakibbutz Hameuchad, 1994).

Tolstoy, Leo. *Master and Man and Other Stories*, trans. Ronald Wilks and Paul Foote (London: Penguin Classics, 2005).

Vasmer, Max. *Russisches Etymologisches Wörterbuch*, vol. 1 (Heidelberg: Carl Winter Universitätsverlag, 1953).

Versas, Shmuel. "Beʻin tohakha le-apologetica: *'Be-ʻir ha-haregah'* u-misaviv la" in *Be-mevoʻei ir ha-haregah: mivʻhar maʻamarim al shiro shel Bialik*, ed. U. Shavit and Z. Shamir (Tel Aviv: Hakibbutz Hameuchad, 1994).

Wisse, Ruth R. *The Modern Jewish Canon* (New York: Free Press, 2000).

Wolin, Richard. *Walter Benjamin: An Aesthetic of Redemption* (New York: Columbia University Press, 1982).

Zipperstein, Steven. *The Jews of Odessa: A Cultural History 1794–1881* (Stanford, CA: Stanford University Press, 1986).

INDEX

Abramovitsh, Sholem Yankev, xix, xxvi, 121; Aleichem and, 22; allegory used by, xxx, 28–30, 35; Bialik and, 22, 43; critics of, 30, 38–39; Kishinev pogram and, 43; towns described by, 34–35
Abramovitsh, Sholem Yankev, works of: *The Book of Cattle*, 39–40; *Fishke the Lame*, 21, 35; *From the Memoir Book*, 39; *The Mare*, xxix–xxx, 21–30, 33–41, 90–91, 105; *The Tax*, 35, 142n14; *The Travels of Benjamin III*, 21
acedia, 109
Adorno, Theodor, 76, 103
Agamben, Giorgio: on *bios/zoë*, 136n27; on "kenomatic state," xxii; on "the open," 89; on shame, 78; on werewolf, xiv–xv, xvii
Agnon, S. Y., 151n17; *Only Yesterday* by, xix, xxx, 103–121, 129
Aleichem, Sholem, xix, 22, 33–35
Alexander II, Russian tsar, 24, 35, 43
allegory, 121; in Abramovitsh, xxx, 28–30, 35; in Agnon, 105, 106, 117–119; Walter Benjamin on, xxiv–xxv, 125; in Bialik, 66; in Celan, 121–122, 128; de Man on, 60; in Greenberg, 66–67; in Heine, 8, 11, 14–15, 17–18; in Kafka, 76, 91, 92, 121
Alter, Robert, 104
animal cruelty: Abramovitsh on, 22–28, 34–40; in Dostoevsky, 31–32; Jerusalem society against, 105; Russian society against, 22–27, 142n11
animal rights, 23–24, 27, 105
Animal Studies, xi, xxiv
anthropocentrism, 91, 96; of Descartes, xiii; of Hobbes, xv
anti-Semitic stereotypes, xvi, xxviii, 1, 16
Arpaly, Boaz, 104
attentiveness, 128–129, 132–133

Bachofen, J. J., 75
Baer, Ulrich, 126, 152n17
Bar Giora, Simon, 68–70
Baroque era, 74, 109
Barzel, Hillel, 146n11
Baudelaire, Charles, 16–18
Bauer, Felice, 87
"becoming-animal," 85–87
ben adam ("son of man"), 54
Benjamin, Andrew, xii, xxviii–xxix
Benjamin, Walter, 138n39; on allegory, xxiv–xxv, 125; on attentiveness, 132–133; Celan and, 123; on Kafka, xxvii–xviii, 40–41, 73–75, 84, 98, 121, 128, 131–133; on melancholia, 151n15; *Origin of German Drama* by, 74, 109, 125; on spatialization of the historical, 137n36; *Theses on the Philosophy of History* by, 131–132
Ben-Zvi, Yitzhak, 44
bestiality, xiii
Bialik, Hayim Nachman, 70; Abramovitsh and, 22, 43; Kafka and, 73; prophetic tradition and, xxx, 51, 54–61, 66, 71–72

Bialik, Hayim Nachman, works of: "In the City of Killings," xix, 29, 43–60, 66, 70–72, 98, 119–120; "On the Slaughter," 43–47, 56; "Radiance," 60; "A Short Letter," xix, 68; "Surely the People Is Grass," 56–58; "Through Clouds of Fire," 60
bios/zoë of animal existence, xxii, 136n27
Book of Lamentations, 53–54
Börne, Ludwig, 1–5
Brenner, Y. H., 62
"broken men" (*shiv'rei adam*), 54
Büchner, Georg, 124–128

Cain/Abel, 47
Campe, Julius, 7
Canetti, Elias, 95
Caspi, Joseph, 38
Celan, Paul, xix, 95, 121–129; "Meridian" speech by, xxx, 103, 123–128; "Todesfuge" by, 122
"centaurs" (*susei adam*), 49
Chowers, Eyal, 57
Chrysostom, John, xiii
civic law, xx–xxi
cockroaches, xvii–xviii
Coetzee, J. M., 40

Daoism, 131
de Man, Paul, 60
defamiliarization technique, 93–94
Deleuze, Gilles, xi, 64, 108; on "becoming-animal," 85–87
Derrida, Jacques, xi, xv, 136n13
Descartes, René, xiii
Desmoulins, Lucile, 124–125, 128
Dinezon, Yankev, 30, 143n23
dogs, xiii; in Abramovitsh, xix; in Agnon, 104–119; in Bialik, xix, 44–47, 56; as emblem of melancholia, 109; in Greenberg, 63–72, 69–70; in Heine, xviii, xxvi, 15–17, 101; in Kafka, 73–101, 112–113; myths of, 111–112; in Shakespeare, xvi–xviii; in Tieck, 75
Dostoevsky, Fyodor, 31–33, 143n28
Dubnow, Simon, 43

Ezekiel, 54

Felstiner, John, 122
Fogel, David, 151n6
Foucault, Michel, 17
Frank, Joseph, 33
freedom, 116; in Celan, 125, 128; in Kafka, 84–86
French Revolution, 2, 124–125, 128
Friedlosigkeit, 135n12
Frishman, David, 26–27

Gadamer, Hans-Georg, 137n32
Gans, Eduard, 1, 4
Gilman, Sander, 1, 139n1
Goethe, Johann Wolfgang von, 6, 12
Gordon, A. D., 62
Greenberg, Uri Zvi, 61–72; prophetic tradition and, xxx, 61–62, 65–72; Zionism of, 61–62, 71–72
Greenberg, Uri Zvi, works of: *A Great Fear and the Moon*, 63–64; *House Dog*, xix, xxx, 61–72; "In the Depths," 67–68; "Messiah," 68–69; "The Third Millennium," 63–64
Guattari, Félix, xi, 64, 85–87, 108
Guizot, François, 9
Gutzkow, Karl, 138n1

Hameiri, Avigdor, 61
Hanssen, Beatrice, xv, 132
Hareuveni, David, 67, 69, 70
Harshav, Benjamin, 90, 104
Haskala, 37. *See also* maskil; Abramovitsh and, xviii–xix, 21; Russian Jews of, 25
hatzir (hay), 55–57
Hegel, G. W. F., 10

INDEX 167

Heidegger, Martin, 89, 90, 94; *Fundamental Concepts of Metaphysics* by, xi, 89, 138n42
Heine, Heinrich, 1–20; allegory in, 8, 11, 14–15, 17–18; illness of, 6–8; on *Merchant of Venice*, xviii, 15; Platen on, 2; on republicanism, 4–5
Heine, Heinrich, works of: *Die Bäder von Lucca*, 18–19; "Die Götter Griechenlands," 3; "Die Romantik," 3; *Die Romantische Schule*, 3; *Geständnisse*, 8–9; "Hebräische Melodien," 11–20; "Prinzessin Sabbat," xviii, xxv, xxix, 14–20, 101; *Romanzero*, 7, 11; *Über Polen*, 2; *Zur Geschichte der Religon un Philosophie in Deutschland*, 3
"Hellenic mentality," xxix, 1–13, 15, 20
Hever, Hannan, 62, 63
Hirshbein, Peretz, 44
Hobbes, Thomas, xiii–xvi, 136n13
Holocaust, xxx, 120–121, 152n17; aftermath of, 103, 121; Celan on, 122–123, 126, 133; Pick on, 120
hyenas, 114–117, 121

infrahuman: Agnon on, 106; Celan on, 123–124; definition of, xii, xv; Derrida on, xv, 136n13; Kafka and, 98–99, 103; *Übermensch and*, 72
inhuman: in Bialik, 56; in Kafka, 78–79, 85–87

Jabotinsky, Ze'ev, 44, 61
Jaubert, Caroline, 7
Jerusalem Society for Prevention of Cruelty to Animals (JSPCA), 105
Jewish diaspora, 56–57
"Jewish Thought," xxvi

Kafka, Franz, xxx, 73–101; Adorno on, 76, 103; allegory in, 76, 91, 92, 121; Walter Benjamin on, xxvii–xviii, 40–41, 73–75, 84, 98, 121, 128, 131–133; Bialik and, 73; Canetti on, 95; Celan and, 123; Deleuze on, 64, 85–87, 108; freedom in, 84–86; Heine and, xviii; infrahuman and, 98–99, 103; Norris on, 84; parables of, 73; on shame, 77–84, 88, 95
Kafka, Franz, works of: "The Animal in the Synagogue," xxvi; "Before the Law," 73–74; *The Castle*, 90; "In the Penal Colony," 86; "Investigations of a Dog," 90–92, 95–98, 106, 112–113; "The Metamorphosis," 75–76, 85–86, 95, 100; "The New Attorney," 40–41, 41, 131–132; "A Report to an Academy," 85; *The Trial*, 73, 75–86, 91–92, 95, 98
kahal (community councils), 35
Kanyuk, Yoram, xix
kiddush hashem (sanctification of God's name), 51
Kishinev progrom (1903), 43–54, 58–59, 70
Klingenstein, Susanne, 141n1
Klozner, Yosef, 44
Kurzweil, Baruch, 104

Lachower, Yeruham Fishel, 38–39, 44, 146n11
Lacoue-Labarthe, Philippe, 125
Lasker-Schüler, Else, xviii
Laub, Dori, 152n17
Levinas, Emmanuel, 77–78, 133
Levy, Yitshok, 73
Lilith, 113–114, 116, 117, 121
Lithuanian yeshivas, 21
Livak, Leonid, xiii
Louis-Philippe, king of the French, 9
Lufthunde, 91, 92
Luftmenschen, 91–92
Lupton, Julia, xxi–xxiii

madness, animality of, 17–18
Maimonides, Moses, 37–38
Malebranche, Nicolas, 128, 132
Mallarmé, Stéphane, 126
martyrs, 51, 62
Marx, Karl, 10
maskilic writing, xviii–xix, 22, 142n14. *See also* Haskala
"medusoid" art, 127, 128
melancholia, 151n15; in Agnon, 109–110, 116–117, 120
Menzel, Wolfgang, 2
Mintz, Alan, 51
Miron, Dan, 73; on Agnon's *Only Yesterday*, 104; on Bialek's "In the City of Killings," 44, 59–60

Nägele, Rainer, 91
Nahmanides, 37–38
Napoleonic Code, 4
"Nazarene mentality," xxix, 1–13, 15, 20
Nekrasov, Nikolai, 143n28
Nevo, Gidi, 28
New Testament, Jews of, xii–xiii
nomos/physis, xv
Norris, Margot, 84, 138n37
Novalis (Friedrich von Hardenberg), 12–13
Nussbaum, Martha, 17

Odessa pogrom (1871), 25–26
Odessa Society for Sympathy to Animals, 26
Ovid, 133
Oz, Amos, 104

Pale of Settlement, 21, 24, 35, 43
Palestine: under British Mandate, 61; under Ottoman rule, 104–105, 118
parables, 73, 106, 114–116, 121
Paul (apostle), xii–xiii, xxvi–xxvii, 138n39

Pensky, Max, xxv
Peretz, Y. L., 44, 143n22
physis/nomos, xv
Pick, Anat, 133; on "creaturely poetics," xxiv, 40, 137nn30–31, 151n17; on Holocaust, 120
Platen, August von, 2
Plautus, 136n13
pogroms, 29, 51; Kishinev, 43–60; Odessa, 25–26, 29; topoi of, 53–54
"poverty in world" (*Weltarmut*), 89–92, 94, 97, 99
"primitives," xiv
prophetic tradition: in Bialik, 51, 54–61, 66, 71–72; in Greenberg, 61–62, 65–72
Pythagoras, 109

Quint, Alyssa, 30

rats, xvii–xviii
retzach ("murder"), 45–47
Reyzen, Avrom, 143n22
Robertson, Richie, 149n35
Roskies, David, 45, 60
Rousseau, Jean-Jacques, 136n13
Russia, 25; emancipation of serfs in, 23–25; Society for the Protection of Animals of, 22–27, 142n11

Sadan, Dov, 104
sadomasochism, 80–84, 88
Saint-Simonism, 3
Saltykov, Mikhail, 34
Santner, Eric, 76; on "creaturely life," xx, xxvi–xxvii; on state of exception, 73–74
"savages," xiv
Schmitt, Carl, xxi–xxii, 74, 136n13
self-alienation, 119
self-hatred, xvi, 1–6, 16
Shaked, Gershon, 36, 142n19
Shakespeare, William, xviii; *Merchant*

of Venice by, xvi–xviii, xx–xxv, xxvii–xxix, 15, 125
shame: Agamben on, 78; Kafka on, 77–84, 88, 95; Levinas on, 77–78
shechita: in Agnon, 120; in Bialik, 45–47, 49, 52, 59, 70, 120; in Kafka, 73, 84, 95
Shimonovitch, David, 62
Shklovsky, Victor, 93, 144n33
Shlonsky, Avraham, 61, 62
Shylock, xvi–xviii, xx–xxv, xxvii–xxix, 15, 125
Singer, Isaac Bashevis, 121
Singer, Israel Joshua, xix
Social Contract, xiv–xv
son of man (*ben adam*), 54, 59
Song of Songs, 34
spiders, xxvi, 52–54
Stach, Reiner, 82, 91
state of exception, xxiii; Celan on, 122–123; Kafka on, 74–76, 86; Santner on, 73–74; Schmitt on, xxi–xxii
state of nature: Bialik on, 50–51; Heine on, 17; Hobbes on, xiv–xvi; Kafka on, 101
Stow, Kenneth, xiii
susei adam ("centaurs"), 49

talush ("uprooted"), 57
Taoism, 131
Taubes, Jacob, 138n39
taxidermy, 114–117, 121
telishut ("disconnectedness"), 57, 60
Tertner, Shmuel, 146n11

Tieck, Ludwig, 75
Tolstoy, Leo, 32, 92–94
tsaʿar baʿalei hayim ("sorrow of living beings"), 37

Übermensch, 72
Umkehr (reversal), 132–133

va-yirdu, xix–xx
Volynsky, Akim, 143n22

Weil, Simone, 137n30
Weltarmut ("poverty in world"), 89–92, 94, 97, 99
werewolf, xiv–xvii; Agamben on, xiv–xv; Derrida on, 136n13; Heine on, xviii; Hobbes and, xv
Wermel, Samuel, 143n22
Wilda, Wilhelm Eduard, 135n12
Willis, Stacey Maryl, 142
Wisse, Ruth, 21, 141n1

yeshivas, 21
Yiddish, xix, 1, 21
Yishuv, 61, 62, 147n18

Zealots, 68–70
Zevi, Sabbatai, 67, 69, 70
Zionism, xix; Agnon and, 103–104, 117–120, 129; Celan and, 128–129; Greenberg and, 61–62, 71–72
Zipperstein, Steven, 25–26
zoë/bios of animal existence, xxii